TWENTIETH-CENTURY WRITING AND THE BRITISH WORKING CLASS

Twentieth-century Writing and the British Working Class

JOHN KIRK

UNIVERSITY OF WALES PRESS
CARDIFF
2003

© John Kirk, 2003

All rights reserved. No part of this book may be reproduced, stored in a retrieval system, or transmitted, in any form or by any means, electronic, mechanical, photocopying, recording or otherwise, without clearance from the University of Wales Press, 10 Columbus Walk, Brigantine Place, Cardiff, CF10 4UP.
www.wales.ac.uk/press

British Library Cataloguing-in-Publication Data
A catalogue record for this book is available from the British Library.

ISBN 0–7083–1813–4

The right of John Kirk to be identified as author of this work has been asserted by him in accordance with sections 77 and 78 of the Copyright, Designs and Patents Act 1988.

Typeset by Bryan Turnbull
Printed in Great Britain by Dinefwr Press, Llandybïe

Contents

Acknowledgements ... vii

Introduction ... 1

1 'Unbending the springs of action': from poverty to affluence in the narrating of class ... 32

2 Class, community and 'structures of feeling': a 'sense of loss' revisited in some working-class writing from the 1980s ... 78

3 Figuring the dispossessed: the negative topographies of class ... 103

4 Recovered perspectives: women and working-class writing ... 135

5 Mapping difference and identity: race, class and the politics of belonging ... 161

Conclusion ... 190

Notes ... 194

Bibliography ... 207

Index ... 217

Acknowledgements

I would like to thank the following editors and publishers for permitting me to reprint work that previously appeared in their respective journals. The Introduction is a modified version of my article 'Changing the Subject: Cultural Studies and the Question of Class', which appeared in *Cultural Logic: Journal of Marxist Literary and Cultural Theory*, Fall 2002. Sections of chapter 2 are taken from 'Class, Community and "Structures of Feeling" in some Working-class Writing from the 1980s', first published in *Literature and History*, 8, 2 (Autumn 1999), and reprinted by permission of Manchester University Press. Chapter 3 is part of an article published in *English: The Journal of the English Association*, 48, 191 (Summer 1999), titled 'Figuring the Dispossessed: Images of the Urban Working Class in the Writing of James Kelman', and I am grateful to the editors and the English Association for permission to use the article. Chapter 4 was originally published as 'Recovered Perspectives: Gender, Class and Memory in Pat Barker's Writing', in *Contemporary Literature*, 40, 4 (Winter 1999), and has been considerably reworked for the purpose of this book. My thanks go to the University of Wisconsin Press. Finally, parts of chapter 5 are drawn from 'Invisible Ink: Working-Class Writing and the End of Class', in *European Journal of Cultural Studies*, 5, 3 (2002), reprinted by permission of Sage Publications, and from 'Urban Narratives: Contesting Place and Space in some British Cinema from the 1980s', first published in *Journal of Narrative Theory*, 31, 3 (Fall 2001).

Many influences have contributed to the writing of this book. In particular I would like to express my love and thanks to my parents for their constant support and encouragement over the years, and extend this to my two brothers Dave and Freddie, who in their own ways helped me think through some of the ideas explored here. My friend, Geoff Hemstedt, supervised an earlier version, and helped get the ball rolling during those early-morning discussions together. I remember those meetings with fondness. I must acknowledge, too, my friend Glenda, for all those valuable conversations in the pub about, among other things, distances travelled. I have been lucky enough to work with students, at a range of institutions, who have helped illuminate some of the concerns examined here, and I would like to thank them also. I am grateful to the people at the University of Wales Press for their help and hard work; in particular, a special word of thanks to Duncan Campbell, who got the project on the road. But my biggest debt must go to my partner, Alison, who was there from the start, and whose support, love and friendship helped make the writing of this book possible. So I dedicate the book to her, with love.

Introduction

Representations of working-class life abound in British culture. They come to us via the cinema, they circulate on the television in the shape of soap opera and sitcoms and the occasional documentary; they are commented upon and unpacked in the pages of 'serious' newspapers, or constitute the more lurid bits in tabloid gossip; they are the staple stuff of much advertising, they are the subject of novels and poems (though somewhat less frequently here) and of plays. They are in the stories we tell other people, the stories we tell ourselves, the stories which tell us. Class, more generally, is implicated in all manner of lived experience: shopping, going on holiday, playing and watching sport; class is what we eat and the way we eat it, where we live, how we work, or not, how we fall in love, how we die. Class is always in some sense present: whether in our refusal to accept it, our inclination to acknowledge it or insist on it or, as in some cases, our being privileged enough not to have even noticed it. On a different register, class is what is meant when one speaks of a relation to the means of production, or historically produced structures of feeling; it is present when one talks of roles determined by the ideology of domesticity and the stratification of gender difference, or the accumulation and differential relations of cultural capital, or the demise of master-narratives – class resonates eloquently in the current prime minister's recent remark, that we are all middle class now.

Despite the fact that ideas and understandings around class are seemingly ubiquitous, and that representations of working-class life are generated in a wide range of discourses – certainly within the field of popular culture – recent times have witnessed the emergence of a new 'common sense' which insists on the death of class, and in particular the demise of the working class. Of course, these arguments, too, are predicated on some notion – some *representation* – of who/what the working class is. Their origin in this case, however, is less popular culture than mainstream politics; less the broadsheet press, than the halls of academe. Here 'common-sense approaches to class amongst the contemporary intelligentsia insist that it is irrelevant to both the public and private spheres'.[1] Although the notion of the disappearance of the working class is no new or recent phenomenon, as I show later in my discussion of the discourse of affluence emergent in the late 1950s, current assertions claim to be more conclusive. The 1980s, and the politics of Thatcherism, saw the 'deconstruction' of the British working class, through a decade or more of economic, political and social change, often defined by commentators as the shift from a Fordist industrial economy to the age of post-Fordism and the rise of the information society. Critics quarry further supporting evidence from the fallout of 1989: the demise of 'official' communism and its historical association with the working class. Then there is the development of globalization and the emergence of postmodernism and postmodern cultural theory. Added to this, a renewed wave of feminist thinking has challenged a whole range of traditional methods of viewing class.

Postmodern cultural theory has made a particular contribution by questioning notions of class through its overwhelming focus on 'difference' and alternative modes of cultural identity. In the proliferation of new identities predicated of the postmodern condition, class becomes just one way of seeing or being among others, and not a particularly good one on some accounts. This fluidity of boundaries, the argument goes, spells the end of class, at least as it has customarily been conceived. These positions influenced a range of disciplines throughout the 1980s, particularly in the field of Cultural Studies and cognate areas. They found a place too within political discourse, arguably evident today in the trajectory of the British Labour Party. From 1980 onwards, the political terrain on which these developments coalesced was dominated by the New Right: most notably, Thatcherism in Britain and Reaganism in the United States. Powerfully articulated as a key strand of these ideological discourses was the emphasis on the subject as consumer rather than producer; a shift designed in part as a way of eroding class identities or identifications. Prioritized instead was a stress on a type of radical individualism conducive to a reinvigorated consumer capitalism and a market-orientated politics; a position oddly commensurate with poststructuralist/postmodernist suspicions of class as a master narrative purportedly homogenizing all identities under its sign.

This study is concerned with examining some of those arguments and positions on class arising from the 1980s, with a specific focus on writing which takes as its main subject matter working-class life and experience. The key stress here will fall on the historical conditions present at the time which seemingly render the question of class – here, specifically debates around the working class – suddenly essential for discussion. The greater part of the book therefore focuses on representations of the British working class in the 1980s and 1990s. To accomplish this in any effective sense, however, calls for a much wider historical perspective, and to provide this I compare, in chapter 1, two other formative periods from the twentieth century where class – and those always present, if sometimes 'submerged', corollaries of, culture, politics and power – looms large: the 1930s (the perceived period of 'proletarian literature' and turbulent class struggle) and the 1950s and early 1960s, or the 'Age of Affluence'. The arguments within the wider culture around the significance of class, in each of these moments, are intense ones, and it is in and through what Raymond Williams called 'the multiplicity of writing' that I want to scrutinize some of the effects and outcomes. The task of analysing the ideological work of representing the working class means engaging with a range of writing, and while I concentrate chiefly on cultural fictions in the shape of novels, films, poetry and plays, I also examine documentary, autobiographical writing and theoretical propositions which articulate working-class narratives, or narratives of class.

This study is deeply informed by Raymond Williams's writing on culture and society, and particularly his concept 'structure of feeling'. Theoretically, then, the book is grounded very much in the tradition of British Cultural Studies: the curious paradox here, however, is that much of the scholarly emphasis in this field over the past twenty years or so has been on anything but class. I highlight some notable exceptions to this later in the introduction. But it seems that Andrew Milner is right, when assessing trajectories in the discipline, to note a radical decentring of social class 'by an increasing preoccupation with the cultural effects of other kinds of cultural difference – gender, race, ethnicity, sexuality'[2] where class then becomes quite quickly the forgotten identity of new identity politics. One of the book's objectives will be to explore the reasons behind this and the subsequent ramifications, as well as to examine other writing which problematizes those seemingly dominant and dominating discourses propounding the end of class.

Indeed, the gradual rejection of class analysis within cultural studies and political discourse in the 1980s can be identified quite clearly in the work of Stuart Hall. His 1988 article 'Brave New World', published in the journal of the British Communist Party, *Marxism Today*, sought to enlighten readers as to the exigencies of 'New Times', a term popularized by the journal to describe the altered political, cultural and economic conditions of Thatcher's Britain.[3] Pointing to post-Fordism as the economic base of the postmodern moment, Hall described its characteristics in terms of fragmentation and pluralism, leading to the 'weakening of older collective solidarities and block identities and the emergence of new identities associated with greater work flexibility, the maximization of individual choices through personal consumption'.[4] Hall argued that this resulted in a fundamental shift in the self-perception of the individual – 'the self is more fragmented and incomplete' – thus enabling a proliferation of autonomous identities which find political expression (if at all) in new social movements. Hall ends by insisting that 'the correspondence between the political and the economic is exactly what has now disintegrated'.[5]

Hall elaborates a move here from class politics to new identity politics, a view given greater theoretical sophistication in Laclau and Mouffe's influential *Hegemony and Socialist Strategy* (1987). The argument developed there posits 'no logical connection whatsoever'[6] between class and politics, and asserts that such talk represents an unacceptable essentialism and should therefore be rejected by the Left. Undoubtedly, the re-election of a right-wing Conservative government in the 1980s (with some level of working-class support) determined many of these developing arguments. Thus, identity, for Laclau and Mouffe, is a far more conflictual, contradictory and overdetermined process, and consciousness is never a simple reflection or determination of being. But more significant in their argument, perhaps, is their out-of-hand rejection of any notion of objective interests at all, until those interests become articulated in and through discourse. In this logic, class identity becomes a contingent one, one potentially radical position among others, and these were frequently regarded as *essentially* incompatible with one another. These positions, symptomatic of a rejection of class as agency for change, shaped an emerging politics of identity focusing, as Milner pointed out, on gender, race and sexuality. In this context, identity is seen to be formed entirely in the sphere of culture. Working-class identity and class consciousness, if viewed as a political and economic category, becomes displaced, located comfortably in some other, earlier, phase of history, to be forgotten about or appropriated and reified as part of the burgeoning heritage industry.

Yet other analyses seemed to contradict this (as did actual practice, if we take into account the 1984–5 miners' strike, for instance), with sociologists finding in one nationwide survey conducted in 1988 that 'social class is to the fore among conceptions of collective identity. It is still the case that important differences in shared beliefs and values are structured more obviously by class than by other sources of social cleavage.'[7] Thus it seems that while the intelligentsia strove to theorize away notions of class identity, lived experience suggested something else. It is only in more recent times that noises have been heard within Cultural Studies and elsewhere which begin to address these contradictions. A recently published collection of essays – to which I will be referring extensively in this Introduction – has argued forcefully for class to become again a central focus for Cultural Studies, so as to re-explore and re-engage with 'sites of [working] class experience, and theorize out of them, as situated knowledges'.[8]

The call is to be heeded. However, my own 'revisiting' of the issue of class in this book turns not so much on a focus of working-class cultures or cultural expression, as on a concern with *representations* of the British working class. The centre of interest is to do as much with writing *about* the working class, as with writing *by* the working class – although a good deal of the work presented here has been produced by those who can be defined, and in some cases have defined themselves, as working-class writers. Historically, literature has been a mode of expression chosen by working-class people to articulate their experiences, even if such writing has on the whole been sidelined within mainstream institutions, or completely ignored within the formation of what Williams terms a 'selective tradition', one which serves to marginalize or incorporate dissenting or alternative voices.[9]

My focus on representation allows a number of important questions to be asked in relation to the range of writing under discussion, questions which form the core of this book. For instance, who speaks in these texts, for whom and in what circumstances? To whom are these texts addressed and, crucially, what historical conditions shape and influence production and reception? What are the ideological perspectives articulated in these discursive acts – expressed both explicitly and implicitly – and what are their effects and functions? These narratives – as with all other representations which circulate in our culture – are both shaped by and, to some degree, help to shape the prevailing socio-economic and cultural contexts of their time. They are determined, too, by the available conventions, narrative strategies and rhetorical devices always already present for speaking about class. Some challenge established orthodoxies – society's dominant ideological perspectives, or aesthetic forms – while others reaffirm them. Alan Sinfield has spoken about the hegemonic function of stories – *representations* – which become naturalized as society's 'common sense'; as just the way things are. Other stories, or what he terms cultural productions, present different ways of seeing.[10] It is such acts of discursive resistance and contestation which are central to some of my arguments. Raymond Williams insisted that 'the arts of a period . . . are of major importance. For here, if anywhere, [the structure of feeling] is likely to be expressed.' This may or may not be a conscious articulation; nevertheless, in the production of literature, 'the actual living sense, the deep community that makes the communication possible, is naturally drawn upon'.[11] This concept of structure of feeling remains essential as part of Williams's theorizing on culture, and it occupies a central place in the following chapters. I elaborate more fully on the concept below in the course of considering some more recent writing focused on the British working class, attempting to place this work in the wider context of the book's overall objectives and concerns.

I Writing the self: the 'personal' politics of class

My opening comments suggested that there are different ways of thinking and talking about class. There are ways of doing this, however, that might seem to be foreclosed in advance, and I want to consider one of those ways. One critic has suggested that those 'speaking of a working-class upbringing, certainly in a British context, [are] liable to find themselves accused of sentimentality'.[12] He goes on to posit that this is no surprise: speaking and writing about class can be emotional; it can be a painful and difficult process in which feelings of belonging and un-belonging often pull in deeply ambivalent and hurtful ways. The prejudices and privileges which go along with class leave marks. Here, Andy Medhurst speaks of the marks of transition: the peculiar difficulties of moving from one class to another, and the dilemmas then of recognition, affiliation, alignment. The implication, then, is that class is something one might leave behind, or forsake for some position that is (impossibly) classless. The possibility of classlessness harbours a myth; in the transition narrative referred to here, classlessness means becoming middle class, which is to be classless only in as much as it is the 'norm', the authoritative and authorized place to be. So, Medhurst asks, how do you deal with feeling working class when you get paid a middle-class salary and do middle-class things?

The question insists we view class not simply as an objective entity (relationships within the means of production), but as an issue of affinity and identification. In any understanding of class this represents a very important way to think about class experience and its narrativization, and Medhurst flags up the uses of autobiography as a major form for articulating configurations of class and self-identity. In later chapters of this book I analyse some pertinent uses of this approach, from both the 1950s and the 1980s. It is worth mentioning here, however, that this mode has a respectable pedigree in working-class writing, and is indeed the main generic tendency of one of the key post-war working-class narratives. Richard Hoggart's *The Uses of Literacy* – that founding text of British Cultural Studies – attempted to think in just this way. In my analysis of writing from the so-called Age of Affluence, Hoggart's text is central for understanding some of the developing arguments, extant at the time, on class affluence and mobility. My conclusions differ somewhat from those of Medhurst; for Medhurst's advocacy of the approach taken by Hoggart is an attempt to rescue *The Uses of Literacy* from the enormous condescension of posterity. He is aware of the limitations of some of Hoggart's arguments, describing it as a 'pained and contradictory book' which nevertheless 'moves me, prompting intense jolts of recognition that few other texts can match'.[13] Hoggart's resort to aspects of the autobiographical in the writing of *The Uses of Literacy* – which results in a hybrid combination of the personal and public, objective and subjective, individual and collective – lend it acute insights on working-class life. The writer strives to legitimate working-class culture during a period when the working class was seen to be disappearing as a distinct presence, at the same time attempting 'to confront and understand the painful contradictions of his own cultural position'.[14] That position is a kind of 'cultural cusp', an in-betweenness derived from the scholarship-boy experience. This is most clearly exposed at the end of the book, where we find a structure of feeling striving to combine what we might call the cognitive and emotive: what Raymond Williams tried to figure in the term 'thought as feeling, feeling as thought'. To be 'uprooted and anxious' is no small matter; the idea of uprooting suggests an almost organic process, a vicious wrenching from native soil. Through this the working-class boy is 'progressively cut off from the ordinary life of the group'; increasingly isolated 'from the intense gregariousness of the working-class family'.[15] The description represents the event as a crude act of social engineering, the benefits of which are seemingly ambivalent. But in recalling these feelings, Hoggart is calling upon *experience* in an effort to evaluate and comprehend the objective structures which scooped him out of his class background and habitus, and into an alien social environment. Such strategies of writing constitute a forceful approach both to understanding cultural identity, and the concept of agency, as well as in defining and comprehending wider social and cultural change. The importance of *experience* remains central to some of the arguments addressed in the following pages, as does an insistence on the need to remain alert to the fact that experience is never the ultimate, unquestioned authority.

The questions raised here are both epistemological and ontological. Autobiographical discourse on class becomes significant as a mode of knowledge about working-class life (not unimpeachable), its articulation taking the view put by one critic that 'class could be something in the blood, in the very fibre of a man or woman; a way of growing, feeling, judging, taken out of the resources of generations gone before'.[16] It recovers lived experience – in part what Raymond Williams was pointing to in the phrase 'structures of feeling' – in all its potential contradictoriness, as a counter-hegemonic principle. In this sense, such an emphasis may take us some way beyond the prejudice (and the hint of pathologizing) which constructs an identification with a working-class upbringing, a working-class past, as mere 'sentimentality'.

Re-reading *The Uses of Literacy*, I wonder, too, how many scholarship boys and girls of that period can read the chapter quoted from above without pained twinges of recognition. Much of what is written in the book has always in some significant sense rung true to me, more so in relation to childhood memories of my own parents' experiences, attitudes and beliefs. It is perhaps appropriate to come clean here about my own working-class upbringing, the son of a factory worker and a hospital cleaner. However, the scholarship experience was never mine. I never knew for sure whether or not I had passed my eleven-plus exam, which was the stepping-stone to 'higher' things (I have always presumed not), ending up at an establishment that was somewhere between grammar school proper and the local secondary modern (it had two 'higher' streams and a sixth-form stream you could be levered into with the right results, though I stubbornly refused to go). My eventual entry into university and to the margins of academia was much more circuitous. Yet Hoggart's thoughts and feelings here still ring true to my own later (and continuing) experiences of 'class mobility'. There I was, the working-class man – somewhat older than Hoggart the scholarship boy and later academic and writer – entering the (*still* largely) middle-class environment of the university and beginning to do what I had always perceived to be middle-class things. Even at a more mature stage, however, and with years of work and life experience behind me, the excitement of being able to 'find things out', to acquire knowledge (and cultural capital), was tempered by the awareness that I was somewhere I perhaps had no right to be. The voices in whom I was asked to place trust – my tutors – were also the voices of the 'Them' Hoggart so clearly describes in *The Uses of Literacy*. I knew the tones only too well: they judged, disparaged, stood aloof, patronized, exploited. But they had something I wanted; something I felt, somehow, I could put to use. The battle was sometimes difficult: both a struggle with myself (as out-of-place proletarian) and with a particular institutional context from which I felt at times alienated. In the end I did get what I wanted and was helped enormously, too, by some of those same people with the annoying accents. But my subsequent research focused on aspects of working-class culture as a way – I understand now – of attempting to 'link the two environments'[17] or, as Annette Kuhn describes it, 'heal the split'.[18]

So when Medhurst insists on the analytical usefulness of experience in speaking of working-class subjectivity we should listen, recognizing that a focus on the experiential might facilitate an awareness of *some* of the 'common experiences . . . and interests' through which class happens and which get handled in 'cultural terms: embodied in traditions, value-systems, ideas and cultural forms',[19] and which may be characterized by both change and/or continuity. Yet a powerful move in recent times to *theory* – part of the 'linguistic turn' in studies of culture – has cast deep suspicion on experiential modes of understanding. Medhurst shows that a fixation with theory – as this body of knowledge has been constructed and developed alongside concerns of gender, race, sexuality – sidelines class and rejects almost outright the dimension of experience (rightly questioning it; wrongly abandoning it), consequently promoting a 'depersonalizing' approach to culture in the name, purportedly, of greater analytical rigour which, however, precludes important understandings and insights into working-class life. According to Annette Kuhn in *Family Secrets*, this leads all too often to 'a failure to imagine how social class is actually lived on the pulse, how it informs our inner worlds as it conditions our life chances in the outer world'.[20] But the shift to theory (and its concomitant anti-humanism) produces its own interpretative shortcomings and analytical silences. What Medhurst labels the 'hyper-theorizing' of much recent Cultural Studies has left us with a large hole where matters of 'expressivity, locality, communality and class' used to be.[21] The approach somehow denies that it is feasible to make sense of self and history 'emotively' – as it is lived 'on the pulse' – rather than cognitively. We lose *feelings*: those of solidarity, justice, hope. These experiences construct possible interpretative frameworks and ways of seeing, should we accept the concept of experience as 'a key category of everyday knowledge, structuring people's lives in important ways'.²²

Williams's idea of structure of feeling attempts to grapple with this, defining structure of feeling – and its traceable presence in cultural texts and historical periods – as 'specifically affective elements of consciousness and relationships; not feelings against thought, but thought as felt and feeling as thought: practical consciousness of a present kind, in a living and interrelated community'.²³ Williams himself never rescinded the importance of the experiential in his work, as I show in chapter 2, where I discuss in much greater detail the analytical usefulness of Williams's concept in relation to writing from the 1980s and 1990s. This is also Medhurst's point: seeking forms to express (represent) lived processes and relations highlights the value of the autobiographical and personal dimension for finding ways to talk about working-class life. It is not a case of falling into sentimentality or, as Virginia Woolf once suggested, indulging in a kind of 'special pleading'. Woolf here seems to be identifying a type of distortion in writing about working-class life, a view which Carolyn Steedman has been quick to upbraid. Indeed, Steedman suggests that any evident tensions in working-class narratives of self derive essentially from the difficulty of placing the self at centre stage as hero or heroine, when the feelings described fall outside the 'proper set of feelings' for working-class people. For Steedman, any tension or distortion is one 'that matches the distortion of what it is that is observed and expressed in the writing'.²⁴

Thus, with such prescriptions in evidence, we could argue that writing about the working class, within the contemporary context, remains very much writing from the margins. Significantly, what sustained work there has been on the subject of working-class culture over the past two decades has come from women: both female academics and writers of fiction. In some of the academic work, a stress can be found once again on the autobiographical: on writing the self, to 'write in' others. Female scholars like Carolyn Steedman, Beverley Skeggs, Annette Kuhn and Valerie Walkerdine have all explored the borderlines between class and gender, belonging and un-belonging, inside and outside, often in relation to their positions within academia, but also to their locations on the class cultural cusp. The cultural theory and practice developed by these women writers is informed to a very important extent by their own working-class backgrounds, and rehearses the familiar feminist notion that the personal is political, offering a take on class that resists the colder probings of a more distanced traditional Marxism and ideas of economic determinism, as well as questioning the poststructuralist ideology of the 'death of the subject' and the end of class. The emotional politics of class identity become a central concern, allowing for explorations of structures of feeling that revolve around painful encounters of loss or lack. Steedman's *Landscape for a Good Woman* (1986) – which I discuss in relation to writing about class and gender in chapter 4 – is an obvious paradigm case, in which she questions a range of theories and positions which claim to 'speak' the working-class subject. This involves castigating some of the more reductive writing on working-class life in Hoggart's *The Uses of Literacy*, while at the same time shaping her own text along similar narrative and generic lines. If Hoggart strove to validate a resilient and respectable working-class culture that he felt to be under threat of a fatal penetration by commercialism (I choose the metaphor consciously), Steedman's text aspires to legitimate her mother's (commodity) desire as perfectly proper, in a world which withheld from her what she identified as the necessary trappings of the good life – mostly small comforts; not too much to expect, the kinds of comforts and securities taken for granted by the higher-class women she had had to service most of her working life. Central to *Landscape for a Good Woman* is *memory*, and how the past remains active and pressing in the present. Memory, of course, is a crucial component of autobiographical discourse, and for Steedman (as evidenced in her other books) life writing is about understanding self and relations with others. It represents a way of narrating difference and sameness, and the memory texts mobilized in *Landscape for a Good Woman* recount and reshape the lived experience both of herself and her mother, and give form to the story she tells.

'Recovery', then, may well be a key theme in writing about aspects of working-class life, and I make this a central concern in chapter 4, examining the work of Pat Barker, among others, whose work has firmly *gendered* writing about working-class culture. From what I have said so far, it is possible to argue that autobiography and the meaning of memory stand as appropriate vehicles of expression and a strategic approach for exploring feelings: feelings of loss and lack, but also of pride and commonality. Or perhaps *autobiographical fragments* is a better term here, because the uses of memory and experience by both Hoggart and Steedman do not represent autobiography as it is conventionally accepted – there are no neat linear narratives of hurdles jumped, ladders climbed and dilemmas neatly resolved. The past is not just back there, but ongoing, still present, *interrupting*; typically, fragments of memory flash up in an almost Benjaminian sense at a moment of danger and stand as a mode of intervention or interrogation. Annette Kuhn describes the objective of such writing as attempting to tread 'a fine line between cultural criticism and cultural production'.[25] Thus her own work on memory and class in *Family Secrets* has to do 'with the ways memory shapes the stories we tell, in the present about the past – especially stories about our own lives', and 'with what makes us remember: the prompts, the pretexts of memory: the reminders of the past that remain in the present'.[26] My discussion of 'memory-texts' in relation to Pat Barker's fiction suggests that this type of trajectory might represent an antidote to the kind of 'year zero' theorizing of postmodernism: the end of *everything* – master-narratives, the subject, history, hermeneutic depth.

This emphasis is found, too, in Valerie Walkerdine's work. Writing about her own working-class background and experience, she talks in terms of 'coming out', as though her past stood under the sign of shame compared to where she is now located in middle-class academia. As gays and lesbians have felt the need to disguise their sexuality, so in alien environments in which they want to succeed the working-class subject will smother their identity, those give-away signs which are evident in verbal utterances and are found written on the body – what Bourdieu has referred to as the subject's *disposition*.[27] But attempting to pass as middle class involves more than masquerade, a change of outfit. In the same way as the middle-class subject can rarely get away with 'slumming it', so the working-class man or woman will eventually slip up in an arena where the rules of the game have changed. Class is deeply ingrained in lived experience, it is profoundly embedded in institutional practices. I am always taken aback when someone says, 'you've come a long way'. It is an innocent enough phrase and often meant well, but the connotations are pretty appalling. What is this journey I have supposedly made, and why is the trip invariably worthwhile or wholly positive? What dark forest have I left behind? And why is there the slightest hint of surprise or admiration in the utterance when it is addressed to the working-class kid? In many important respects, it is inaccurate to refer to Walkerdine as writing of her class *past*, as class (as she makes clear) is still for her a very present and active thing, so that her 'coming out' has meant relinquishing silence and being able to proudly call herself an 'educated working-class woman'.[28] This represents the kind of 'strategic essentialism' referred to by Spivak, vitally important for acts of emancipation; it enables Walkerdine to 'assert my education and my power with pride and claim back my education, not as alienation and a move to another class but as part of a narrative which allows me a place from which to struggle, a sense of belonging'.[29] So she expresses feelings of loss and lack, of pride and commonality – not uncommon themes in writing about working-class life. But rejection constitutes an alternative response also, because there is no essential need or reason for the class-mobile individual to want to identify in this manner. Acts of dis-identification may be more common, in fact.[30] At a conference I attended recently a woman academic stood up during a discussion which moved to the subject of class and stated: 'I was working class, I'm not any more. I'm an academic now.' This was greeted with general assent; she had got something off her chest. It tied in with her Lacanian paper, delivered earlier. In a sense, she too was 'coming out'. But is this what is currently meant by classlessness? Why didn't she define herself as 'middle class now'? Surely that would have been closer to the mark. How can anyone be class*less*, which her comment seemed to imply?

Difference dominated conference discussions, though class difference failed to get much of a look-in. Constant reference to the proliferation of new identities predicated of the postmodern condition structured the whole event, and this purported fluidity of ontological boundaries seemed to seal the fate of the working-class subject. Some days later, when I came to write up notes on the conference for an article, perhaps, on class, I sought out a quiet place of retreat outside the office. I appropriated an empty seminar room, early in the morning, at around 8.30. Outside, a cold winter wind lashed rain against the third-floor windows; my trousers were still damp from the walk from the railway station, through streets teeming with commuters about their daily routines. The room I occupied was a bit of a mess: some event had occurred the evening before, tables and chairs were strewn around the place, paper plates contained remnants of buffet food, plastic cups lay on their sides. I found an uncluttered space, set out bits of paper with my scribbled notes. Not long into my ruminations, a group of university cleaners came in. There were three women; I was on nodding acquaintance with one of them, so we exchanged greetings. Usually they were gone before most academic staff arrived. The animated banter with each other dried up on seeing my presence. The papers and books in front of me were giving away my academic status. Now *I* was one of Them. They began work at the far end of the room, cleaning up someone else's mess. Whatever the conversation was about earlier, it was not for my ears. They worked systematically, as a unit, reinstating order, a job that they had probably done hundreds of times; a woman of Asian extraction, a white (English?) woman and, the one I knew slightly, a woman of Irish descent. They were not old: young women, maybe one nearing middle age, and all in the uniform of domestics – the overall, rubber gloves, hair pinned back to keep it from falling over your face as you bent and scrubbed or hoovered – the diaspora workforce of various origins (that fluidity of boundaries) and quite clearly, working class. Very probably, they had other jobs to go to when they left this one – two or three part-time jobs, to 'make ends meet'. Were they being quiet on my account, not wishing to disturb my work? Were they intimidated by my presence? Were there things that they simply did not want me to hear? I tried not to watch them work; they tried not to watch me. Of course, they were women doing 'women's work'; those feminist readings were nudging me, reminding me. And I should not really have been there and was in their way. I offered to go. 'No, no need.' They would have cleaned around me, but I got up and shifted everything to the other end of the room, the now clean bit. The best I could manage was to thank them when they had finished. But why and for what?

That woman academic's remark was symptomatic of the powerful supposition that class no longer matters in any significant sense, that it belongs to the past, is at best a historical curiosity. But then, looking back risks nostalgia, and nostalgia, we are often reminded nowadays, is a bad thing. This represents an oddly undialectical approach to the topic: as Raymond Williams pointed out long ago in the pages of *The Country and the City*, nostalgia can be politically *enabling* as well as potentially *dis*abling. Memory, or what I have called in chapter 4 'nostalgic memory', represents a symbolic act of recovery, so in this context, negotiating nostalgia is a necessary thing: in fact, the only alternative to this – as Walkerdine implies – might well be silence. Joanne Lacey is insistent on the viability of personal narratives and 'memory-texts', which in turn can illuminate wider structures and questions around class identity and difference; and she contends that working-class academics should continue 'to rework the tension between Marxism, political economy and the study of social class in Cultural Studies . . . making class matter again'.[31] Some feminist writers whom she credits with accomplishing this (some of those I mention above) draw on a range of approaches to explore these questions, including aspects of poststructuralism to posit class as, among other things, 'performance'. This might offer interesting insights on subjectivity, though I am not completely certain that this emphasis alone can help class 'to matter again'. I find the idea of 'passing', for instance, finally weak and inadequate for exploring configurations of class. Thus, as Beverley Skeggs points out, 'class passing rarely works, where sexual passing frequently does'.[32] Class cannot be reduced to its performances, nor 'reduced to surface inscriptions of ritual and repetition, and it cannot be subverted by parody'.[33] Meanwhile, the politics of recognition or difference (or the dominant ideology known as identity politics) disenfranchises class through its embeddedness in the discourse of individualism and its curious sense of closure, a kind of essentialism it seeks at other times to disparage.

But here a curious paradox begins to emerge, recently highlighted by Andrew Milner in his book, *Class*. The paradox is that the new movements which constitute identity politics, and which have tended to eclipse concerns of class in the present, are grounded materially in class interests. Milner concedes that feminism, ideas of ethnicity and the gay movement have 'effected a quite unprecedented "decentring" of traditional (white, straight, male, middle class) cultural authority' – and he is quite correct to suggest that this is a good thing, too. Yet these movements are empowered by a professional, well-educated middle class in whose interests they are developed. They are, in fact, what Milner denotes as 'middle-class movements'. And, like all dominant classes, they disclose a blindness, a symptomatic silence, with regard to their own social positioning. These movements, with increasing influence in governmental circles and in key cultural institutions, 'derive their primary identities from an intelligentsia which is itself socially privileged'.[34] If Milner is correct that this shift has been driven by a class fraction located in the middle class, his argument finds echoes in bell hooks's recent remarks that 'the class-based academicization of American feminism created the context for its deradicalization and for the takeover of gender studies [and we could add ethnic studies to this] by opportunistic men and women who were simply not interested in radically changing society'.[35] There is no attempt to alter the social order fundamentally, but there is a call for recognition within it, and if that recognition and participation generally occur through processes of market commodification and consumption, then so be it.

II Screening class: recent film and representations of the British working class

So far I have considered how class might be spoken in autobiographical (or hybrid-autobiographical) writing, with its pertinent tropes of memory and remembering, its interrogation of gender categories and its inscriptions of the experiential as a mode of cognitive mapping. But what of other regimes of representing the working class?

When the subject of social class – which is used generally as a synonym for working class – comes on to the political agenda it is in the form of pathologization: a problem. In cultural theory (postmodern in hue) it belongs to the quartet of race/class/gender/sexual orientation and thus becomes the sin of 'classism'. Terry Eagleton has offered a plausible critique of this position.[36] It is a way of seeing class as an unequivocally bad thing, which to a large degree Marx also believed. But he saw class as a good thing too, as it constituted the motor-force of history. And, of course, it was the economically exploited working class who represented the agents of change and the gravediggers of capitalism. There is a long tradition of writing about the working class within this context, and one obvious example explored later is the writing and representation from the 1930s, a period of class polarization and class politics. It is one, it needs to be noted, that warrants only a kind of ghostly presence haunting current commentaries on the working class. Aside from this position seeming enormously 'old hat' at the moment (it appears that few Marxists embrace the notion seriously any longer), there are, of course, good historical (as well as theoretical) reasons for the omission.

In a recent article, Roger Bromley touches on some of these reasons and this brings us in many respects to the central concerns of this book. The background to his argument, and its exploration of representations of the British working class in film, is the Thatcherite 1980s, a period which saw the relation between capital and labour (to use the old language for a moment) alter fundamentally in favour of the former. A radical remaking of the British working class got under way with the election of Thatcher's Conservative government in 1979, as the country's industrial base was eroded and the lived experience of whole communities (particularly in the north of Britain) was transformed rapidly. Some of these developments form the central themes in chapter 2, where I examine a range of writing concerned with these historic changes, focusing in particular on Alan Bleasdale's highly successful television drama, *Boys from the Blackstuff*, seeing the work as a seminal text which defines and explores this altering working-class landscape. These newly emergent conditions, in fact, represented an important determining factor influencing the end of class debate in Britain, as elsewhere. As might be expected, a good deal of working-class writing from this period encodes a deep pessimism as a response to the defeats of Thatcherism and the disintegration of working-class communities based around steel, coal, shipbuilding and textiles. In this restructuring class formations alter, but do not disappear. Yet, as Bromley insists, class is the resounding silence in all contemporary political debate, revealing itself instead, if ambiguously, in popular film. Contemporary British society, variously labelled 'Blair's Britain', or 'Cool Britannia', lays claim to the status of a meritocracy, replacing old privilege and those limits set in place by class structures. Our rulers invent a new language to reinterpret the presence of poverty and exclusion. In the thrall of technological determinism (entranced by the 'new' economy meant to transcend 'old' manufacturing and, somehow, the capital/labour relationship), captive to globalization (enabling the language of inevitabilism or, rather, the old

Thatcherite mantra of 'no alternative'), Blairism invokes a classless society operating, paradoxically enough, through the hegemony of middle-class values, driven by laissez-faire economics. In this context, working-class identity re-emerges in any significant sense only in certain key films from the period: it is here, Bromley suggests, that 'class-belongingness', though hesitant and unsure, constitutes a powerful structure of feeling. The films in question are *Ladybird, Ladybird* (1994), *Brassed Off* (1996), *The Full Monty* (1997) and *My Name is Joe* (1998). Bromley contends that the tentative representations of class found here, and in particular class relations, stem from the increasing difficulty in figuring these relations in terms of available representational strategies: historical change has rendered the given set of conventions used to talk about this no longer appropriate in current conditions, when the 'enemy' is invisible. The 'unrepresentability' of the ruling class (or power bloc) has obvious ramifications for any understanding of the condition of class consciousness: how do groups become class conscious without some sure and stable identification of the Other? The argument is similar to the one laid out by Fredric Jameson some time ago in his 'Class and Allegory in Contemporary Mass Culture', hence Bromley brings a symptomatic reading to the films under discussion.

Bromley's article touches on many of the concerns I develop in greater depth in later chapters: in particular, issues around the importance of historical change in the altering forms and conventions for narrating class. For Bromley, a major question to address at this stage is how one talks about *the* working class, in a period of class fragmentation and remaking. Bromley suggests that Ken Loach attempts to deal with this by introducing a subtle shift of emphasis in his work, which involves a 'move away from any attempt to depict *the* working class' to a focus upon 'a social issue or problem confronted by "negatively privileged" individuals for whom their class position is a crucial dimension of their experience'.[37] Frequently then workers are seen as work*less*. We know by now the reasons for this: capital flight to locations where labour is cheaper, profits greater. The images proffered by the films tend, then, to be profoundly negative; characters struggle to find, or re-state, an identity coming 'under erasure' (we will find similar structures of feeling in the narratives of James Kelman in chapter 4). The figures who occupy the housing estates in Loach's films,

Bromley describes as 'social victims';[38] or viewed from another angle they are close to the underclass category pinned on them by sociologists of the Right (and not only the Right, it might be added), who prefer this terminology to the more accurate description of working-class poor. Chris Haylett argues that in the term 'underclass' lies the objective to divide and rule: 'distinctions between groups of working-class people is the key tenet of the hegemonic discourses of the underclass . . . the deserving and the undeserving, the married couple and single parent, the male and the female, the young and the old'.[39] What we witness in the films is an exploration of powerlessness, an inability to nail the 'enemy', because they are camouflaged by the servants of the state. Struggles are carried out in opposition to those agencies who *manage* (social workers, for instance, in *Ladybird, Ladybird*), controlling and coercing institutions which legitimate the dominant order at the same time as they operate to alleviate the costs of its domination.

The tensions involved in the explorations of working-class identity here are necessarily inflected by issues of gender. As I have shown, one major strength of the recent work by scholars which has attempted to address class has been the attempt to examine the intersection of class with other identities of race, gender and sexuality. Bromley's concern lies with masculinity, especially in relation to the two films *Brassed Off* and *The Full Monty*. One major fallout of de-industrialization, flexibility and the casualization of the workforce has been a radical shift in the demarcation of gender roles within the working class. It is perhaps the central thematic concern of *The Full Monty* and a significant subtext in *Brassed Off*. Signifiers of working classness permeate both films; they are strongly gender-loaded in terms of working-class manhood and ideas of work, and they are written as somehow 'residual'. Men are seen as occupying enclosed or empty spaces – the fraternal comfort/compensation of the band-room in *Brassed Off*'s mining community, derelict steelworks in *The Full Monty*, where the redundant men 'work out'. Paid work is absent, or about to be: working-class masculinity can no longer be reaffirmed in older codes linked to collective agency within the public sphere, and the 'unspoken' of these films becomes not merely the tensions present for understanding working-class identity, but the future direction and prospects of class politics in the new dispensation. It is by no means insignificant that in both films the men are seemingly forced in the end to become simply consumerist spectacles. I will return to this later.

Gender and class, then, are inseparably linked in any understanding of subjectivity. In Glen Creeber's close analysis of the Gary Oldman film *Nil by Mouth* (1997), he focuses on working-class masculinity/machismo, viewing the film from within the context of British cinema and social realism, invoking what he identifies as the dominant aesthetic of the 'male norm'.[40] The relevance to Bromley's analysis is obvious, I think. The 'male norm' refers to the tradition of film about the working class dating back to the late 1950s and 1960s: the New Wave and 'social problem' films of the period which took as their central thematic emphasis aspects of working-class life. I discuss in chapter 2 some of the literature of this period, out of which a number of these films emerge. Terry Lovell has stated, '[t]he basis on which the British New Wave staked its cinematic claims was a realism defined in terms of its working-class subject, and a more open treatment of sexuality'.[41] However it is from the perspective of the male working-class subject that the narrative is organized; female subjectivity is subordinated to male desire and fantasy. Women are positioned as 'enablers': either as sexual object and conquest, or comforter and nurturer. According to Creeber, *Nil by Mouth* differs in significant ways. Ostensibly, the film sets out on the 'male norm' pattern, figuring male characters as central, subordinating women to this male gaze – or, in the case of this film, *rage*. But the aggressive male culture which defines the early part of the film is undermined as the narrative unfolds and, collectively, the female characters take control of their own lives. Consequently, the film prompts a consideration of the culturally constructed nature of working-class masculinity, at the same time showing female characters claiming 'space and the power to overturn and reinvestigate the narrative through which they would have been previously constructed and contained'.[42] By initially prioritizing the male trajectory, then dismantling it, a female working-class voice emerges, marginalizing the 'male norm'.

In *Nil by Mouth*, all this takes place within the domestic sphere (or the domain of culture: the social club/pub). Work is not an issue: Ray's vicious aggression and alcohol dependency Creeber links to little more than an 'oppressive male culture', where the character seemingly defines himself in relation to anything 'feminine' (women, gays). In early social realism films of the New Wave, work remained significant in defining identity for the working-class male, as it does in *The Full Monty* and *Brassed Off*. So, in these films, male authority is shattered by economic restructuring: essentially it is in this way that gender roles are disturbed, even reversed. In *Brassed Off*, it is the miners' wives who picket to save the jobs and the community; when this fails, it is a woman again (the insider/outsider, Gloria) who provides the necessary capital to enable the band to compete in the finals in London. In *The Full Monty*, the gender reversal is at times almost surreal (women piss standing up!); they are the breadwinners who enjoy nights out at the club entertained by male strippers. Of course, all this is in an important sense recuperated at the end of the film, with the men's reinstatement at centre stage at the working-men's club; this makes *The Full Monty* a more problematic film, ideologically, than *Brassed Off* (though highly entertaining). An emphasis on community resistance (if somewhat residual) is the active structure of feeling evident at the end of *Brassed Off*. This is defined or established in *displaced* class antagonisms: the north/south divide; the metropolitan/periphery border; the geopolitics of place/space. In fact, the end of the film represents an attempt at what Fredric Jameson labels 'cognitive mapping': we see closing shots of Big Ben and the Houses of Parliament as 'Land of Hope and Glory' plays ironically in the background, and as the closing credits tell of the number of jobs lost in mining since 1984 (an almost Brechtian alienating device). Here, the audience obtains a glimpse of the power bloc which oversaw and instigated economic reconstruction and the decimation of communities. As a class analysis this is no doubt inadequate and pessimistic: it reinforces Bromley's suggestion of the 'unpresentability' of the bourgeoisie in postmodern capitalism and the dissolution of working-class identity and political formation. But Bromley's view that the film 'suggests no continuities', but is 'an end-stopped, terminus film',[43] a film that is an epitaph to a dying way of life, misses some important points. The film's 'double ending' suggests two things: rejecting the prize in the brass-band finals tells us that the miners and their culture are unwilling to become mere heritage spectacles, icons of an industrial past; secondly, the route past the Palace of Westminster, while speaking evasively and ambiguously about class power and its figuration, also compels us to rethink class struggle for the future (it would have been far more appropriate to take this trip through London's financial centre, however).

Other points need to be made, too, about both films, in terms of imputed audience reception. Raymond Williams's term 'structure of feeling' — which is to do with modes of reception as much as with textual production and cultural analysis — remains acutely relevant here. What made the films successful, it could be argued, is their focus on lived, *historical* experience, rather than political analysis (for which Bromley seems to be asking). As I suggested in relation to *Brassed Off*, there is a residual structure of feeling in evidence — this formation evokes notions of community, or communality, as part of the film's class-belongingness. To a lesser degree the same claim can be made for *The Full Monty*. By the close of this film, the men's 'reinvention' of themselves implies not only their re-emergence or renewed dominance: the working-men's club — itself 'reinvented' by the working-class women — stands also as a metonym for community, identity, place. In both films there is no question that things have changed and will never be the same again, but this does not constitute a 'terminus' point. Change is acknowledged, but within a certain set of continuities. What we need perhaps to consider here, in terms of how the films are read and experienced, is Terry Lovell's idea of the 'pleasure of identification', where she suggests that 'the pleasure of a text may be grounded in pleasures of an essentially public and social kind . . . pleasures of common experiences identified and celebrated in art, and through this celebration, given recognition and validation; pleasures of solidarity to which this sharing may give rise; pleasures in shared and socially defined aspirations and hopes; in a sense of identity and community'.[44] To some extent, this returns us to the earlier discussion of nostalgia: in this case, I would suggest that the nostalgia Bromley attributes to the films represents an act of celebration and affirmation, rather than a valediction, or exercise in sentimentalism.

Williams spoke about structure of feeling as comprising 'dominant', 'residual' and 'emergent' forms. *Brassed Off* and *The Full Monty*, it has been argued, articulate a *residual* structure of feeling. Residual, however, does not imply archaic. Bromley makes this point in a final defence of the films, insisting that they signify that class can now be treated not as some 'obsolete economic classification', but indeed as a condition of 'pre-emergence'.[45] He goes on: '[w]hile appearing to be addressing residual characteristics of class, the films are . . . indicative of emergent symptoms of the contemporary which are "active and pressing but not yet fully articulated" '.[46] Bromley in a sense is flagging up the political unconscious of these films; that problematic which seems to be circling the theme of class politics, class struggle and working-class identity. But another point can be made here about our sense of the residual and ideas of 'pre-emergence'. Residual forms of culture stand in opposition or as alternatives to a dominant culture and formation which will not accommodate the others values or needs. They need not be radical, though they can be. A residual structure of feeling is, nevertheless, what Terry Eagleton calls 'an active element in the present'. Moreover, Eagleton implies that in recent times there 'is an increasingly close interweaving of all three of Williams's categories', in that the 'dominant culture . . . increasingly undermines traditional identities, thus pressurizing the residual to the point where it reappears as the emergent'; stirring 'a movement which in challenging the dominant culture of the present, lays claim to what might lie beyond it'.[47] Both these films to some extent pose the residual in the process of rethinking itself and, potentially, refinding itself as the emergent.

A very evident absence from the films is the question of ethnicity and race, though ideas of national identity are always bound up with conceptions of class, as I argue later in this book. Some might view these narratives as *white* working-class films, in the sense that they present communities which historically were never characterized by a large multi-ethnic presence (this is particularly the case with the south Yorkshire mining community of *Brassed Off*). The cultural politics of race found prominence in the 1980s, fired by a renewed stress on national characteristics and character as part of the ideological matrix that was New Right politics, and I examine this at some length in chapter 5. What Jim McGuigan has described as the 'politicization of difference'[48] on the Left was in part a response to this, but was also the result of a general drift towards positions aligned to the politics of postmodernism. McGuigan suggests that,

> Such discourses, inspired by post-structuralism and deconstruction, share a critique of essentialism in all its manifestations. Specifically, notions of essential race or ethnic identity are rejected. Social reality is

fluid and provisional from this perspective, which has inspired the 'new cultural politics of difference' so admirably theorized in the USA by Cornel West and which has a powerful resonance in the work of British writers like Stuart Hall, Paul Gilroy and Kobena Mercer.[49]

An important critique of categories like 'Englishness' or 'Britishness', as they are articulated in conservative discourse, with their attendant strategies of closure and exclusion, this argument is less persuasive when dealing with the political economy of class, or with associated notions of community or solidarity. This is a development I address in chapter 5, by looking at a range of writing by black writers concerned with the politics of diaspora, hybridity and belonging.

None of the films discussed above necessarily presents an 'imaginary resolution' to the dilemmas experienced by the working-class characters – even *The Full Monty* refuses the suggestion that the men somehow go on to scale the heights of the male-stripper circuit and achieve a kind of fame. And the same is true of *Nil by Mouth*: Val wins some autonomy and respect on her own terms, on her own 'patch', thereby changing herself and the world around her, maybe irreversibly. *Escape*, it seems, is not necessarily an option here, although the theme of escape has been a potent one in much working-class writing and representation, and in theorizing about working-class life. It was there in our earlier discussion on educational mobility – being 'educated out'. It has a powerful resonance in the founding texts of Cultural Studies, Hoggart's in particular, as it has in the fictional works of the late 1950s and 1960s. The wave of British proletarian writing in the 1930s encoded the narrative of escape in terms of emancipation from a purely negative material existence: exploitation, deprivation, shame. The writing spoke of a desire for respectability and recognition: even for social revolution to alter a system which naturalized inequality. Here it was not simply the case of a fortunate individual climbing the ladder, but of a class rising collectively to claim a proper inheritance. Such structures of feeling (intensified by the sacrifices of war) laid the ground for establishing the post-war welfare state; a forceful theme, then, in writing about the working class. But what is this border crossing meant to signify? In purely material terms, a chance to better yourself economically, perhaps. Aspirations: the parents' hopes for their children – a 'better' life; away from the council estate that carries the stigma of failure – what Diane Reay has referred to as 'negative emplacements'.[50] Here, then, is the sense of place or space as circumscribed: places marked out in dominant culture as 'Other', and lived and experienced in a condition of alienation by those within. The intensity of the metaphor as it has been applied to working-class life – one is rarely literally escaping, unless it is from an abusive relationship of some kind – speaks to some considerable degree of loss or fear, but also of shame and humiliation. It legitimates one mode of existence, as it maligns another. More often than not the trope of escape emphasizes the individual (often seen as special) over the collective, or class: this being the mode of life from which it is necessary to liberate oneself. Looking at this particular representation of working-class life – the escaper paradigm – I will close by examining that most recent contribution to the form, the hugely successful film *Billy Elliot*.

The film is set in a mining village in County Durham during the miners' strike of 1984–5. At the centre of the film is eleven-year-old Billy Elliot, son of a striking miner. During a boxing lesson Billy becomes fascinated by a ballet class conducted in the same hall: he joins in and shows real talent which is then fostered – against his father's wishes – by the ballet teacher, Mrs Wilkinson. She secretly prepares him for an audition for the Royal Ballet School (and by implication, for his ticket out of the strike-torn world where he lives). Having seen Billy dancing with his friend Michael in the village hall, Billy's father comes to recognize his son's talents and determines that he should attend the audition, even if it means strike-breaking to raise the fare. To prevent him from doing this, his fellow strikers raise the money between them: Billy goes south, is successful and, in the final scene, some fifteen years on, Dad and brother Tony travel to London to see him perform in *Swan Lake*.

This film has much in common with both *Brassed Off* and *The Full Monty*, and stands in that tradition of British social realist films dating back to the 1960s – in fact it quite subtly references Ken Loach's *Kes* on more than one occasion: the relationship between the two brothers, the scene where Billy steals a library book, even (to stretch it a bit) in the significance of *flight*. As with *Brassed Off* and *The Full Monty*, themes of masculinity, working-class identity and community are important. And, as with those films, *Billy Elliot* focuses on the culture industries (rather than the 'traditional' industries) as a way for the working class to refind or, rather, reinvent itself. To do this Billy will have to enter the more privileged spaces of the middle class: acquire the cultural capital which will enable him to reap dividends on his innate skills and talent. Sport, a traditional escape route for the working-class kid, is replaced by 'art', high culture substituted for low, though there is a definite sense that the film sets out to deconstruct this binary, as it sets out, too, to problematize ideas about masculinity and the 'male norm'. Thus, at the close of the film, as Billy warms up in the wings prior to performance, boxing and ballet merge.

Notably, however, it is the working-class *individual* – something the title of the film reinforces – who occupies the central focus of this working-class narrative of refashioning. Billy is the exceptional individual who, in a theme that goes back at least to Lawrence, can fully express himself only outside the stifling confines of the enclosed and embattled community. Though Billy's story could quite easily have been set in the present (as much as at any time in the past, for that matter), choosing to set it during the miners' strike seems only to emphasize the imperative of escape from an aggressive and disintegrating landscape – the 'negative emplacement' referred to earlier. In some respects the strike is the exotic backdrop in which Billy defines his Otherness, only connecting ambiguously with the cross-dressing Michael, as they stand isolated in a world of male violence and threat. That Michael learnt his cross-dressing from his father is a good joke, but the total absence of his father or mother in the film further accentuates the boy's isolation, or *difference*, as well as the sense that here is a culture that cannot nurture, and that the good, the true life, must lie elsewhere. In many respects this typifies the escaper paradigm in some forms of working-class writing and representation: Billy becomes emblematic of the necessity to escape the restricted codes of working-class life. Amid the aggression, there is also a kind of *muteness* about this culture, it is inert: Billy's father seems unable to express emotions that are clearly damaging him, the grandmother has trouble putting together a single, coherent sentence and Billy's brother tends to resort to angry, helpless tirades or demands for silence from his brother. On one level there are evident reasons for these behaviours – the death of Billy's mother, the tensions of the strike, the onset of senility in the old woman. But these all contribute to a certain sense of closure, which represents far more powerfully the terminus point suggested by Bromley in his discussion of *Brassed Off*. Billy escapes south to become William, the film jumps fifteen years, and we never come to learn how well he negotiated his border crossing (we assume he did OK), or how the community he left behind coped with economic and social decay. Recoding the escaper paradigm to suit postmodern times conveys the 'New' Labour message of meritocracy and classlessness as the film's overriding ideological point of view.

Arguments that class no longer counts have always constituted a position taken by those usually unaffected by its exclusions and deprivations. As Diane Reay points out, 'contemporary discourses of both widespread social mobility and classlessness are myths which operate to ensure dominant class hegemony and perpetuate social inequalities'.[51] This introduction has examined conditions and arguments which have signalled the demise of class, while pointing to significant works which have, in different ways, attempted to contest this position. I have suggested that analysing the importance of the lived experience of class can illuminate our understanding of the complexity of class identities. Raymond Williams once argued that there was 'no getting beyond class politics', and that the issues raised by new social movements would inevitably lead 'into the central systems of the industrial-capitalist mode of production and . . . its system of classes'.[52] But it is important now (and possibly always was) to understand class identity in a plural sense – as *identities*. Class is complex, class changes, class is multidimensional. The reifying of class – *the* working class – or seeing class merely as an economic category or, for that matter, as essentially a cultural identity, have been contributing factors in the rejection of class from much contemporary debate: here has been an easy exit sign for those who do not want to 'do class' any more. An understanding of working-class identity and experience has to be firmly grounded in an acceptance of this multidimensionality, of the fact of class altering over time and in space. Yet incorporating an awareness of the 'reality that classes are internally stratified along race, gender and ethnic lines',[53] need not mean succumbing to the logic of *difference*, but striving instead for reciprocal modes of identification in the construction of complex solidarities.

In the concluding part of this introduction I will outline in greater detail the specific contents of the subsequent chapters. Chapter 1 provides a broad overview, focusing on representations of class at two important historical conjunctures, and this provides a necessary historical backdrop for my later analysis. The 1930s saw a surge of working-class writing, often by working-class people, as a response to the political developments of the time, and to the harsh socio-economic conditions characterizing the period. I look at some of the literary responses to such conditions by proletarian, or working-class, writers, including Robert Tressell, Lewis Jones, Walter Brierley, Ellen Wilkinson, Walter Greenwood and Lewis Grassic Gibbon. Certain tropes and themes emerge as dominant and sometimes conflicting structures of feeling: the tension between the individual and the collective, the metaphorical and literal exploration of the idea of entrapment, the significance of work and its absence, representation of gender difference and, finally, what I perceive to be the dichotomy between radicalism and reform found in many of these texts.

'Affluence and after' flags up the second section of the chapter, and offers an analysis of working-class representation following the wake of the Second World War. I examine the post-war affluence debate as a main thematic concern. This is influenced by some of the central arguments explored by John Hill in his book, *Sex, Class and Realism*, a consideration of the British New Wave films of the 1950s and 1960s. Richard Hoggart's *The Uses of Literacy* will be a central text here, with its influential take on the altering nature of British post-war working-class life, or structures of feeling. The work of Raymond Williams, and the fiction of Colin MacInnes, John Braine, Alan Sillitoe and others will be used to examine the influential position outlined in Hoggart's thesis. The significance of this focus is that it not only enables an exploration of some key working-class fictional writing of the period, writing which both affirms and contests the discourse of affluence, but it also provides space to address the importance of Williams and Hoggart in contemporary understandings of class and class formations and this will then partly inform the subsequent sections of the book.

Chapter 2 uses a range of fiction writing from the 1980s to explore working-class experience, and this work will highlight what I perceive to be some of the central themes governing writing about working-class life during this time, themes I pursue in greater depth in subsequent chapters. The chapter then stands as a lengthy preamble to the long final section of the book. An emergent theme will be a sense of loss and fragmentation, a profound response to socio-economic change, articulated most vividly in the massively popular television drama by Alan Bleasdale, *Boys from the Blackstuff*. I analyse this text alongside writing by Tony Harrison and Barry Hines. To illuminate these themes, I expand some of the major theoretical insights of Raymond Williams, positions already employed in earlier analysis, though here and in later chapters I seek to position the relevance of Williams's ideas to formations of gender and race.

Chapter 3 looks at a range of writing which deals with what we might refer to as the spatial displacement of working-class experience. This is to do with representations which articulate the disorganization of working-class life and community in the shape of urban redevelopment, and most profoundly through processes of de-industrialization. Hence, a sub-theme will be that of work, which in turn provides a focus on representations of working-class men in the context of 'worklessness', figured within what is often seen as the empty public sphere of the post-industrial landscape. My main focus of attention will be the writing of James Kelman, but I also look at work by Irvine Welsh and Christopher Meredith.

The key theme in chapter 4 will be the 'feminization' of working-class writing. Pat Barker's early novels are central to the chapter, suggesting that the trope of memory plays a vital part in her work and in her desire to recover through fiction hidden female histories and working-class subjectivities. Annette Kuhn has argued suggestively that '[m]emory work is a method and practice of unearthing and making public untold stories'.[54] Such representations can articulate 'the lives of those whose ways of knowing and ways of seeing the world are rarely acknowledged, let alone celebrated, in the expressions of a hegemonic culture'.[55] A similar point is made by Carolyn Steedman, in her important *Landscape for a Good Woman*, which I read alongside these novels, seeking to examine and insist upon the central importance of gender in considerations of working-class subjectivity.

The 1980s in particular witnessed the emergence of black and Asian film-makers intent on exploring black experience in Thatcher's Britain. This was accompanied by new theoretical perspectives within the discourses of post-colonialism and postmodernism, emerging as the 'politics of difference'. Race and ethnicity here become central concerns in understanding identity, and my aim in the final chapter is to consider the dialectic of race and class within the specific context of 1980s Britain. The cultural fictions examined there include film, the novel and autobiography, seeking to explore how working-class experience and working-class identities are filtered through ideas of national belonging and of race. At the same time I attempt to contest some of the positions developed within 'the politics of difference', highlighting their often contradictory relation to class, and suggest instead the development and nurturing of what I referred to earlier as complex solidarities, as a way of confronting the challenges ahead.

1
'Unbending the springs of action': from poverty to affluence in the narrating of class

This chapter lays the foundations for later discussions of individual texts from the 1980s and 1990s. There are two main aims: first, to establish some of the wider socio-historical conditions shaping the narratives of class discussed here; second, to define the thematic concerns, narrative devices and textual orientations characterizing the writing. As my overall emphasis is on post-war class narratives, I present here a rather attenuated discussion of 1930s' proletarian fiction. This is not to undervalue its significance as a formation of literary work; indeed, it is as good an example as it is possible to find of counter-hegemonic discourses oriented to social change. Here the work from that decade helps to illuminate important and, to an interesting extent, recurring problematics in working-class fiction and representations of class. Primarily, it serves as a significant marker of some of the fundamental changes perceived to have taken place in the experiences of working-class life between the period of the 'Hungry Thirties' and the 'Age of Affluence'.

I Revolution or reform: from the 'painters' bible' to proletarian fiction

Any discussion of literature which takes as its focus the British working class would have to acknowledge the importance of one novel in particular in the 'canon' of working-class writing: Robert Tressell's *The Ragged Trousered Philanthropists* (1914). Tressell's novel, described by one critic as the 'master-narrative' of working-class fiction,[1] opens with a manifesto statement in which the author outlines his intentions for writing the book. Tressell's purpose 'was to present . . . a faithful picture of working-class life – more especially of those engaged in the building trade – in a small town in the south of England', exploring class relations and class difference, and describing the workers' 'circumstances when at work and when out of employment; their pleasures, their intellectual outlook, their religious and political opinions and ideals'.[2] Here, Tressell's concern is with representations – 'faithful' ones – and this preoccupation is evident throughout the novel, with specific reference to the place and the politics of culture. As Gary Day has suggested, the 'relation of culture to a possible politics of change is a key element in *The Ragged Trousered Philanthropists*', and the novel foregrounds the significance of representations through the way the *Daily Obscurer* and the *Daily Chloroform*, in the articulation of ideas and attitudes, are seen to influence the workers' ways of seeing the world.[3] As one of the main aims of the novel is 'to indicate what I believe to be the only real remedy'(p. 13) for poverty and unemployment – namely, socialism – the narrative endeavours to expose the ideological work of the capitalist press in preventing this outcome, and in the process to put forward alternative stories in its place. The novel itself fulfils this function of course, in its writing and dissemination; but Tressell also employs the strategy within the text's structure, in the shape of young Bert's presentation to family members and friends of his 'Pandorama'. Here a story of exploitation unfolds for the reader, mocking notions of 'Merry Hingland', while exposing how 'Thirteen million of peoples in England [are] always on the verge of starvation' (p. 303). Contrasted to this are the fine banqueting halls of Europe and England, and these representations of class relations operate to 'show that this is not the ordering of providence, but a particular economic arrangement'.[4]

Tressell's text is remarkable in the way it deconstructs the dominant paradigm of the bourgeois novel, appropriating the form and reworking it to articulate working-class experience and feelings, through a discontinuous narrative interrupted by anger, sentiment, lectures and didactic role-play. For Raymond Williams, this constitutes the text's radicalism, the innovations 'sitting uneasily with the other writing, but there it is, extraordinarily successful . . . [narrative] interventions which do what, to this day, the fiction books tell you you can't do'.[5] Thus, *The Ragged Trousered Philanthropists* offers an exemplary depiction of the potential for radical working-class resistance; but it is also a narrative which speaks with exasperation of a perceived conservatism within workers' culture which thwarts this agency. Tressell shows the dispossessed as partly agents of their own dispossession, downtrodden by economic conditions, while in thrall to ideological forces intent on pacifying them. Conflict and conciliation constantly pull against each other throughout the novel. If it is the metatext of working-class fiction, it is one, however, which resists idealization of its subject, refusing any easy narrative resolution to the issue of class consciousness, and leaving the path clear for other writers – either of working-class origin or not – to solve the riddle of history.

Wim Neetens argues that the overriding objective behind Tressell's project was to challenge dominant representations of the British working class extant in a range of discourses throughout the Edwardian period, and he suggests that the novel stands as 'an example of how a fictional text may become a vital part of a popular political consciousness on the side of counter-hegemony'.[6] Stedman Jones has pointed to a renewed interest and concern with working-class life at the turn of the twentieth century; a concern driven by fear and anxiety signifying, for Jones, the deepening existential divide between the increasingly affluent middle-class and the London poor. Thus he writes of the 'slum literature' of social explorers, who set out to discover the nether regions, the 'abyss', in which the working class live 'unknown', virtually unknowable, lives:

> Knowledge and rumours about the conditions of the working class came not from personal experience, but from parliamentary enquiries, from the pamphlets of clergymen and philanthropists and from the sensational reports to be found in the press. From these reports it could be learnt that workers were infidels, politically seditious, immoral and improvident.[7]

Paradoxically, however, his argument attempts to dispel this ostensible threat. Though workers consistently rejected middle-class attempts to 'civilize' them during this period, the working-class culture which did develop was, for Stedman Jones, in any case one which was not politically combative, but instead was characterized by 'an enclosed and defensive conservatism'.[8] Some of this conservatism is certainly echoed in Tressell's novel – in fact, in the very title. In particular, what Stedman Jones identifies as the culture of consolation – the private sphere of leisure or the home – earns sustained rebuke in the *The Ragged Trousered Philanthropists*, as the workers are distracted by the pub, gambling and the gutter press from understanding the real conditions of their existence.

Much has been written on this novel in recent times, so I will not dwell on it in detail here. My interest is in the way it depicts the working-class subject, and particularly the way the narrative understands, or reflects, the importance of discursive struggle in the field of culture. We could argue that one factor, which does indeed render the novel the master-text of working-class fiction, is its absolute insistence on class struggle as the driving force of social and political life, and the innovations the author sets in place to articulate this structure of feeling. Such a perspective, of course, radically determines the way Tressell represents the working class as the revolutionary subject in waiting. Clearly, not all working-class writing, nor writing about the working class, approaches its subject in the same way.

Indeed, according to Peter Keating, it has been generally at times of social and economic distress that 'any significant number of English novelists have attempted to write fiction centred upon working-class life.'[9] Keating refers to the middle-class novelists of the nineteenth century who used the novel form to explore the question of class and class conflict, attempting to articulate what Williams called 'knowable communities' in rapid transition as a result of the Industrial Revolution. My purpose here is to examine representations of the British working class – mostly by writers from the working class, or with working-class origins – at two key historical moments in the *twentieth* century: the Depression period of the 1930s, and the span of years from the late 1950s and into the 1960s which came to be termed by commentators the 'Age of Affluence'. The working-class presence earned high levels of attention during these periods, though for contradictory and contrasting reasons.

The Hungry Thirties, as they came to be known, stand as a period when the politics of class was given much prominence as a result of a deep and enduring economic crisis, so that much of the iconography of class – whether in fiction, ethnography or political discourse – was often inscribed in antagonistic or dichotomous terms. This sentiment was expressed even within the political establishment; a young Harold Macmillan, surveying the social and political terrain of the 1930s, commented:

> Now, after 1931, many of us felt that the disease was more deep-rooted. It had become evident that the structure of capitalist society in its old form had broken down . . . The whole system had to be reassessed. Perhaps it would not survive at all . . . Something like a revolutionary situation had developed.[10]

The anxiety spoken in this comment echoes a widespread unease, whether warranted or not, of social upheaval; open social conflict seemed a genuine possibility. That such tensions found articulation in the literature of the period did not satisfy everyone. Indeed contemporary commentators found it difficult to regard such writing as 'literature' at all. In an article written for *Scrutiny* in June 1940, surveying the literary scene of the previous ten years, F. R. Leavis concluded that it had been 'a very barren decade'.[11] The 1930s had failed to produce anything to match the genius of T. S. Eliot or D. H. Lawrence, instead bequeathing a literature marred by 'political distraction', which proved 'very bad for creative work'.[12] The article evinces a familiar and insistent division between politics and art, and Leavis's blanket judgement anticipates all those later assessments that came to regard the period in general as a 'low dishonourable decade'. Leavis was not alone in his emphasis. George Orwell, writing on the inimical effects of politics upon literature – Orwell equates the Party-line with politics – reduces the writing of the period to propaganda. A misguided capitulation to Marxist dogma had resulted in 'practically no fiction of any value at all'. Moreover, Orwell adds with characteristic hyperbole, 'no decade in the past one hundred and fifty years has been so barren of imaginative prose as the nineteen-thirties'.[13] For some commentators, then, it seems that by the decade's end the wide variety of literature produced during the thirties could be effectively written off, as it was to be later by some who were most prominent and productive during the period, most notably W. H. Auden.

In his survey of socialist fiction of the 1930s, H. Gustav Klaus listed something like seventy publications, mostly by working-class writers, despite the inevitable problems of time, education and outlets these writers faced.[14] This writing emerged out of a time of acute hardship and distress, but also during a period when the politics of the Left was beginning to find an audience with large sections of the working class. There emerged a tendency for literature to be harnessed to political ends, as some later critics suggest. Thus narratives exhibit an emergent, and historically produced, structure of feeling, offering representations which in some striking instances contest the period's dominant ideological perspectives, exploring different ways of seeing the place, the potential – in fact, the *fate* – of the working class at this time.

The epigraph to Walter Greenwood's 'Depression novel', *Love on the Dole* (1933), opens: 'The time is ripe, rotten ripe for change. Let it come.' Greenwood's novel has attained something of a classic status in the formation of working-class fiction. Set in Salford, Manchester, the novel tells the story of young Harry Hardcastle's search for work during a period of economic slump; it explores the existential misery which poverty breeds; it reveals the withering of hope produced by conditions seemingly beyond people's control. These themes would preoccupy much working-class writing and representation of this period. In the closed environment of Hanky Park (the novel's setting) work is an absent presence – it exploits the men when the economic cycle is good, and abandons them completely when that cycle takes a downturn. The life of the community is fully determined by these processes, which might be understood (or withstood), but seemingly cannot be challenged or changed.

This level of understanding is articulated in the novel through the male autodidact, Larry Meath, a figure clearly constructed in the mould of Tressell's autodidact hero, Owen. The purpose of the autodidact figure – who emerges in a number of working-class texts at this time – is to enlighten his fellow workers, offering an alternative view of the economic system to the one they have come to accept:

> And to find the cost of the present system you have only to look at your own lives and the lives of our parents. Labour never ending, constant struggles to pay the rent and to buy sufficient food and clothing; no time for anything that is bright and beautiful. This existence is what is fobbed off on to us as life. And Hanky Park is not the whole of

England. In every industrial city of the land you will find such places as this, where such people as us who do the work of the world are forced to spend their days.[15]

This radical epistemology of working-class experience barely registers with the community, however, beyond Harry's rather adolescent hero-worship and his sister Sally's romantic attraction. His fellow workers at the factory regard Larry as a crank. The narrative implies that their real interests lie in gambling and beer, while the local women prefer to consult the oracle to discover what the future holds for them. The problem, then, of class consciousness – which was a major preoccupation of Tressell's *The Ragged Trousered Philanthropists* – becomes a central narrative thread here. Collective mystification thwarts working-class agency; instead they are 'discontented and wondering why they are discontented . . . each putting on a mask of unconcern, accepting his neighbour's mask as his true expression' (p. 24). Larry Meath's death, following a means-test march, sees the voice of 'revolt' and figure of agency effectively silenced altogether, which then compounds this condition, suggesting there is no way out.

Images of entrapment recur throughout the novel. Valentine Cunningham has identified entrapment as a repeated motif in 1930s writing, and he describes *Love on the Dole* as presenting 'a closed economic circle, ending as it began with the knocker-up clattering along at 5.30 a.m. to rouse the people for work'.[16] Individuals and their families must wait for the economic cycle to pick up and for better times. Greenwood's intention, then, seems primarily to be with depicting the working class as victims of an iniquitous, even irrational, system which breaks lives. At this level, the narrative succeeds. One reviewer at the time wrote: 'as a novel it stands high, but it is in its qualities as a "social document" that its great value lies.'[17] Here the novel is viewed from an almost ethnographic perspective, the 'Otherness' of working-class experience depicted in all its abjection.

Love on the Dole stands alongside those nineteenth-century novels of reform in terms of both form and overall structure of feeling. The desire to generate a sympathetic response towards the working class predominates, and this is orientated towards an inferred and attendant middle-class readership with whom agency lies. Hence the stress on individual experience over collective action, a device which dilutes the text's still barely submersible message of the need for radical change, even revolution, to alter what are depicted as almost insupportable conditions of existence. It is working-class women who are then forced to bear the burden of representation. Working-class women emerge in various guises, signifying feisty rebelliousness (Sally Hardcastle) or abject depravity (Helen's mother's crude, almost animalistic, sexuality). That Sally has to prostitute herself by marrying bookie Sam Grundy following Larry's death, thus securing work for both her brother and father, is the novel's ultimate moral condemnation of the economic system. Sally's entrapment, however, differs only in degree from the other women of Hanky Park:

> Slatternly women, dirty shawls over their heads and shoulders, hair in wisps about their faces, stood in groups congregated on the pavements in the shafts of light thrown from the open doors of the public-house. Now and then they laughed, raucous, heedless of the tugs at their skirts from their wailing weary children. (p. 14)

Working-class women, finally, signify the very depths to which working-class life can sink.

Increasingly, for those on the political left during this period, cultural production was viewed as a necessary conduit for raising class consciousness. The Communist-influenced *Left Review* became a key apparatus for the publication of writing about working-class life, with an appeal in 1934 for writing by working-class writers who 'desire to express in their work more effectively than in the past the struggles of their class'.[18] This developing formation of writers was aided, too, by radical publishers like Gollancz and organizations such as the Left Book Club. These interventions into the cultural and political life of Britain constitute what Raymond Williams would call a 'cultural formation' attempting to define alternative and/or oppositional regimes of representation, which contest dominant or hegemonic ones.[19] Greenwood's text falls under the alternative heading: it is deeply critical of the system, but sees no way of altering it. The working class are not agents of their own emancipation, but generally worthy recipients of pity or aid from outside. These structures of feeling emerge in other writing from the period, as do more strictly oppositional stances.

Walter Brierley's *Means Test Man* (1935) is another example of 'Depression literature'. Pamela Fox has identified the theme of class shame as a constitutive and reiterated motif in such writing.[20] Partly, this is the product of the narrative focus on male experience, particularly in the context of unemployment. Exile from the public sphere of work – man's proper place – leads to a crisis of masculinity. Harry Hardcastle's father, and Harry himself, repeatedly echo these feelings. The inference is that without work the male protagonists have no role or function: unemployment in effect 'feminizes' them, suggesting how some aspects and examples of this writing reaffirm gender ideologies as they contest other dominant ideological meanings and representations. Such representations affirm the ideological division between the social and domestic; but this is not always the case. Writing into these narratives the dramatic effects of the means test on working-class lives during the Depression deconstructs this divide. The monthly arrival of the means-test inspector highlights the tensions and the deep resentment this violation engendered in working-class families. C. L. Mowat notes how the means test was 'hated and loathed by the working classes';[21] and George Orwell, in *The Road to Wigan Pier*, says 'the most cruel and evil effect of the Means Test is the way in which it breaks up families'.[22] Walter Brierley's *Means Test Man* (1935) follows Greenwood in depicting the misery of the long-term unemployed. It presents a week in the life of Jack Cook – three years unemployed – and his wife and child. Brierley employs psychological realism to explore the effect of the Cooks' sense of exclusion and entrapment. Two worlds exist, the 'real' world for those with work, and the un-real world which imprisons the unemployed, and the theme of entrapment is once more a key note.

> He was in prison again, freedom and independence mocking him [. . .] He shuddered as he sat by the window. Hemmed in he was, and four walls were the right place for him. He was not ordinary, he had no home, just a place where they let him and his family live and sleep if they could.[23]

Ideas of representation and reality are central to the novel. The 'real world' is mediated through the pages of the daily newspaper, though the front-page headlines – 'Hitler sold storm troops to

France', 'Premier wants to meet with Roosevelt' – seem to have little relevance to Jack's condition. Turning to the inside page he reads on:

> All Made with Remnants article . . . the *Washing Day Adventures of Some Tiny Animals*. Jack turned to the last page and looked at the pictures of Pearly Kings and Queens and donkeys . . . and the picture of a starling sitting on a horseshoe nailed to a post – the illustration to an article on rural things. (p. 148)

There is an absurdist register here: clearly these things have no relevance to Jack's life or the life of his family, and Brierley asks us to question their significance. Thus any normative 'real world' in this novel is almost an 'absent subject'.[24] Despite employing a naturalist mode, *Means Test Man* is not out to reflect the real at all, but to deny the reality on offer through the pages of the press. For some people 'reality' – the reality of newspaper reports, politics, work and social life – simply does not exist outside ideology, therefore highlighting the contradiction between official representations of the 'real', and the actual experience of those excluded from it.

Like Harry in *Love on the Dole*, the withholding of work produces for Jack Cook a moment of existential crisis: 'He had worked there ten years, the place was part of him, he was part of the place . . . It rejected him. Such was infinitely worse than love-rejection, this was being-rejection' (p. 87). For Jack, the crisis is one of masculine identity, too. Since he cannot fulfil the role of breadwinner, his social and psychological alienation is intensified. Jack feels fear and shame, knowing that he may not have the money for medicine for his son, and despairs at the small allowance from the Public Assistance committee, which barely allows them to live. Their Co-op savings-book offers another mode of representation to remind them of their decline: 'the book was the very calendar of their existence for the last three years, showing all the steps down in the losing fight against conditions' (p. 260). Towards the end of the novel, Jack consoles Jane after the visit of the means-test inspector:

> If all the women in England could feel for a minute what you've gone through this morning, there'd be no more of it, no more homes upset.

Still, no one would understand who hasn't gone through it; it's like the war only worse. The women are in the line as well and are being tortured and starved instead of being shot outright. (p. 267)

The book speaks of a state of siege, clearly intent on addressing a much wider audience – 'all the women of England' – and urging change. Contesting prevailing views that unemployment was the result of individual fecklessness, the novel presents the working-class subject as victim of the system. *Love on the Dole* and *Means Test Man* thus centre on a moral critique of the system that produces such hardship, rather than a political interpretation which might provide the insights needed to change it. In Brierley's writing the motif of entrapment paints a 'dark' picture, and the very naming of the two characters – Jack and Jane (and son John) – suggests some gruesome parody of the fairy-tale, one for which a happy ending would be inconceivable. But in the end, what the narratives discussed fail to propose (Tressell aside) is any sense of working-class agency as a way out of the dilemmas facing the working class at this moment in history.

This is addressed in John Sommerfield's *May Day* (1936), 'the best collective novel that we have yet produced in England; the real protagonist is the London working class . . . the true London, smelt, seen and understood'.[25] *May Day* has been described as a 'deliberately de-centred and open work, with only the barest of characterizations, no central plot and hardly a hero to speak of'.[26] The novel covers barely three days, culminating in the factory strike and the May Day march through the London streets. The narrative reach discloses a panoramic view of London, sweeping the rooftops of the city, moving from the working-class East End to the well-heeled in Mayfair hotels, suggesting all the time a sense of connected experience, so that 'Beneath these immediate connections and making sense of them is the structure of social and economic relations which is focused by the involvement of many of the characters, at a variety of levels and in a variety of roles, in one particular factory.'[27]

In *Love on the Dole* the factory represented a negative space, the site of alienation where people suffered as individuals the monotony of machine operating, or from where a person was excluded altogether and left to waste. In *May Day* the factory regulates and determines individual lives in this way, but it is also, crucially, the site of struggle and solidarity, 'magnetic points attracting vast converging streams'.[28] Thus Sommerfield offers two conflicting views of subjectivity – of individuals, and of individuals within, or as part of, the mass. The narrative is concerned to explore the utopian possibilities of the latter position: 'Taken individually they were just a lot of ordinary, silly, laughing girls, some noticeably prettier or uglier than most . . . But also the whole lot of them together shared a group consciousness; beyond their own individuality was their individuality as a mass' (p. 149). This constitutes a different structure of feeling with regard to working-class agency to those examined earlier. The factory owner, Langfier, recognizes the potential strength there; it is one that 'fascinates him and yet one that he half fears – when they are together, in a mass, they exhale a sense of their own power, that deeply disturbs him' (p. 19).

The May Day march is the culminating point of the text; it is when the 'body politic' of the working class finds expression, in an image of collective agency which transgresses the boundaries of bourgeois order in what becomes a reversal of society's power relations. The march, then, represents a celebration in which the ordered body politic of the bourgeoisie is overturned:

> The police have been withdrawn. The marchers have won the streets.
> The blood is running fast in their veins, they feel heroes, still filled with the sharp joy and anger of fighting. They feel something strong within them, something huge and strong, an emotion that transcends their separate individualities and joins them in a single conscious mass. (p. 241)

The narrative remains open and inconclusive to the last. There is no sense of resolution, of a return to familiar ground, old formations. The workers hold the streets, the authorities gaze sternly upon them and the final words are 'Everyone has agreed on the need for a big change' (p. 242). The image produced here contains the idea of the 'utopian impulse' which constitutes a significant feature of such writing, a way of figuring the future. Representations of the working-class protagonist embodied in these modes are produced as much through an emphasis on the writing's 'rhetorical effect' as through any consideration of the 'reality effect' of such tropes. The symbolic value is essential in its articulation of a liberated future time.[29] The utopian impulse in narrative acquires greatest effect when not thwarted or contradicted by subsequent events – such as the degeneration of the potentially liberating protest march into chaos and tragedy in *Love on the Dole* – but allowed to act upon the readership both as a mode of cognition or demystification, and as a politically enabling rhetorical device. In this sense it contributes to the 'pleasure of the text', which I referred to in my introduction, producing possible modes of identification, solidarity and hope and embedding within the representations alternative and oppositional structures of feeling.

Lewis Jones's two mining novels, *Cwmardy* (1937) and *We Live* (1939), set in a Welsh mining district, clearly aspire to this condition. As with Sommerfield and Tressell, we encounter in the work a proletarian and socialist consciousness, derived from Jones's own background as a miner, trade unionist and Communist activist; these determinants ensure that within the writing the 'community, and more crucially the class . . . becomes the central "character" '.[30] In both of Jones's novels the collective finds a voice through common experiences of work and community life. In the foreword to *Cwmardy*, Jones tells us that 'All the events described, though not placed in chronological order, have occurred, and each of them marks a milestone in the lives and struggles of the South Wales miners.'[31] Finding a form to record this history is Jones's objective, and it is largely within the documentary realist mode that the narratives are told. But Jones is not content merely to record these things. Instead the work strives to present 'a powerful image of a possible future society, rather than an accurate record of a society that was'.[32]

Expressing the collective force of the working class is vital to both novels. During the people's march in *Cwmardy*, '[they] lost their individual identities in the vibrating rhythm of the tune which impelled their emotions into expressions through bonds of vocal unity' (p. 154); and these utopian gestures are reproduced in *We Live*, as the villagers gather to march against the means test, 'covering the hills with black waving bodies . . . "Good God," the man next to Mary whispered, "the whole world's on the move"' (p. 243). The utopian impulse predominates, one in which reality and fantasy are collapsed into one another.[33] Constructing the collective in a struggle against political and economic hegemony in this way also represents the real history of the Welsh coalfields during this period. Interestingly, the struggle is not coded as a purely masculine affair. In *Cwmardy* Len complains angrily of hearing his friends 'talk about women exactly as if they were cattle' (p. 202), foregrounding here the politics of gender. In *We Live*, Mary's own political development is described as a series of rational choices, often in tension with the emotional ties linking her to her father (a Labourite, rather than a Communist, as Mary becomes), thus emphasizing the uneasy relationship between the personal and the political, the private and the public sphere. In contrast to Sally in *Love on the Dole*, and Jane in *Means Test Man* – who both, in the end, are made to signify a kind of hopelessness and despair – Mary is at the forefront of political struggle, often, along with the women of Cwmardy, taking the initiative:

> She looked at him and the other women slyly, then replied loud enough for them all to hear: 'The women are going in to see the chief unemployment officer.'
> The men stood stock-still for a moment, amazed at the casualness of the statement and the implications involved in it . . .
> 'You can't do that,' said one . . .
> Mary changed colour . . . 'The Government isn't only a number of people in London. Government is of no use and can't act unless it has agents and officers and staff in every village in the country.' (*We Live*, p. 245)

Mary demonstrates an astute political awareness, and the narrative betrays no specific demarcation of the sexes, no inclination to write women out of the political struggle.

That it is a male author writing Mary into the political struggle in *We Live* is deeply symptomatic of the absence of published working-class women writers during this period. A notable exception to this, however, is Ellen Wilkinson. Her novel, *Clash*, published in 1929, takes as its subject the 1926 General Strike and the effect of the strike on mining communities in particular. Class politics in this novel is resoundingly 'feminized' by placing the central protagonist, Joan Craig, at the heart of the story. Focalized through Joan, the novel offers not only an insight into the course of the strike and its eventual collapse, but a perspective on the politics of class conciliation, or collaboration, itself. Working-class Joan, a trade unionist, has close ties with the mining communities; she is also close to a middle-class Bloomsbury set in London, and embarks on an affair with a member of the group, Anthony Dacre. The novel's romance plot, mobilized to reinforce Joan's central role in the story, also suggests the tensions and sacrifices needed when the personal and the political come into conflict.

In a number of respects the novel is about contesting representations: in this case, the dominant version of the strike, which attempted to represent the strikers as political subversives. Prime Minister Baldwin, on the eve of the action, stated that:

> Constitutional government is being attacked. Let all good citizens whose livelihood and labour have been put in peril bear with fortitude and patience the hardship with which they have been so suddenly confronted. Stand behind your government who are doing their part, confident that you will cooperate in the measures they have undertaken to preserve the liberties and privileges of the peoples of these islands . . . The General Strike is a challenge to Parliament and the road to anarchy and ruin.[34]

Thus Wilkinson, through Joan, exposes the real hardships suffered by workers, the crucial underlying economic motives which had paved the way to 1926.

As the strike gets under way, Joan is joined by Mary Maud, Anthony Dacre and the slightly more class-ambiguous figure of Gerald Blain, who help organize and aid the strikers against the government and the middle-class volunteers who make up the Organization for the Maintenance of Supplies. The narrative's attitude to class politics wavers between a clear class-versus-class stance, to one of class collaboration and/or conciliation. Joan remains the go-between, torn between one side and another, seduced by the bohemianism of Dacre and his set, yet politically drawn to the suffering miners and the working class. This is mirrored in the narrative's alternating shift between a radicalism that pins its hopes on workers' power and a politics of compromise that attempts to accommodate everyone. Yet Wilkinson's understandable tendency to show the miners (the men, at any rate; miners' wives are treated differently) as victims in the end denies their agency, instead tapping into a latent middle-class conscience with representations of (unnecessary) working-class victimhood and suffering. This becomes part of the novel's strategy to educate the middle class about life on the other side of the tracks.

This is reflected in an important moment in the novel which finds Joan putting right the establishment activist, Captain Bowyer-Blundell, on the miners' butty-system. The fifteen pounds per week (he had seen the company's pay cheques, being a shareholder) which Bowyer-Blundell had previously waved triumphantly in Mary Maud's face to disprove assertions of poverty conditions, is put in its proper context by Joan, who goes on to inform the Captain that, as part of the system, the pay cheque will be shared among five men.

> The soldier took it handsomely. 'I grovel, I bow to the judgement of Portia, but honestly, I gave the case in good faith.' 'Of course, I know that', said Joan, sympathetically . . . Bowyer-Blundell was grateful, and the table greatly appreciated the tact which did not follow up an obvious advantage.[35]

In this exchange, Bowyer-Blundell learns the 'truth'; as do the other diners, and so too the readers. By presenting the strike from a perspective foreign to most readers, and by representing the condition of northern working-class life in ways which might undercut prejudices and preconceptions, Wilkinson figures the workers – whether striking or not – as dignified victims, cautious of violent conflict, organized but not doctrinaire. Early in the novel we learn the relative weakness in England of the Communists, or of communist sentiment among the working class: ' "A General Strike . . . ! Things like that don't happen in England. It's not as though the Communists had any influence now, and the best of them are in jail, anyway. British revolutions are made by British churchwardens" ' (p. 9). Any outright revolutionary threat – in the guise of Communist Party activism or workers' control – is shown to be an aberration from, or anathema to, the true nature of the working class. But it is a position not easy to maintain. As Joan begins to see, Labour's constitutional stance (and the Trades Union Congress's acquiescence in it), its acceptance of the status quo and the mechanisms and restraints of the political system, pose a threat to its own activists: not only one of inevitable collaboration but also one of potential betrayal, incorporation or embourgeoisement. But this is displaced somewhat by being couched in terms of the north/south divide: the 'fleshpots' and bourgeois delights of London, as opposed to the 'real' world of the north. This recurring feature in the text implies, among other things, that class is based upon regional differences rather than relational ones. Increasingly, Joan becomes aware of her own compromises, derived from her close attachments in London and with constitutional Labour. In fact this tension is written into the very language she uses: a divide, or split, which manifests itself in the tones and inflections of middle-class London, and the slippages of pronouns which haunt Joan's conscience: 'Already influential London was "we" in Joan's mind . . . She was already unconsciously on the path to those who draw a distinction between "we" and "they"' (p. 250). Gerry Blain, renegade middle-class socialist (slightly along the lines of Barrington in Tressell's *Philanthropists*), explains this to Joan in explicitly class terms:

> you'd become one of their circle. It's not what their class consciously does to the workers . . . It's easy to fight against that, but it's the mass of ideas which they take for granted, the atmosphere they create that is so difficult to fight against . . . All their class privileges are bound up with not being converted [to ideas of socialism], not seeing the ugly truth. You've only two things to do, keep out and fight them, or go in and accept all they have to give – and it's a lot if you are worthwhile. But you can't go in with them and fight them at the same time. (p. 294)

This is a dilemma which Joan must face and, by choosing to marry Gerry Blain, rather than continue her affair with Dacre, it is one, the narrative suggests, which she manages to resolve; combining both the personal and political and maintaining, if a little tenuously, the integrity of both.

Many of the themes and concerns discussed so far come together in striking terms in Lewis Grassic Gibbon's epic trilogy, *A Scots Quair*. *Sunset Song* (1932), *Cloud Howe* (1933) and *Grey Granite* (1934) present the historical transformation of the Scottish people from a rural peasantry into an urban proletariat. In *Sunset Song* we witness the decline of a particular peasant tradition, which leads to the key female protagonist, Chris, moving into the small town of Seggett and to her marriage to a socialist minister, narrated in *Cloud Howe*. *Grey Granite* sees Chris, and her son Ewan, in the industrial town of Duncairn. Gibbon uses the trilogy to document history from below, and is thus centrally concerned – as in those other texts discussed – with challenging dominant representations of reality. Gibbon's trilogy is a work of real complexity and scope, in both form and content, speaking of a radical resistance which insists on the inevitability of class struggle as the motor of historical change. Though I will focus here on the third book of the trilogy, *Grey Granite*, this emphasis runs throughout all three sections. It is highlighted by now familiar devices: protests against the means test and unemployment, strike actions and hunger marches.

The narrative trajectory of *Grey Granite* angles away from Chris as focalizer towards her son, Ewan, and a working-class politics articulated through the Communist Party. Ewan's radicalism can be read as a response to social and economic conditions, dire in Scotland in the 1930s. Initially introduced to socialist ideas by his girlfriend Ellen Johns, he is driven to a closer association with the workers when he witnesses police brutality during the means-test march. Later, arrested by police after leading a strike, Ewan is tortured in the cells. As Ewan comes to experience the real nature of the system, the narrative makes the reader equally aware of the ideological work carried out to uphold the powerful. In *Grey Granite*, Ewan ponders angrily in the city's museum galleries upon those who have been conveniently forgotten by 'official' history:

> Why did they never immortalize in stone a scene from the Athenian justice courts – a slave being ritually, unnecessarily tortured before he could legally act as a witness . . . Why not the head of Spartacus? Or a plaque of the dripping line of crosses that manned the Appian Way with slaves – dripping and falling to bits through long months, they took days to die, torn by wild beasts.[36]

Ewan wants to rewrite the history books; in Walter Benjamin's terms, 'brush history against the grain'.[37] Like Benjamin, too, he recognizes that to survey cultural treasures is to contemplate horror, aware that there 'is no document of civilization which is not at the same time a document of barbarism'.[38]

Alternative, or oppositional, stories are then seen as suppressed by hegemony. Figuring the dispossessed is inscribed in the text dialogically, contesting dominant scripts. In *Grey Granite* the unemployed are seen in the Royal Mile: 'aye plenty of them, yawning and wearied with their flat-soled boots and their half-shaved faces' (p. 368). While the apprentice, Alick, worrying about his future, realizes that 'when his apprenticeship was up . . . they were sacked right off . . . chucked on the Broo' (p. 370). All this while the *'Daily Runner,* the rag . . . said you never looked for work, you that tramped out your guts day on day on the search' (p. 395).

Gibbon saves much of his sarcasm for the press. This is Valentine Cunningham's point, when he argues that proletarian novels 'sought deliberately to oppose the worker's voice to the voice of the undemocratic and hostile media'.[39] We see this, too, in Walter Brierley's implicit disdain for journalistic mystifications and in Tressell's blistering attacks on the press. Gibbon pours vitriol on the machinations of the media, as they misrepresent strike action, means-test marches and police brutality in favour of officialdom. In some ways, in the final two parts of the trilogy, Gibbon allows the medium of journalism to replace the ideology of religion – so remorselessly attacked in *Sunset Song* – as 'the opium of the people'. Towards the end of *Cloud Howe,* as the means test begins to take effect, Gibbon writes:

> Would you find that news in the *Mearns Chief*? The *Chief* said week by week we were fine, and Scotland still the backbone of Britain, and the Gordon Highlanders right gay childes, not caring a hoot though their pay was down, and Progressives just the scum of the earth, that planned to take bairns out of the slums and rear them in godless communes . . . Ay, the *Mearns Chief* was aye up-to-date, and showed you a photo of Mrs MacTavish winning the haggis at a Hogmanay dance. (p. 341)

A report of the police brutality during the means-test march in Duncairn is distorted in the *Daily Runner,* blaming 'the Reds who had fought the bobbies with bottles . . . The poor police had just tried to keep order, to stop a riot, and that's what they got' (*Grey Granite,* p. 397). Representation and reality are in constant conflict. The narrative foregrounds class struggle refracted through language, dialogically inflecting discourse through a bitter irony which laughs at official rhetoric and challenges dominant representations. Debunking the powerful is a utopian impulse too, through which the 'high' are made 'low' and the 'low' lord it over them, in a mode reminiscent of Bakhtinian carnivalesque. Through such rhetorical devices, the reader comes to understand the importance of storytelling and representation, which constitute a vital site of ideological struggle itself. Cairns Craig has argued that 'what Scottish novelists have had to do again and again in recent times is to link their novel to some moment of historical dynamism which intrudes upon the historyless Scottish community: Scotland can only be known through narrative in those moments when narrative possibilities are forced upon a society that has lost all sense of its own narrative.'[40] This necessity may be true not only for Scottish writing, but for representing working-class experience as well; it represents a way of making space for narratives which have been suppressed, silenced or discounted within the dominant culture.

Of the working-class narratives considered here it is Walter Greenwood's *Love on the Dole* which has become perhaps the most successful working-class novel of the period. It is not surprising that one of the least radical novels of the 1930s, in both aesthetic and political forms, should outlive the decade. Both then and now, *Love on the Dole* is more acceptable to the dominant culture and its literary institutions, recuperable to a liberal reading which robs the narrative of any oppositional class discourse. This is not so easily done with some of the other writers considered in this chapter. The work of Tressell, Jones, Sommerfield, Grassic Gibbon and Wilkinson would far more tenaciously resist such readings.

In this section I have attempted to highlight some of the main concerns of some key working-class narratives of the pre-Second World War years. By 1940, George Orwell felt able to proclaim in a radio interview that 'Proletarian literature is mainly a literature of revolt. It can't help being so.'[41] Orwell suggests that such writing constitutes acts of resistance to cultural hegemony, potential alternative or oppositional stories to those dominant within society at the time. As we have seen, this is only partly true. And for Orwell, in the end, it is a passing moment; he foresees English society becoming progressively classless, therefore the working-class writer will have nothing more to write about. This idea of classlessness receives greater articulation in the years following the war; it is to this period we now turn.

II Affluence and After

Since George Orwell published *The Road to Wigan Pier* in 1936, Wigan has changed from barefoot malnutrition to nylon and television, from hollow idleness to flush contentment. In the market-place commerce ('brisk buying and selling') had replaced politics ('angry speakers' and 'hungry listeners'). A former mayor felt that 'the working class have come a long way . . . There's not far to go now.'[42]

That George Orwell's *The Road to Wigan Pier* is the reference point for these observations is not surprising; for many writers on working-class culture, Orwell represented '*the* chronicler of the older northern working-class world of deprivation and poverty against which post-war accounts were to be measured'.[43] Orwell's book was published in the middle of the Depression years, its objective to disclose how the northern working class were coping with hard times. The book took on a hybrid form: part ethnographic survey, part political tract. Contrasting views of working-class life emerged there: from the degraded domestic space of the Brookers' lodging house with 'the full chamber pot under the table', to the warm and cosy comforts of the 'typical' working-class home, with father, in shirt sleeves in his rocking chair, 'reading the racing finals', and mother darning socks by the fire while keeping a watchful eye on the children.[44] Orwell describes the heroic labour of the miners, whom he could not 'watch without feeling a pang of envy of their toughness', and the abject hopelessness of the young Wigan woman he spots from his departing train, 'on the slimy stones of a slum back yard, poking a stick up a foul drain-pipe'.[45] Indeed, some of these perspectives shaped the fiction discussed in the previous section, and Orwell's book is often savage in its condemnation of the poverty experienced and endured by the working class at this time. One purpose of the book is to help eradicate such inequities by exposing them. That people should live this way, Orwell makes clear, is unacceptable; that the working class should possess the self-determination to alter their own conditions, however, is a prospect Orwell's narrative also firmly denies.

The quotation which opens this section was written twenty years after the publication of Orwell's famous tract, but Wigan is used again as the characteristic social landscape on which to define a particular class experience and habitus. But now affluence had arrived, and in terms of consumption we have shifted from 1930s' 'barefoot malnutrition', to 1950s' 'nylon and television'; in terms of politics and economics 'commerce ("brisk buying and selling")' prevails, in place of the want and misery which had prompted those old bogeys 'angry speakers' and 'hungry listeners'. At this historic juncture, with the grinding poverty of the inter-war years – described by Orwell and others – in the past, 'flush contentment' constitutes the overriding structure of feeling of the working class; as a final and unanswerable proof of the facts, the writer/explorer produces a former mayor of the town, a Labour man, who confirms that the workers 'have come a long way . . . there's not far to go now'. Quietly, and without much fuss it seemed that the revolution had arrived.

The previous section examined writing whose main purpose was to insist on the working-class presence; here I examine post-war debates on its disappearance. By the late 1950s the notion of the 'affluent society' had become hegemonic, accepted by many on both Left and Right, and it is this view of Britain that will form the context of my discussion of representations of working-class life. Specifically, I will ask how work from the period, which takes as its central focus working-class experience, deals with the twin issues of affluence and classlessness (and its related term, working-class embourgeoisement), and how this finds articulation in the altering iconography of class.

British society experienced profound changes following the Second World war. After the malaise, the austerity and the rationing of the late 1940s there was almost uninterrupted full employment from 1951 to 1964, with rapid increases in productivity. Average earnings and consumption both rose; and ownership of cars and televisions rose from 2¼ million to 8 million, and 1 million to 13 million, respectively.[46] Politically, the Conservatives were the real beneficiaries of these developments. Instead of dismantling the reforms put in place by the Labour Party in the period 1945–51 (reforms on which the structures of post-war welfare capitalism was founded), the Conservatives kept them largely intact, signifying to observers the convergence between the two parties on matters economic, and registering on the ideological barometer the first indications of the politics of consensus, a dominant political practice and discourse until the arrival of the Thatcherite neo-liberalism of the late 1970s. Moreover, it was argued that affluence meant stability and the perceived erosion of class distinctions. Indeed, Harold Macmillan asserted: 'the class war is over and we have won'.[47] This view seemed to be supported on the Left: 'the changing character of labour, full employment, new housing, the new way of life based on the telly, the fridge, the car, the glossy magazines – all have had their effect on our political strength.'[48] Hugh Gaitskell's sentiments were widespread, compounding the image of the affluent worker and the developing myth of classlessness, so that 'one has only to cast the imagination back to those days [pre-1939 Britain] to appreciate the extent to which things have changed . . . The day is gone when workers must regard their stations in life as fixed – for themselves or for their children.'[49]

Themes of affluence and mobility became a dominant strand of political discourse, and there seemed no point preaching class consciousness if class relations no longer existed. Anthony Crosland argued that 'capitalism is undergoing a metamorphosis into a quite different system, and . . . this is rendering academic most of the traditional socialist analysis'.[50] That metamorphosis was in the direction of a more managed system, rather than a transformed one; state intervention would mean that the worst excesses of the market were at least ameliorated by welfare provisions (paid for, of course, by the workers themselves). There was to be no return to the 1930s, and the advances made through welfare provision signalled a new prosperity for all. Hence classlessness and 'affluence' became full-blown ideologies, discourses which, according to one view, work to 'cover over the gaps between real inequalities and the promised utopia of equality-for-all . . . the "affluence" myth aimed to give the working class a stake in a future which had not yet arrived', ensuring that 'the ideology of affluence reconstructed the "real relations" of post-war society into an "imaginary relation"'.[51]

It was also perceived to produce an 'I'm all right, Jack' individualism, rendering the collective historical agency predicated of the working class by those on the Left, and feared by others on the Right, redundant. For some writers this was the essential problem and the great tragedy – and in some writing a sense of loss emerges, as the workers are seen to have 'sold out', accepting the materialism which constructed them essentially as consumers rather than producers, thus ensuring their exit from the historical stage. Whether in the writing of the Frankfurt School or Richard Hoggart, in the novels of John Braine and Alan Sillitoe or the plays of Arnold Wesker, this position is variously explored and articulated. Yet to homogenize working-class experience under the sign of affluence, and to suggest that the class rose en masse from a position of penury to one of plenty (as was the dominant representation) is to distort the picture. This tension emerges in contradictory ways in cultural and literary production.

John Hill has argued: 'If it was classes that were presumed to be disappearing there can be little doubt that it was "youth", by contrast, who were making an appearance.'[52] A range of novels, films and plays of the period affirmed this. Young people now had jobs and money to spend, and this was accompanied by celebration and anxiety on the part of the establishment. Though it could be regarded as a crucial signifier of the dissolution of class, these developments also represented a fragmentation of 'tradition'. Thus, as Hill suggests, youth culture – with its apparent rejection of traditional ties – 'came to serve as a metaphor for the "underside" of the "affluent society": its slavish devotion to consumerism, allegiance to superficialities and absence of "authentic" values'.[53] Nonetheless, it also added to the theory of the demise of class, despite the view that, as Hill asserts, the 'teenage phenomenon [was] almost exclusively working class'.[54] The 'telly', glossy magazines, cinema, fashion: the post-war explosion of these material and cultural goods represented 'progress' (affluence) and, conversely, decline (erosion of traditional values). On the one hand British people were told that they had stepped into the future, whilst on the other that they should continue to live in the past.

As I pointed out in the introduction, one seminal text defining these changes was Richard Hoggart's *The Uses of Literacy* (1966 [1957]), which presented a sustained analysis of the implications of social and economic changes characterizing the post-war period, with a sharp emphasis on culture. Hoggart's text was to become a key reference point for others working in this and complementary fields of analysis, and a number of significant themes and positions explored by Hoggart found articulation too in literary forms. Hoggart's focus was on these widespread changes and how they were reflected in, and altered important aspects of, working-class life. His narrative strategy established a contrast between the pre-war period and the post-war, and the thrust of the narrative is to assert that the changes wrought in the period of welfare – in particular, the explosion of mass cultural forms directed at an 'affluent' working-class audience – was in the process of eroding the fundamental values, and moral economy, of working-class life.

Hoggart invoked 'personal experience' as the measuring rod for his findings. His 'authentic' working-class background was thus trailed as an index of the purported validity and accuracy of his views, analyses and observations. Such an intervention, with its primary focus on working-class culture, worked to confirm both the existence and disappearance of class.

Then and since the book has been much discussed and, though history has illuminated some of its shortcomings, its influence cannot be discounted. If its authenticity and assurance derived from Hoggart's own background and upbringing, the book's authority was further reinforced by its geographical location: 'The setting and the evidence as to attitudes are drawn mainly from experience in the urban North, from a childhood during the twenties and thirties and an almost continuous if somewhat different kind of contact since then.'[55] Thus Hoggart's credentials are set out: born into, and reared by, the working class at a particularly evocative period (the Hungry Thirties), a continued, if tenuous connection with his background still some twenty to thirty years later and, a powerful confirmation this, an existence in the very heart of the working-class landscape – the north of England. Constructing this working-class past in explicit contrast with the present (the massification of culture and experience in the late 1950s), we detect a claim to objectivity in conflict with a barely checked nostalgia for the 1930s – a period, as we have seen, of extreme hardship. As with George Orwell's exploration of working-class life in *The Road to Wigan Pier*, there emerges in the writing a kind of sentimentalism. Ironically, then, whilst accusing Orwell of seeing the working class 'through the cosy fug of Edwardian music-hall', Hoggart himself reproduces stereotypes of his own, such as the mythical working-class wife or mother (the ideological flip-side of the working-class women as abject, denoting class shame, as we have seen), always on hand with a hot meal, kind words, a welcoming home, and a ready gossip 'over the washing-line'.[56] Such representations occupy both landscapes (the 1930s and the 1950s), though Hoggart states that the inter-war setting which these people occupied – and in which a cultural and moral economy prospered – was giving way in the 1950s to damaging cultural and ideological impositions from outside.

The age of economic affluence – this 'candyfloss world' – is thus seen as the moment of cultural decline for the working class, and the narrative is then taken up with a critique of mass cultural forms (advertising, pulp fiction, the cinema) unfavourably compared with examples of superior production (the novels of George Eliot, for instance); the working-class consumers of these contemporary products thus appear as undiscriminating, uncouth, unsavoury and uninformed. Thus:

> Inhibited now from ensuring the 'degradation' of the masses economically, the logical processes of competitive commerce, favoured from without by the whole climate of the time . . . [is] ensuring that working class people are culturally robbed. . . . [T]his subjection promises to be stronger than the old because the chains of cultural subordination are both easier to wear and harder to strike away than those of economic subordination.[57]

It is the threat of ideological manipulation and assimilation that troubles Hoggart here, and it represents a very familiar theme in writing about the working class. Hoggart seems to believe that economic exploitation of the workers has been removed, to be replaced instead by their cultural impoverishment. The portents are not good for culture generally: 'The hedonistic but passive barbarian who rides in a fifty-horse-power bus for threepence, to see a five-million dollar film for one-and-eightpence, is not simply a social oddity: he is a portent.'[58] What Hoggart regards as the specificity of working-class culture prior to the Second World War, is crushed out of existence by the influx of a commercialized 'Other': quality is replaced by quantity. Thus the image is of a working class easily penetrated and absorbed by the culture industry, which in many respects seems radically at odds with Hoggart's initial insistence on a vibrant and autonomous (self-fashioned) habitus.

Raymond Williams was to be one of the earliest critics of Hoggart's position, rejecting the view of working-class 'materialism' as debased, and upbraiding Hoggart for marginalizing working-class political activism as a 'minority' case. Thus the argument over the existence, the 'condition' of the British working class was taken up again in *Culture and Society*. In the long, final chapter Williams addressed himself most directly to working-class culture, and cultural formation.

The material advances of the working class in the period under discussion, no matter how uneven they will be seen to be on closer analysis, have to be viewed in a positive light, Williams asserts. The accompanying mass culture and mass communications, which had been defined as a consequence of this expansion in economic terms, and which Hoggart had identified as the reason for a certain cultural loss within the working class, Williams described as 'at best neutral'.[59] Interrogating the concept of mass, or masses, Williams considered that it now represented, in terms of social and cultural meaning, a familiar elitist disdain for popular habits, and constituted a replacement word, or signifier, for the older word 'mob'. 'There are no masses,' Williams insists, 'there are only ways of seeing people as masses.'[60] As a coded refutation of Hoggart's pessimistic homogenization of working-class culture, Williams's position echoes arguments he had set out in a condensed form a year earlier (1957), in a review of *The Uses of Literacy*. Rejecting the formula 'enlightened minority, degraded mass', Williams questioned Hoggart's findings, the chief one being Hoggart's symptomatic silence in relation to the political:

> He picked up contemporary conservative ideas of the decay of politics in the working class, for which I see no evidence at all. The ideas merely rationalise a common sentimentality – the old labour leaders were noble-hearted, less materialistic, fine figures of men, but they are seen thus because their demands are over.[61]

The idea of affluence is again articulated here, suggested in the final clause of the sentence, but the key emphasis for Williams is to try to define the cultural in political terms. So we read in *Culture and Society*:

> Working-class culture . . . is not proletarian art, or council houses, or a particular use of language; it is, rather, the basic collective idea, and the institutions, manners, habits of thought and intentions which proceed from this . . . Working-class culture, in the stage through which it has been passing, is primarily social (in that it has created institutions) rather than individual.[62]

This basic collective idea – the dominant structure of feeling characteristic of working-class culture – was not swamped by a new ethos of individualism, and for Williams, the possibility of spreading the 'collective idea' throughout society was still a very real one. What Williams presented in *Culture and Society* was a different way of seeing the working class of this period; a way of seeing which, while registering the many changes in working-class life since the end of the war, highlighted the crucial continuities also. Thus he comes to an idea of culture generally, which rejects Hoggart's notion of the massification of culture, and propounds a view which suggests an *expanding* culture – a more neutral position, wary of the negative value-statements manifest in the writing of other observers. Williams identifies but discards many of the conservative responses in this period in relation to class, whilst accepting the evidence of change within a new, and historically important conjuncture.

As a cultural intervention it was a powerful one, though commentators since have been critical of his views, holding that the argument is undermined by an organicism which in some ways denied struggle between classes, and represented working-class communities as unproblematically embraced in the collective ethos of solidarity. Nevertheless, the arguments of both Williams and Hoggart (perhaps more so the latter) constituted defining contributions to the overall discursive context of the 1950s and early 1960s, which was dominated by the vexing question of the disappearance (or not) of the British working class. *Culture* now becomes a key arena for contestation: if the political and economic had appeared settled facts by the middle of the 1950s, the cultural became increasingly a place of discursive struggle. Class as economic category, or political entity – strongly expressed in 1930s' writing – yields to class as primarily cultural identity, thus the insistence by both Williams and Hoggart on the validity of working-class culture. The danger here, however, lies in the eclipse of the political economy of class, which traditionally stresses conflict between capital and labour, and foregrounds structural inequality and exploitation as key definers of lived experience. This formed the contradictory moment in which classlessness emerged as the 'common sense' of social and cultural commentary, at the same time as the working class continued to be a real cultural presence and focus of discussion. But the 1930s' stress, say, on the working class as a political reality with the potential to transform society, became increasingly subordinated to the mass-marketed sense of class as 'style'.

Colin MacInnes's *City of Spades* (1957) and *Absolute Beginners* (1959) articulate this position with succinctness. *Absolute*

Beginners represents a homage to 'youth', and shows a preoccupation with attempting to define the subversive potential of emergent sub-cultures, which materialize in the text as the site of a new dissident exchange. Hence, the themes of race and racial prejudice are key elements of *Absolute Beginners*, and the overriding focus of MacInnes's earlier novel, *City of Spades*.

In this novel, liberal England comes face to face with the ramifications of its colonial past. Montgomery Pew – civil servant and welfare officer at the Colonial Department – stands as a kind of Forster-type creation out of *A Passage to India*, identifying at some personal cost with the emerging black sub-culture, and specifically with the Nigerian-born Johnny Fortune. The novel documents Montgomery's rapid disillusionment with his job in the face of official corruption and racial prejudice and shows, chiefly through the character of Johnny, the inequities and humiliations encountered by immigrants coming to Britain at this time. As the main concern of the narrative revolves around attitudes in an emergent post-colonial society, class is not an obvious presence, despite the novel being set generally in a lower-class milieu. Indeed, there is a strong sense in the novel that class-specific issues have in fact been displaced by racial ones: that the black sub-culture, oppressed by white bigotry, now stands in place of the working class Other once subordinated to and struggling against the structures of capital and the imperatives of the state. Post-war society in Britain is regarded by Montgomery Pew as 'monolithic', social conflict resolved by state intervention leading to a stability which merely produces a stifling sameness. Black sub-culture represents a rearguard action to this, opposed not only to residual colonial attitudes and assumptions, but also to the mundane and pedestrian culture of metropolitan massification. We hear that:

> these boys seemed incapable of a vulgar gesture! And as they danced, they were clothed in what seemed the antique innocence and wisdom of humanity before the Fall – before the glory days of conscious creation, and the horrors of conscious debasement, came into the world. These immensely adult children, who'd carried into a later age a precious vestige of our former life, could throw off their twentieth century garments, and all their ruthlessness and avarice and spleen and radiate, on the stage, an atmosphere of goodness! of happiness! of love! And I thought I saw at last what was the mystery of the deep attraction to us of the Spades – the fact that they were still a mystery to themselves.[63]

Nature versus culture; the shallow materialism of modernity opposed by the natural expressiveness and freedom of its historically despised Other, a group who are then seen to reject white society's values and beliefs and slip the straitjacket of conformity. Though we do glimpse this black sub-culture in the guise of a new, super-exploited proletariat (labouring on building sites, for instance), MacInnes's novel privileges cultural transgression as the key trope, resulting in the romanticization of sub-cultural expression in a world rid of the problem of class. The novel then insists upon a new emphasis on style, or performance, as constitutive of subjectivity:

> I [Montgomery] went upstairs sadly, and changed into my suit of Barcelona blue . . . As I drank heavily of Theodora's gin, the notion came to me that *I* should visit these haunts against which it was my duty to warn others: the Moorhen, the Cosmopolitan dance hall and perhaps the Moonbeam club. But first of all, I decided, adjusting the knot of my vulgarist bow-tie (for I like to mix Jermyn Street, when I can afford it, with the Mile End Road), it was more imperative to inspect the welfare hostel. (p. 36)

Self-fashioning is the keynote: significant is the hybrid stylistic combination of Jermyn Street and the Mile End Road, a symbolic collapsing of class codes, suggesting not merely Montgomery's fashion preferences but a new paradigm where style and performance, rather than structure and society, shape identity and self.

This position acquires greater articulation in MacInnes's later novel, *Absolute Beginners*. The myth of classlessness forms the ideological cement of the text, transposing class structure into the cultural performance of 'youth', or the teen-cult, which severs all ties with tradition (class or otherwise) and places youth at the vanguard:

> Youth has a kind of power, a kind of divine power straight from mother nature. All the old taxpayers know of this . . . but they are so jealous of us, they hide this fact, and whisper it among themselves. As for the boys and girls, the dear young absolute beginners, I sometimes feel that if only they knew this fact . . . namely how powerful they really are, then they could rise up overnight and enslave the old taxpayers, the whole damn lot of them . . . even though they number millions and sit in the seats of strength.[64]

The energy and style of 'youth' – its fledgling strength and identity in the affluent world of late-1950s' welfare capitalism – represents the potentially revolutionary class (or caste) waiting in the wings to sunder tradition and conformity and remake the world in their own image. Firmly anti-establishment, the Boy (notably a freelance photographer, working within the culture industries) rejects the politics of the mainstream, and the two main Party dispensations, as anachronisms.

> 'You mustn't despise politics,' he told me. 'Somebody's got to do the housekeeping.'
> Here I let go of my Rolleiflex, and chose my words with care.
> 'If they'd stick to their housekeeping, which is the only backyard they can move freely in to any purpose, and stopped playing Winston Churchill and the Great Armada when there's no tin soldiers left to play with anymore, then no one would despise them, because no one would even notice them.' (p. 25)

The disdain is specific, a result of Britain's post-war colonial pretensions, and Suez is the actual event signalled. But the sentiment is general: politics, like class, is a non-starter, a kind of ruse which the Boy, and his acquaintances, have seen through.

Such a novel could have been set only in London, and the city is perhaps the key to it. It represents the 'scene', a potentially fluid site without borders or boundaries, populated by the young, the talented or the hopeful, by advertising executives and record-company bosses feeding parasitically off others in this emerging society of the spectacle. Youth and affluence here connotes liberation; the race riots – the novel is resolutely topical, with references to Suez, Wolfenden and, in particular, the Notting Hill clashes – reveal the emerging tensions between black and white and provide the Boy with the opportunity to state his support for the ethnic sub-culture, increasingly part of the cosmopolitan mix and style of the metropolis. And London provides the space to articulate a new mobility, starkly contrasting with pre-war images of the city, and with those representations of class and urban life in the 'provincial' novels examined in greater detail later. Mobility, classlessness and style: the novel is replete with the 'performance' of youth:

> If you know the contemporary scene, you could tell them apart at once . . . Take first the Misery kid and his trad. drag. Long, brush-less hair,

> white stiff-starched collar (rather grubby), striped shirt, tie of all one colour (red today, but it could have been royal-blue or navy), short jacket but an old one (somebody's riding tweed, most likely), very, very, tight, tight trousers with wide stripe, no sox, short boots. Now observe the Dean in the modernist number's version. College-boy smooth crop hair with burned-in parting, neat white Italian rounded collared shirt, short Roman jacket very tailored (two little vents, three buttons), no turn-up narrow trousers with 17-inch bottoms absolute maximum, pointed-toe shoes, and a white mac lying folded by his side, compared with Misery's sausage-rolled umbrella. (p. 63)

The rise of youth, founded on affluence and a suspicion of the past and of authority, constitutes a kind of 'universal' identity in the text; conversely, this universal is based upon internal difference, upon individual performance and projection – upon the cultivation of personal style. As Alan Sinfield has noted, however, 'the experiences of the boy were only open to a minority of people' from the lower classes, thus the novel in the end contributes to 'the fallacy of the classlessness of youth'.[65]

It is worth noting the quite alternate structure of feeling to be found in Trinidad-born Sam Selvon's *The Lonely Londoners* (1956). Not only does this work provide early examples of the theme of diaspora, but it attempts to bring together the concerns of race (or ethnicity) and class, seeking solidarities between black settlers and the white working class. This is both a political and a cultural question for Selvon, and one about which the narrative is quite explicit:

> Wherever in London that it have Working Class, there you will find a lot of spades. This is the real world, where men know what it is to hustle a pound to pay the rent when Friday come . . . It have a kind of communal feeling within the Working Class and the spades, because when you poor things does level out, it don't have much up and down.[66]

Even so, the narrative shows little evidence of this coming together, and constitutes rather a 'utopian impulse' than a reality.

MacInnes's emphasis on youth and affluence is given different inflections too in Shelagh Delaney's *A Taste of Honey* (1958).[67] *A Taste of Honey* focuses on the relationship between teenage Jo, and Helen, her mother. In this single-parent family, the various strains between mother and daughter are articulated within a setting which is primarily domestic, but which is empty of any of the 'traditional' maternal comforts suggested by Hoggart. Notions of the family are disorganized in the play: this family appears 'dysfunctional', and ideas of female sexuality and moral probity are rewritten in a number of interesting ways. For instance, Helen is hardly the self-sacrificing, nurturing mother of myth; she is generally selfish, uncaring and drunk. The family itself is not part of a working-class community (though the play is set firmly in a recognizable working-class area: Salford, Manchester, location of Greenwood's *Love on the Dole*); it is uprooted and seemingly isolated, living out of dingy rooms, on the edge of penury and squalor. The opening scene takes place in what is described as a 'comfortless flat'; the mother squarely represented as a semi-prostitute, and the promise of affluence undermined in the first dramatic exchange:

HELEN Well! This is the place.
JO   And I don't like it.
HELEN When I find somewhere for us to live I have to consider something far more important than your feelings . . . the rent. It's all I can afford.[68]

Such stark economic necessity cuts against the grain of the ideology of affluence assimilated in mainstream discourses. And here the domestic interior is inscribed within a framework of destitution: metonymic markers suggest the absence of comfort (the peeling wallpaper, Jo's leaking shoe, a view of the gasworks as an index of this inner-city 'community'); and the bottle of booze Helen seemingly always has on hand represents her careless mothering and suggests her free and frank sexuality. Early in the play, Helen abandons her daughter to marry her latest boyfriend, Peter, and later discloses scant sympathy for her daughter when she falls pregnant.

Appropriately, perhaps, youth culture in the quintessential working-class north is not quite what it is presented to be in MacInnes's cosmopolitan south. Jo does not circulate with the 'in-crowd' in anything like the sense with which the boy does in *Absolute Beginners*; and though race issues figure in the character of Jo's boyfriend – and the father of her child – any tendency to celebrate the vibrant sub-cultural identity found in *City of Spades* is absent (interestingly, Jo's boyfriend has no name until two-thirds into the play, when she finally refers to him by his given name). Homosexuality is represented, though a curious asexuality emerges in the figure of Geof, who comes dangerously close to exhibiting those maternal instincts scholarship boys of the time were keen to predicate of working-class mothers per se. Thus youth revolt here is framed by meanness and deprivation (only a *taste* of honey, after all) and shaped by class inequality. When Jo tells Geof that they 'are a couple of degenerates' (p. 52), our response might be one of pity rather than anxiety. Helen, the mother, is the active, sexual one, transgressing what might be termed the moral codes of the 'respectable' working class. Jo's sexuality is ambiguous, a point signalled in the exchange with Jimmie, when he begins to arouse her:

JO   Don't do that
JIMMIE Why not?
JO   I like it.
            (p. 32)

In fact both Helen and Jo, as working-class women, exist on the margins of society and of working-class culture – at least as it is figured in the landscape painted by Hoggart in *Uses of Literacy*. This is something to which we will return much later in relation to women's writing in the 1980s.

Stuart Laing has suggested that representations of working-class life in fiction tended to break decisively with pre-war modes of writing about working-class experience. He identifies the emergence of a particular 'post-war genre, that of the young male hero on the make in the fluid social situation of a post-war Britain'.[69] MacInnes's writing reflects this view, though Laing is more interested in the working-class fiction of John Braine, Stan Barstow and Alan Sillitoe. It is to two of these chroniclers of working-class life, Braine and Sillitoe, that I will now turn.

John Braine's *Room at the Top* was first published in 1957 and tells the story of Joe Lampton who represents, as the blurb of a recent reprint puts it, 'the original "angry young man"'. It is a novel concerned with the perceived social mobility of post-war Britain. The cover of the Mandarin edition of Braine's text is interesting in itself. We are presented with a blurred image of our hero looking rather shiftily over his shoulder and into the distance where, indistinct but still definable, are grey images of terraced back-to-backs and smoky chimney-stacks – the archetypal image of the industrial north. Joe's expression suggests relief (at his 'escape', presumably) and a certain anxiety (his possible return?). This backdrop is Joe's past, then, an index of how far he has come.

This is a story of embourgeoisement. The opening section of the novel speaks of the theme of departure – both literal and metaphorical – from one world to another. Braine's early descriptions are marked out by the metonymic, or synecdoctic, mode; the narrative cluttered with material objects which work to signal Lampton's new environment, and symbolically to signify his upward mobility. His place of lodging with the Thompsons discloses a range of middle-class markers:

> It was a drawing-room furnished in what seemed to me to be very good taste with Sheraton-type furniture, thin-legged and graceful but not spindly or fragile, and pale yellow and cream wallpaper in an arrangement of colour rather than pattern. There was a radiogram and a big open bookcase and a grand piano: the piano top was bare, a sure sign that it was used as a musical instrument and not an auxiliary mantlepiece. The white bearskin rug on the parquet floor was, I suppose, strictly Metro-Goldwyn-Mayer, but it fitted in.[70]

There is evidence of a certain cultivated style here, even though the bearskin rug very nearly disturbs the scene with its intimations of MGM and popular culture. Joe's own room offers a starker contrast to his previous dwellings in Dufton, adorned as it is with 'fitted cushions ... a divan bed ... two armchairs and a dressing-table' (p. 11), a far cry from the brass-railed bed and hard-backed chair which occupied his bedroom at his aunt's house. The descriptions constitute a comment upon 'taste' and symbolic capital rather than a discourse upon relative affluence; finally, the mark of high culture lends its own sign of authenticity to Joe's impending 'transformation':

> There were small pictures hanging on the far wall: *The Harbour at Arles*, a Breughel skating scene, and Manet's *Olympe*.
> 'Especially chosen in your honour,' Mrs Thompson said, 'Medici reproductions. We have quite a library of them ...'

'I like the skaters,' I said, meaning I liked it best. It wasn't true; even as I said it, I was looking at Olympe, white, plump, and coldly self-possessed. But my upbringing held me back; I couldn't bring myself to admit to a woman that I liked a nude. (p. 12)

The exchange reveals a reassessment or critique of his own origins, that closed culture from which he has escaped. Much later in the novel, when Joe has begun his relationship with middle-class Susan, we see them together on a bus. As they pass through a working-class district, a couple board the vehicle and sit near them:

A young man and a girl of about nineteen got in at the next stop. At least I though she was about nineteen; her face, like the young man's, had a settled look, as if she'd decided what was the most respectable age to be, and wasn't going to change in a hurry. She had a round flat face with lipstick the wrong shade and her silk stockings and high heels struck an incongruously voluptuous note; it was as if she had been scrubbing floors in a transparent nylon nightie. The young man had a navy-blue overcoat, gloves and scarf, but no hat; he was following the odd working-class fashion which seemed to me now, after Alice's tuition, as queer as going out without trousers. I felt a mean complacency; with that solid mass of brilliantined hair and mass-produced face, bony, awkward, mousy, the face behind the requests on Forces' Favourites, the face enjoying itself at Blackpool with an open-necked shirt . . . which Wilfred Pickles might love but which depressed me intensely – Len or Sid or Cliff or Ron – he'd never have the chance of enjoying a woman like Susan, he'd never explore in another person the passion and innocence which a hundred thousand in the bank would alone make possible. (p. 153)

It is worth quoting this passage at length, because it not only captures Joe's attitudes now to working-class life, but also highlights a number of assumptions pertinent to the emergent mass commercial culture and to attendant ways of seeing the 'new' working class. For Joe, this working-class couple symbolize all he is escaping from and it is significant that they are young rather than old – products of the widespread affluence but, more succinctly, of the mass cultural milieu. These two are ground down, it seems, not by poverty or scarcity, but by a certain *excess*. Signifiers of consumer culture litter the description, from the boy's brilliantined hair to the girl's lipstick: she, in particular, represents mass culture, the cheap, the ineffable and the disposable. Her 'voluptuousness', purely artificial, sits uneasily with an 'essentialized' proletarian demeanour. They signify what working-class life has become. Joe makes no connection between himself and them, and his 'escape' is palpable and complete.

The representations of working-class life in *Room at the Top* encode Hoggartian themes, some of which have been flagged above. Braine represents the new tokens of mass commercialization as life-denying, or inauthentic; and classless affluence seems to have sapped any moral, political or spiritual fibre from those older working-class communities of Joe's origin. Towards the end of the novel, he returns briefly to his home town, this hybrid world (signs of 'old' and 'new' everywhere) he now despises. The traditional pubs exist still, as do the familiar drinks and songs, and after a few glasses, Joe soon finds himself sitting alongside a local girl:

> I think that it was about half past eight when I was aware of a nasty silence over the room. I looked up; a young man was standing scowling over us. He had the sort of face that one's always seeing in the yellow press – staring-eyed, mousy, the features cramped and shapeless and the mouth loose. He was wearing a light blue double-breasted suit that was so dashingly draped as to look decolleté and he had a blue rayon tie of an oddly slimy-looking texture. At that moment he was enjoying what a thousand films and magazines had assured him to be righteous anger: His Girl had been Untrue. (p. 227)

Here is the generalized product of better times, with his staring eyes, loose mouth and cramped features. The description operates to justify Joe's escape from this manufactured life, shaped by media representations and a superficial affluence. Yet, the affluence discourse emerges in a particularly ambiguous form: material conditions (found in the description of Dufton) still appear as unremittingly grim, the benefits instead articulated through the consolatory trinkets of the market, with identity fashioned through the ideological appeal of tabloid newspapers and the cinema (also an emergent concern for the 1930s' writers). As Hoggart's thesis suggested, mass-mediated cultural forms now provide this working class with a sense of who they are. Thus Braine's novel is as much a comment upon contemporary working-class life, seen from someone escaping it (the upwardly-mobile writer), as it is a story of Joe's rise to the top. The text endorses the affluence-as-cultural-deficit paradigm and works to undercut any positive representation of working-class life.

The ideological perspectives of Braine's novel place it within the category of the 'escaper novel', a mode examined in earlier discussions. Like a number of 'provincial realist' texts, Braine's novel went on to to be made into a film (and a television series). The same was true of Alan Sillitoe's *Saturday Night and Sunday Morning*. However, Sillitoe's writing discloses a far more contradictory relation to ideas of affluence and class. *Saturday Night and Sunday Morning* (1958) opens on a Saturday night at the pub.

> It was Benefit Night for the White Horse Club, and the pub had burst its contributions box and spread a riot through its rooms and between its four walls. Floors shook and windows rattled, and leaves of aspidistras wilted in the fumes of beer and smoke. Notts County had beaten the visiting team, and the members of the White Horse supporters club were quartered upstairs to receive a flow of victory. Arthur was not a member of the club, but Brenda was, and so he was drinking the share of her absent husband – as far as it would go – and when the club went bust and the shrewd publican put on the towels for those that couldn't pay, he laid eight half-crowns on the table, intending to fork out for his own.[71]

No sense of pre-war penury, here, and Arthur's eight half-crowns signify a kind of freedom. Yet the language of work and the factory is never far away:

> A high-octane fuel of seven gins and eleven pints had set him into motion like a machine, and had found its way into him because of a man's boast. A big, loud-mouthed bastard who said he had been a sailor . . . was throwing his weight about and holding dominion over several tables. (p. 4)

Arthur's 'freedom' is fuelled by the drink he consumes, setting him 'in motion like a machine', a carnivalesque image of excess. The money is, however, part of the deal he has cut to remain anchored five days a week to the lathe. His *individual* revolt against all authorities is thus framed by the rules they impose. This strong sense of individual revolt against the system is found also in *The Loneliness of the Long Distance Runner* (1959). Whose laws are to be obeyed, is the essential question asked in the text, though other, equally interesting ones emerge. The Borstal boy is being trained up to win the prestigious cross-country run for the Institution:

> They're training me up fine for the big sports day when all the pig-faced snotty-nosed dukes and ladies – who can't add two and two together and would mess themselves like loonies if they didn't have slaves at their beck and call – come and make speeches to us about sports being just the thing to get us leading an honest life and keep our itching finger-ends off them shop locks and safe handles and hairgrips to open gas meters. They give us a bit of blue ribbon and a cup for a prize after we've shagged ourselves out running or jumping, like racehorses, only we don't get so well looked after as racehorses, that's the only thing.[72]

If Arthur implicitly accepts that he is a cog in the machine of capital, used merely to furnish profit, the boy is equally aware of his exploitation by the powerful. This reiterates a familiar Sillitoe theme: revolt against authority ('Them'). But also evident in *Saturday Night and Sunday Morning* is a structure of feeling seeking to articulate a sense of loss. This sense of loss is political, often articulated in the narrative's frequent reference to the 1930s, and it explains the curiously anti-political stance (in strict ideological terms) of Arthur Seaton. Though a vibrant product of better times – Arthur is not slow to celebrate his relative affluence, or signify it by dressing stylishly – he still discloses a certain Hoggartian disdain for some of its commercialized manifestations:

> Margaret sat down and told Arthur that she had had a television set installed. 'It's marvellous, our Arthur. I never thought I'd be able to afford one, but Albert don't drink so much any more, and he said he'd pay the thirty bob a week. So whenever he gets on to me, I can just switch on the pictures and forget him!' (p. 178)

Arthur's response is telling:

> Television, he thought scornfully when she'd gone, they'd go barmy if they had them taken away. I'd love it if big Black Marias came down all the streets and men got out with hatchets to go in every house and smash the tellies. They wouldn't know what to do. There'd be a revolution. (p. 178)

This structure of feeling suggests a loss of radical intent on the part of the working class. Articulated here is a view of Orwell's doped (or duped) proles in *Nineteen Eighty-Four*, a view of working-class life as altered by alien (and alienating) forms of entertainment and leisure – reconciling people now to the way things are. Yet, in the end, the regular wages which purchase these consumer goods only reinforce the system which shackles and exploits. This is a double bind of which Arthur is particularly conscious; his riotous carnivalesque behaviour is his response, one which directly counters the passivity of watching television, though he remains uncertain of its efficacy:

> He did not ask whether he was in such a knocked-out state because he had lost the nights of love over two women, or because the two swaddies represented the raw edge of fang-and-claw on which all laws were based, law and order against which he had been fighting all his life in such a thoughtless and unorganised way that he could not but lose. Such questions came later. (p. 174)

This act of self-reflection is revealing and signals the view that Arthur has not stopped searching for possible alternate ways to challenge the system. This possibility is articulated in another of Arthur's inner-voice discourses:

> Once a rebel, always a rebel. You can't help being one . . . And it's best to be a rebel so as to show 'em it don't pay to try and do you down. Factories and labour exchanges and insurance offices keep us alive and kicking – so they say – but they're booby traps and will suck you under like sinking-sands if you aren't careful. Factories sweat you to death, labour exchanges talk you to death, insurance and income tax officers milk money from your wage packets and rob you to death . . . Ay, by God, it's a hard life if you don't weaken, if you don't stop that bastard government from grinding your face in the muck, though there ain't much they can do about it when you start making dynamite to blow their four-eyed clocks to bits. (p. 197)

Class resentment speaks here of a class consciousness rejecting the rules of the game and the correlation of affluence and assimilation, in turn imagining a future condition ripe for revolt. The sense of loss theme I have identified in the novel is tempered by the confidence and security relative affluence brings to Arthur and those around him. But the *dialogics* of the novel – the deep structure and *voice* – remain profoundly contestatory, and such oppositional structures of feeling resisting incorporation can be found with equal force in the discourse of the young 'deviant' in *The Loneliness of the Long Distance Runner*. Peter Hitchcock's study of Sillitoe has argued that an 'understanding of the class specificity of *Saturday Night and Sunday Morning* is primarily to be found in language'.[73] This notion applies to other examples of working-class writing too, and raises much more general and important questions about our understanding of working-class culture and identity. In this novel, Arthur's inner-voice discourse does not merely represent the expression of an individual person's world-view, but emerges as the product of clearly articulated and defined social relationships. The working-class text is defined as such not because it speaks a working-class consciousness in some monologic and unified sense, but because the narrated dialogics – the clashing styles and voices, which represent class relations rather than a single class utterance – signify the existence of class antagonisms. Invoking the 'multi-accentuality' of the sign, Valentin Vološinov argued that 'various social classes will use one and the same language. As a result, differently oriented accents intersect in every ideological sign. Sign becomes a arena of class struggle.' This represents a way of seeing language, described by Williams in *Marxism and Literature*, as both constituting and constitutive, a dialectical process which both enables and determines human identity, or subjectivity.[74] This consciousness of class articulated in the sign produces a novelistic discourse and mode of address orientated towards a working-class readership or audience. I argued this point in my discussion of earlier writing, highlighting narratives orientated towards specific reading formations, whether the implied sympathetic middle-class readership for *Love on the Dole*, or the potentially radical-activist reader of *The Ragged Trousered Philanthropists*. In *Saturday Night and Sunday Morning*, the play of pronouns constitutes one strategy by which Sillitoe interpellates his readership: the shifts from 'you' to 'I' to 'us' and 'Them', for instance, promote modes of identification and solidarity which constitute a call to arms for some readers, and a clear threat to others. Thus, if Hitchcock is correct in his assessment of Sillitoe (and I believe he has a case), what distinguishes Sillitoe's class narratives from some of those others discussed above lies deep in the narrative's mode of address.

At times, Sillitoe's text speaks of disdain for the tokens of affluence – at these moments, the writing depicts the once-classed subject's apathy and cultural colonization by the forces of mass commodity culture, leading to the cultural pessimism found in *The Uses of Literacy*, and in some of the other writing examined above. The fear of incorporation is never far away, and the working-class subject stands forever vulnerable to ideological forces or the dull compulsion of the economic. Arthur, of course, (along with other working-class 'heroes' discussed earlier) has seen through all this. Thus pessimism is undercut by Arthur's optimistic polemic of revolt, as it is alleviated by scenes of communal culture and solidarity which contradict the individualistic emphasis and override commodification, which seemingly threatens everything. For all of Arthur's individualist machismo and bravado, he accepts his place as part of a wider community, and feels no shame in turning to this community, especially in times of need. Arthur signifies his difference from others through 'style'; the snappy dressing allows him to stand out, but not stand outside the community to which he belongs. Here the performance of style carries different connotations to those predicated of MacInnes's sub-cultural location, and the trappings of a 'candyfloss world' do not necessarily check class identity or identification.

Community finds its voice at moments of festivity and carnival (Nottingham's annual Goose Fair), the materiality of sharing, the conviviality of family ties. However, women, in this context, play the subservient role, segregated as they are to the domestic sphere of nurture. Thus in a text focused on work as a central determining factor of life, women are represented in a traditional role within the home, despite the fact that, historically, more and more women were entering the workplace in this period. Arthur sees women as objects, to be conquered, fleetingly possessed, then cast aside; we see a similar set of representations in *Room at the Top*. Their place is to assuage sexual desire and to bolster male ego; for Arthur, by the end of the novel, women come to represent (in the shape of Doreen) a type of 'closure' or defeat: his freebooting, footloose lifestyle stymied, 'caught' and ensnared by the woman he chooses resignedly to marry. Despite this Arthur will not be conciliated; instead he will be 'fighting every day until I die' (*Saturday Night and Sunday Morning*, p. 213).

Though *Saturday Night and Sunday Morning* powerfully addresses the new working-class world of consumer complacency, it is not done with the blanket acceptance and elitist disdain we find elsewhere. Sillitoe's writing instead discloses a quite ambivalent structure of feeling towards working-class life. We see representations of the workers glued to the telly, but we also have images of communal expression, political articulation; the text offers the idea of the affluent young, working-class male on the make, alongside, however, detailed descriptions of the workers at the lathe, in the factory and on the shopfloor. Above all, the narrative suggests that this life is a different one from the hardship experienced in the 1930s, but it is not enough. In a later novel, *The Death of William Posters* (1965), Sillitoe introduces us to another Seaton-like character, though one who has moved a stage further towards a total negation of the system – a retreat which will take him, finally, to the street fighting of Algiers. Consonant themes emerge then: the alienation of work, the seduction of consumerism, and, in this text, a reference to the demise and destruction of community.

Work is a key motif: Posters rails against the alienations of factory work, the processes of which he and his comrades are powerless to control.

> I'm what they used to call a mechanic, but I was beginning to see further than the end of my nose. I was also what the gaffers call 'a bit of a troublemaker', but for years they were baffled by me because I was also a good worker. I could get anybody's tools and take their machine apart as well as the chargehand, and I had many hints that if I stopped being such a keen member of the union, life would be easier for me as far as getting on went. But I saw too much injustice to accept that. I knew which side of the fence I stood on, and still do.[75]

Class politics at the point of production receive very specific articulation here in the shape of a union activist, though it is instructive to observe that Posters gives up the fight for economic justice for some seemingly more 'authentic' struggle to find the self. The alienation of work must be rejected, though Posters's attitudes to life are coloured too by the promises of affluence and the dubious rewards of welfare capitalism. The worker is now defined predominantly as a consumer – of goods, of leisure, of images: here the guarantee of self-worth lies in the possession of things, such as the 'telly', for instance.

I feel as if I'm being strangled . . . I look at all the people around me who have boxed up their future in the telly, and it makes me sicker than that whisky I slung down . . . That's what the telly does anyway, teaches you to despise your fellow man. There's nothing left to believe in in this country, nothing left, not a thing. (pp. 45–6)

As a way of confirming this view, Sillitoe uses in the novel the advertising executive Keith as a signifier of that very system of consumption referred to:

His ability to probe the pseudo-masochistic impulses of the human soul, and lay them out as alluring symbols of acquisitiveness or greed, ought to help in an expedition such as this. He smiled at the thought. Christ, what haven't I sold in my time? Persuaded people to buy? The bonfires of conspicuous consumption had lit up the housing estates, flames dead already, dustbins emptied, ashes cleared away. The world is a furnace, a boiler-house, wheels within dark satanic wheels moaning above the backs of the HP-paying multitude. It would be nice if reality were so stark and clear . . . Simplicity was the oil on the wheels of his chronometer heart, reaching even the poetic cogs of them, the last hope of the divided men who could never really put Humpty-Dumpty together again. (p. 108)

Fear of manipulation and ideological incorporation dominate this image, invoking soulless housing estates as signifiers of a cheap, downmarket materialism, metonymic of a new way of life for the working class. Frank, far less ambiguously than Arthur Seaton in *Saturday Night and Sunday Morning*, holds out against this, and the narrative then reproduces that individualistic perspective found in the earlier novel and in other examples of Sillitoe's writing. The returned-to emphasis on communal experience punctuating *Saturday Night and Sunday Morning* – and undermining, as I have argued, an individualistic structure of feeling – is displaced in *The Death of William Posters* on to the later camaraderie of the Algerian war. The communal, or solidaristic, structure of feeling of the working class, as far as Frank can see, has been destroyed anyway by the 'modernizers' of the welfare state. Traipsing his local streets before his departure abroad, he notes:

Streets in all directions had been cleared and grabbed and hammered down, scooped up, bucketed, piled, sorted and carted off. Where had the people gone? Moved on to new estates, all decisions made for them, whereas he also wanted to uproot himself, but must make his own moves. (p. 63)

The intensity of the feeling here is signified by the collocation of adjectives ('hammered', 'scooped', 'sorted'), and the phrase 'all decisions made for them' aptly defines that sense of loss referred to earlier in this chapter. It is a collective loss ('them/us') and a political loss too (the reference to 'decisions', suggesting loss of *agency* over their own lives) that has eroded the potential of the working class.

There is a sense in some of Sillitoe's early writing that consumerism is seen as a gloss, a sop to the working class. Nevertheless, his working-class figures are rarely wholly enthralled by the delights of the commodity and thus steeped in false consciousness. Moreover, the writing frequently insists that this 'New Britain' does little to alter the place of the worker in the productive process. What stands out, contrary to many of the novels of the 1930s, is the evident lack of a collective political response to alienation and exploitation. This is not merely symptomatic of Sillitoe's preference for individual agency, but constitutes a recognition that collective potential has been stymied by the failed or false promises of welfarism, which had materially improved aspects of working-class life at the same time as it robbed it of any opportunity to instil a political economy and culture more definitively its own.

I have focused in this chapter on two key historical moments in which the working class find a powerful presence in cultural production, even if – in the second instance – that presence is predicated on a kind of absence. The ideology of post-war affluence produced a new rhetoric of class, one linked paradoxically to ideas of *classlessness*. Some of the writing discussed was shaped by this moment and in turn helped shape it; still other narratives contradict or reject the position. Nevertheless, the myth of 'classlessness' came to be contested in the 1960s in a number of studies which rediscovered levels of poverty and need hitherto considered erased by welfare provision. Academic research found echoes in broader cultural intervention into the debate – in particular, Ken Loach's film *Cathy Come Home* (1966), highlighting the significant shortcomings of welfare capitalism. Later writers would argue that ' "affluence" was, essentially, an ideology of the dominant culture *about* and *for* the working class, directed *at* them (through the media, advertising, political speeches, etc.)'.[76] Post-war developments had been more complex than this discourse asserted (as Raymond Williams stated with force in *Culture and Society*), disclosing unpredictable and often contradictory outcomes:

> The overwhelming emphasis in the ideology of affluence on money and consumption may well have had the unintended effect of stimulating an awareness of 'relative deprivation' and thereby contributed to the 'wage militancy' of the 1960s and '70s. The affluent workers in engineering and motor firms pioneered the shift to workplace power, plant bargaining, shop stewards' organization and 'wage drift' – a militant 'economism' which lasted right into the period of inflation and recession, pulling the 'revolt of the lower paid' behind it. These, too, were responses to 'affluence' which its ideologues neither did nor could foresee.[77]

By the end of the 1960s the dominant ideology of affluence no longer held hegemonic sway, and throughout the next decade, certainly by 1979 and the rise of Thatcherism (and more so thereafter), the state's struggle for working-class assent to mainstream values and beliefs would shift decisively from the nurturing of consent to the politics of coercion. The economic recession of the second half of the 1970s witnessed the demise of the post-war settlement. The new political conjuncture was to experience what Raymond Williams described in *Politics and Letters* as 'a real return to class politics'.[78] The age of affluence was slowly and grindingly ending and by the close of the decade, with a new Conservative government in power under Margaret Thatcher, a profoundly different political and economic agenda would be set which would lead to a remaking, and a rewriting, of the British working class.

2
Class, community and 'structures of feeling': a 'sense of loss' revisited in some working-class writing from the 1980s

This chapter seeks to explore some key themes and concerns to emerge in writing about (and by) the working class during the 1980s, issues which will then be taken up in greater depth in subsequent chapters. The sudden rapid rise in unemployment in the early 1980s, the result of Thatcherism's prescription of monetarist economics, heralded for some a return to the grim scenes of the 1930s. In 1989 Alan Sinfield observed that unemployment in Britain was not just a consequence of recession, and that 'of the rise between 1979 and 1983, 40 to 50 per cent has been variously estimated as due to government policies'.[1] Tom Nairn suggested that economic policy – what he termed Mrs Thatcher's experiment – was

> No more than an attempt to utilize the recession to hasten and complete the dominance of financial capital. The apotheosis of 'Freedom' is de-industrialization: southern hegemony permanently liberated from the archaic burden of the Industrial Revolution's relics, the subsidies that prop them up, and the trade unions that agitate for them.[2]

Both writers point to two key developments in the eighties: the start of the long process of de-industrialization, and the emergence of a north/south divide.

The effects of these changes on working-class life would be profound, with a particular impact in the northern industrial districts, which is my main focus here. Statistics reveal the depth of the problem: in 1954, the registered unemployed stood at 260,000; by 1982, the figure was 3,400,000 and unofficial estimates put the total at four million. In Liverpool, 40 per cent of all male workers were jobless; in the east London district of Poplar, 32 per cent were without work (somewhat undercutting the argument that this was a northern problem only).[3] Thus a city like Glasgow experienced a 40 per cent increase in poverty levels between 1981 and 1986, with 28 per cent of its people living below the poverty line. Homelessness had risen by 60 per cent and 16 per cent of the city's workforce remained unemployed.[4] In Liverpool, one writer witnesses on a Birkenhead waste-tip, 'people up to their waists every day in old teabags, cat-food tins and onion skins, sliding and falling on slopes of polythene bags and bacon-rind, scrambling to get the copper wire before the next man'.[5] A sense of decline and disintegration came to represent the dominant structure of feeling in relation to large sections of the working class.

This might be seen as an appropriate context in which to return to Peter Keating's contention that writing about working-class life emerges most strongly at times of socio-economic distress, and thus to ask how some of the developments documented above were mediated in some literature of the time. To do this I will first expand more fully than hitherto the theoretical insights which can be drawn from employing Raymond Williams's notion of 'structure of feeling', applying the concept to the work of three writers whose texts focus on working-class life and experience in the period under discussion. I will argue that this writing explores structures of feeling which correspond to and powerfully define both the individual concerns of these writers and crucial aspects of the broader social, political and cultural context of the period.

I Structures of feeling and the articulation of class

The concept of structure of feeling holds a central place in Williams's work. It relates in key ways to his notion of 'knowable community' – the idea of community being vital to Williams's writing. The working-class writers I discuss here have their roots in the working class, and their writing focuses powerfully on aspects of working-class experience: in this context, articulating structures of feeling which speak of community in crisis and fragmentation, concerns symptomatic of changing social relations and political pressures. In particularly acute ways, these writers struggle to articulate shared meanings and feelings at the level of lived experience, speaking a structure of feeling in conflict with dominant ways of seeing. This is not necessarily to suggest an unproblematic and homogeneous structure of feeling in some simple way related to class: these writers' concerns with working-class life are framed in crucial ways also by pressures of gender and generation. I have tried to make this point in earlier chapters, and will be taking it up again in later analysis, where I will examine structures of feeling which articulate in complex and sometimes contradictory ways the relationship of class, gender and race.[6]

Arguably, one of the most fruitful ways of approaching the theoretical implications of the term is to regard structure of feeling as a kind of riposte to, or critique of, key aspects of poststructuralism. Peter Middleton has argued that the concept is grounded in a notion of experience and 'presence' that runs contrary to the anti-humanism of much poststructuralist thought.[7] One tenet of poststructuralism is that experience cannot emerge pristine and uncontaminated by ideology. Williams accepts this, but still insists that we need not see all experience as ideological, or accept that the subject is merely an ideological illusion. Williams holds on to the difficult term experience, at the same time rejecting the subject of bourgeois humanism, the sovereign individual with the capacity to act in the world unconstrained by structures and ideology.[8] Thus, Middleton suggests: 'The *concept* of experience he would . . . accept as in part an ideological illusion, but what he wants to retrieve is a recognition of the life processes, the praxis, that precedes analysis.'[9] Ideology, for Williams, *does* contaminate experience; but there still occurs the life process, involving an effort after meaning, in the telling of stories and the making of culture. Literature and writing produce a structure of feeling which is open to critical analysis and is privileged as a site where a specific sensibility, or habitus, can be encountered. Elaborating on this in *Marxism and Literature*, Williams states that he is 'talking about characteristic elements of impulse, restraint and tone; specifically affective elements of consciousness and relationships; not feeling against thought, but thought as felt and feeling as thought: practical consciousness of a present kind, in a living and interrelated continuity'.[10]

'Feeling' exists within a framework, or structure, articulated as social *and* personal, the result of intersubjective social relations and processes. Arguably, there is something profoundly dialogic bound up with the concept of structure of feeling; we get the sense that art and/or literature represents something more than the author's individual expression, or 'vision', as it necessarily engages with wider historical structures, discourses or events. Narrative then is a socially symbolic act. In this context, feeling suggests process and unfinishedness – articulation finds uneasy expression through certain images and ideas which for Williams hover at the very 'edge of semantic availability'.[11] This tension may constitute the text as a source of an often quite privileged insight on history.

Williams's own approach in terms of structure of feeling is to identify an experience common to a group of writers in a particular period, writers with no ostensible connection between them, yet who can be seen as expressing in their work common themes or patterns. His own major example is the English novelists of the 1840s. He identifies the emergence of a group of writers, a new generation of novelists, adapting the realist form inherited from Scott to develop what have come to be known as the 'industrial novels', contributions to a wider 'condition-of-England' debate. Williams then sees these writers as adopting or adapting specific conventions to express a structure of feeling focused on the exploration of community, as a response to the force of change which they perceive. Thus 'class relations, including class conflict, [becomes] the conscious material of fiction', even if this dynamic is addressed 'precisely so it can be reconciled or evaded'.[12] Touched on here is the emphasis on intersubjectivity which I have ascribed to Williams's concept – the dialogism expressed when language and experience are recognized (consciously or not) and articulated as a site of class antagonism and struggle, representing a condition we have already encountered in some of our earlier readings of class narratives.

Structure of feeling can help to understand writing's entanglement with historical change. Texts provide evidence about the vital, and lived, experiences or attitudes of a group or of a society in a particular historical period, defining a particular quality of social experience. Interaction occurs between the official consciousness of a period, duly codified and formalized (in the sense of a dominant ideology), and what Williams calls 'practical consciousness' – and this relationship remains a site of potential fracture and contradiction. Any opposition to the period's official consciousness is experienced as a 'kind of feeling and thinking which is indeed social and material'.[13] The term 'feeling' is appropriated to make a distinction from ideology as 'world view' ('the ideology of the working class'), because Williams is keen to identify meanings and values that are actually lived and felt, 'and the relation between these and formal or systematic beliefs'. This connection is variable and can range from assent to opposition; so that 'there are cases where the structure of feeling which is tangible in a particular set of works is undoubtedly an articulation of an area of experience which lies beyond them'. This is 'especially evident at those specific and historically definable moments when new work produces a sudden shock of *recognition*. What must be happening on those occasions is that an experience which is really very wide suddenly finds a semantic figure which articulates it.'[14] Williams's clarification is of primary significance, and articulates structure of feeling to a question of *conventions*. Referring back to Williams's own example of the nineteenth century, and his discussion of the industrial novels, he detects there a recurring convention of absolute primacy: sympathy for the poor, in tension with a view of working-class political *collectivity* as 'mob rule', an open threat to an essentially stable and democratic order. Williams relates this to the rise of working-class politics and to the class's newly emergent visibility, and the potential threat this posed to bourgeois hegemony. At the same time as these writers were encoding such anxieties in their work, they were responding also to a more general, and epochal, societal shift we know as the Industrial Revolution; grasping for an understanding of new social relations in a 'knowable community' increasingly more difficult to define. Thus another category (along with that of conventions) becomes relevant to Williams's formulation of a structure of feeling: that of community itself.

In Williams's work generally, community is a key word. The relationship between self and other forms within community: here the subject acquires knowledge of herself/himself within a wider, and often determining, social context. Structure of feeling is the term which suggests the continuing interaction between the individual and the social, standing as 'socio-historical description and development . . . integral to [Williams's] understanding of community'; stressing at the same time the 'process of communication by which interaction becomes possible'.[15] The concept embodies a structure of past, present and future which leads the text's characters (and, crucially, the audience/readers, too) 'towards a new way of seeing and/or feeling, resulting in the familiar appearing strange or the strange becoming familiar'.[16] At the same time, more than one single, common structure of feeling will be evident; this difference Williams places within a framework of the dominant, emergent and residual. The conflicting levels of consciousness are the moment of articulation that I will examine below; exploring tensions which are based overwhelmingly on an acute perception of change, felt as loss, crisis or discovery.

I have chosen significant working-class writing which can be seen to interact with the dominant structure of feeling of the period. That dominant sensibility was of course the codified – if ultimately contradictory – discourse and experience called Thatcherism. I have defined the work of the three writers discussed as working-class writing, on the basis that the central focus and concern of their production is to do with representing and defining contemporary working-class life. Their work belongs to what we might loosely term a tradition of working-class cultural intervention, other examples of which we have examined in the first chapter and in the introduction. In this case, all three writers come from the working class, and all three are of roughly the same generation, born around the time of the Second World War. This is a point of some significance and one key reason why their separable, yet collective, project to delineate particular structures of feeling relating to working-class experience in the 1980s – the expression of a gradual awareness, barely articulable, of radical change and rupture – stand as important interventions in the cultural and political milieu of the time, both reflecting and shaping our own responses to the historical moment.

II   'Giz a job': unemployment and the crisis of identity

First televised on BBC2 in October/November 1982, the impact of Alan Bleasdale's *Boys from the Blackstuff* was such that it was given an unusually quick repeat transmission in January 1983. It achieved popularity on a national scale, with a total of thirty million viewers watching its BBC1 second showing, and it generated widespread debate within the media, the political establishment and the public at large. Its intervention into the social and cultural field at this time received added thrust in the light of the social, political and economic developments resulting from the election in 1979 of a right-wing Conservative government under Margaret Thatcher. Within the space of three years, the economic policies pursued by the Thatcher government had secured a return of mass unemployment as the industrial base of what was already an ailing economy was stripped away.

The central theme of *Boys from the Blackstuff* is unemployment, and its effects on a number of working-class families and individuals in Liverpool, with a particular emphasis on the male experience of joblessness. Its representations of (un)working-class men (Bleasdale focuses overwhelmingly upon the male experience of unemployment) seems to be constructed in such a way as to counter the official discourse of 'dole scroungers'.[17] This reflects Bleasdale's own belief that

> it is important now to write about the dole as seen from the point of view of those who are on it, and to side with them against the people and papers who would like us to believe, despite the million and a half out of work and mass redundancies at every opportunity, that the majority of the unemployed are malingerers and rogues.[18]

Bleasdale shows working-class Liverpool, its people, and how they cope during recession and economic reconstruction. The stories work within a dynamic that draws together the workplace (or the lack of it), the domestic or familial, and the personal with the political.

The effectiveness and impact of *Boys from the Blackstuff*, 'the TV drama event of the eighties',[19] was in its readiness to deal with the lived experiences of a large number of people faced or dealing with the prospect of unemployment. For one critic, it became in effect the *Means Test Man* of the 1980s.[20] Urban representations in *Boys from the Blackstuff* are predominantly bleak. Community breakdown – a powerful structure of feeling here – is reflected through images of urban decay, be they shots of neglected and rubbish-strewn wasteground, the uniform drabness of run-down post-war housing estates or the derelict docks now devoid of the activity that had previously animated them. The series uses locations easily recognizable to local people: the docks and the Tate and Lyle factory are two examples. Filming in and around housing estates contributes further to this process of identification, or orientation; a deliberate strategy to blur the distinction between fact and fiction, so although *Boys from the Blackstuff* is labelled 'drama', the mode of representation suggests real life – a key component in the genre of social realism. Through Bleasdale's mapping of the city we witness the destruction of the vernacular landscape or social space, processes set in train by industrial collapse. Public spaces become spaces of alienation, which then take on personal and ontological forms in figures like Yosser Hughes (psychologically damaged through the loss of his identity as a working man), or Chrissie's wandering from building site to building site in search of work, or in George's 'last ride' through the dead docks where he spent his early working life and learnt his politics.

Bleasdale's writing exhibits a high consciousness of formal strategies or conventions. I have already suggested that the effectiveness of *Boys from the Blackstuff* lay in its readiness to deal with the lived experiences of a large number of people faced or coping with unemployment. Representations of unemployment, the sense of human life stifled and repressed by outside forces, link Bleasdale's work with some of the concerns of earlier socialist and working-class writers. The realist representations of working people in *Boys from the Blackstuff* found wide popularity through what I term the 'pleasure of identification'; the mobilization of a collective structure of feeling increasingly pressured in a climate of ideologically motivated individualism. What is then depicted is the crisis of a 'knowable community'. But *Boys from the Blackstuff* moves beyond the dominant conventions of realism at important moments, applying strategies which disrupt naturalist representation in a process resembling Brecht's 'alienation effect', a de-centring of the action where the narrative moves from the quotidian experiences of the dole or family life to, for instance, the slapstick behaviour of the dole inspectors, or Yosser's unpredictable head-butting, or the nightmare comic grotesque of the final episode. In this way, contradiction (even absurdity) is foregrounded, evinced in Chrissie's frustrated, and thwarted, attempts to live a normal life (get a decent job). Chrissie then represents 'nothing but an exhibit of the contradictions which make up our society'.[21] In discussing Brecht's Epic theatre, Walter Benjamin argues that what counts, 'is not so much the development of actions as the representations of conditions . . . the truly important thing is to discover the conditions of life . . . The discovery (alienation) of conditions takes place through the interruption of happenings.'[22] This 'interruption' Brecht referred to as the 'alienation effect', which constructs a necessary distance between 'viewer' and 'viewed', effecting a radical discontinuity, and preventing any simplistic identification with the characters, thus decentring the action. The resulting fruitful dialectic of familiarization and defamiliarization characterizes *Boys from the Blackstuff*.

This relates to the sense, broached in the earlier discussion of Williams, of the familiar becoming strange, the strange made familiar. These forms encourage, rather than passive consumption, 'complex seeing' which does not paralyse the audience's critical faculties, but emphasizes the changeable and discontinuous nature of reality and of subjectivity. It is possible to regard Bleasdale's mode of presentation as a process which both confuses and sharpens the act of identification and understanding, calling for some degree of political reflection, placing the viewer in the position of questioning what is happening on the screen and through the characters. *Boys from the Blackstuff*, formally at least, strives for this 'complex seeing'; yet the five episodes express overall an acute political pessimism, a structure of feeling symptomatic of the particular historic conjuncture in which the series was produced. This emphasis is symbolized in the powerful 'semantic figure' of the elderly political activist and trade unionist George Malone, who is so pivotal in the series.

Each of the five episodes focuses on the individual experiences of the 'Boys' and their search for work. These stories, however, overlap in crucial ways to suggest a collective experience, representing the characters as men fallen on hard times, finding it almost impossible to cope with their new conditions of existence. A strong sense of dispossession pervades the stories; their lives, and the communities in which they live, start to disintegrate. Snowy, militant son of George Malone, voices the hard-Left anti-government stance, trying to rally the Boys:

> All I'm saying is, if y'don't fight, if y'know, if . . . like I mean, it was easy to be a socialist when I was growing up in the sixties, an' even f'most of the seventies. Everyone was a friggin' socialist then. It was fashionable. But it's not now. Everything's gone sour, everyone's lockin'

the door, turnin' the other cheek, lookin' after number one. *But now's the time when we should all be together.* Now's the time when we *need* to be together, 'cos . . . 'cos well we're not winnin' anymore. *Don't you see that?*[23]

Despite Snowy's commitment, the discourse is hesitant, unsure, under pressure. And Bleasdale renders Snowy as a symptomatically marginal figure in the series as a whole, hardly a representative voice. That Bleasdale should feel the need to kill off this character so early on (in the first episode) says a great deal about Bleasdale's view of class struggle and class politics in Britain at this time. Later in the series, when George Malone, quoting Dickens, and indeed paraphrasing Marx's argument on surplus value, tells the others that 'We are the most important part of the nation. We are the ones who do the work', we cannot help feeling the irony behind the remark, as the dole queues are seen to lengthen with each passing week. The overall emphasis on the individual and psychological effects of unemployment heightens a feeling of pessimism, even hopelessness; and from the relatively light humour of the first episode, the comedy grows progressively darker until in the latter scenes it verges on the comic grotesque (though this carries its own ideological implications). I want to concentrate on the final episode, because it is here that the structure of feeling receives its fullest articulation.

The final part of *Boys from the Blackstuff* ends the series on a highly ambiguous note. It is an episode of high melodrama infused with what have been described as elements of the 'comic grotesque'.[24] This last story is 'about' George Malone, as in some ways is the whole series. Traces of George, and what he is meant to represent in relation to a traditional working-class culture and politics, are present in various degrees virtually from the outset. He is the figure of working-class mutuality and solidarity; the discursive and historical embodiment of working-class resistance to exploitation and oppression to whom the others might have turned in times past. The figure of George becomes representative of a wider, and largely unstated, problematic in the series as it negotiates at a subtextual level with the current status of class struggle itself. George's death, more than anything else, signals a downturn in this struggle, at least as it has manifested itself in its Labourist guise, or tradition. This has led one critic to argue that

'All that is left is "the world going mad" . . . "an absurd black farce" that corresponds to the cynical humour the "Boys" use as their strength and their only defence against the material oppression visualized in the landscape of urban decay.'[25] At this particular historical juncture it might be argued that it would have been disingenuous for Bleasdale to suggest anything else. Rapid de-industrialization, mass unemployment and working-class demoralization form the context in which *Boys from the Blackstuff* was written. Though it is possible to see the drama opening up a space for protest, a cultural intervention into contemporary politics, critics have also made the point that its overriding structure of feeling is one of despondency, which suggests no way forward, but instead only a debilitating passivity, a sense of acceptance.

The final episode – 'George's Last Ride' – has a profound generational perspective. Blacklisted in 1958 for militant activities, recalled fondly by the doctor son of a docker father who had, as a child, witnessed him speaking passionately at a shop-stewards' meeting of 'one for all, and all for one', the ailing George Malone is shown arguing with his sons about politics in a new era:

> JOHN   It's different now, dad. These days y'go on strike –
> RITCHIE   Whatever the reasons –
> JOHN   . . . before y'can get out of the gates, management are havin' singsongs an' wearing party hats.
> RITCHIE   [*Indicating*] With 'Goodbye Boys' written on the front.
> JOHN   Come back next week to get your cards.
> GEORGE   But what are the men thinking about? Y' not goin' to tell me that they're safeguardin' their future – 'cos they've got none whatever way it goes – so they may as well do what's right an' honest. (p. 151)

The two sons are shop-stewards, union activists, trying to represent their men in a hostile political climate. New trade-union laws and rising unemployment make it increasingly difficult for the tactics George's generation might have successfully employed to carry weight in the present. Exasperated, they try to explain, but neither George nor their mother will have any of it:

> MRS MALONE   I won't have that kind of defeatist talk at my table. Go and eat jelly with the bairns go on. And on your way to work in the morning, buy the *Daily Mail*. (p. 152)

She goes on to invoke the 1930s and past working-class struggles against a system that brought hunger and poverty; a time of greater solidarity which, John argues, no longer exists:

> JOHN   It means the thirties mam, and soup kitchens and hunger marches. You with your father marchin' from the North East, and my dad with his. It means people standing together and fighting. And it means another time and age. (p. 152)

Though it is suggested that the conditions of the 1980s (high unemployment, the roll-back of the welfare state) are beginning to resemble those of the inter-war Depression years, those earlier responses are deemed inadequate. Past and present collide here, in an exchange resonant with working-class history and politics. What is partly spoken is the view that the mass worker of the welfare state represents an increasingly marginal figure, and George stands as a monument to a lost identity. Despite Mrs Malone's argument that the past should inform the present – fuel contemporary struggles, providing insights on a potential future – her sons are fatalistic, feeling sidelined by the bosses and let down by the men who 'don't seem to care or understand about anythin' that hasn't got tits or comes out of a barrel'.

As George symbolizes an era that has passed, the images that surround him evoke a different time of flat caps, old-fashioned furniture, coal fires. His 'last ride' through Liverpool, a sick man being pushed along by Chrissie in a wheelchair, is an elegiac emblem. As they take in the dead docks and the wasteland that surrounds them, George's narrative recounts a history of working-class culture and politics. The scene dramatizes a lack of hope – 'Once upon a time, Chrissie . . . once upon a time' – and the narrative recalls the 'the ship-repair men, scalers, dockers . . . The kids playing alley oh, the little shops on the corner . . . and on the third Saturday an organ-grinder and his monkey'. The camera moves from the derelict warehouses to the new container port as George recalls the arrival of the welfare state, as a time of promise and of 'politics and power and come the day when we'd have inside toilets and proper bathrooms. Of Attlee and Bevan, Hogan and Logan'. The post-1945 settlement that was meant to sweep away the misery working people had faced in the 1930s; the memories of an intimate culture and entertainment; the sense of cohesion, of a class for itself:

GEORGE   Forty-seven years ago. I stood here, a young bull, and watched my first ship come in . . . They say that memories live longer than dreams . . . But my dreams, those dreams, those dreams of long ago, they still give me some kind of hope and faith in my class . . . I can't believe there is no hope, I can't. (p. 193)

George expresses a resonant structure of feeling, speaking across the generations, evoking a specific historical and political condition, in an attempt to reinstate a particular identity for his generation of the working class, or of working-class men (women do not figure large in Bleasdale's writing). He would agree with Walter Benjamin on the need to remember, lest one should be written out of history altogether by the enemy. Thus he is trying to 'seize hold of a memory as it flashes up at a moment of danger'.[26] But the changed political constellation of the present renders him a residual figure. He dies leaving an isolated Chrissie scurrying around the industrial wasteland, directionless.

If George is meant to represent 'a lifetime of discursive struggle against the economic order'[27] then his death must signify *at least* the end of a certain type of working-class political organization and opposition to the dominant. If we are not witnessing the total demise of the meanings and values ascribed to a class, we do see them coming under intense pressure. At the same time, George's very articulation represents a challenge to this threat. This occurs time and again throughout the series, embodied in the dilemmas and disappointments (as well as their struggles to fight back) of each of the Boys and finally encapsulated in George's 'last ride'. This, in turn, brings us up close to Williams's use and meaning of structure of feeling, and its thematic and structural links to a sense of a 'knowable community'. If, in this final episode of *Boys from the Blackstuff*, a particular present is dying, it seems the case also that any utopian impulse towards the future is being stifled too, and the sheer bleakness of the melodramatic portrayal of it all suggests that the 'hope' George speaks of cannot outlive him. The mayhem in the pub at the close of the final episode seems further to emphasize this; yet before the final credits we see Chrissie, Loggo and Yosser turn their backs on the meaningless anarchy in the Green Man to seek solutions of a different kind.

Barry Hines's fiction has traced aspects of working-class life since his first novel, *The Blinder*, published in 1966. He is probably best known for *A Kestrel for a Knave* (1968), made into the successful film, *Kes*, by Ken Loach. In this novel young Billy Casper is seen struggling against the life-deadening institution of school, an unloving family environment and his future destiny as fodder for the pit, which has already contributed to the alienation of his older brother. What truly motivates Billy is his relationship with the kestrel, Kes, and this helps him survive in his impoverished and harsh surroundings. What is suggested by the relationship is that Billy's developing values are not the values of the wider community, and the novel stands as another form of critique of the 'affluence' theory discussed in the previous chapter. In the end, however, Billy is forced to accept his fate as there seems to be no way out. In two novels published much later, we have a different view of work and of community.

The Price of Coal (1979) and *Looks and Smiles* (1983) offer more politicized representations of a working-class experience of work or of no work. It has been suggested that Hines's writings 'span a wide range of possible reactions to class subordination, from Sillitoesque freebooting, through tentative attempts at alternative patterns of life, to the recognition ... of the importance of collective action and class solidarity'.[28] Through a brief analysis of these two novels, it is possible to register an important shift in what I have termed a working-class structure of feeling, and as with Bleasdale's intervention, this represents a shift reflecting the wider socio-economic developments of the time.

Set in the assured solidarities of a south Yorkshire mining community, *The Price of Coal* divides structurally into two parts. Part one, entitled 'Meeting the people', involves a visit by Prince Charles to the colliery. Part two is called 'Back to reality': the reality of deficient working conditions, incompetent management techniques and, finally, a fatal coalface accident. Following later assaults on the mining industry in Britain, we experience now a certain degree of pathos on reading *The Price of Coal*. Hines foregrounds the political awareness of the colliers, and their keen recognition of the class-divided nature of British society, a condition embodied in the imminent arrival of royalty and the often absurd lengths to which management is willing to go to make the visit as comfortable as possible. Work is the central organizing feature of the novel, not only its dangers, but its capacity to engender collective solidarities and a more radical value-system and structure of feeling than that associated with the dominant:

> 'What I mean is, if we were in charge of the day-to-day running of things, and were responsible for setting production targets, safety would be bound to improve, wouldn't it? We'd make sure that safety and production went hand in glove. We'd feel it was more in our interests then, wouldn't we?'
> Tony was listening now because he was thinking about his father. He had heard Syd use the same argument many times, and he remembered him saying that industrial democracy was just as important as the wages battle.
> But he had never been interested before, the debate had seemed too theoretical. But now, with his father trapped underground, it was suddenly relevant and urgent. These ideas had become functional.[29]

Control of the labour process is seen as vital, not at an individual level, but for the community as a whole. Hines suggests that worker control over production would not only make conditions safer, but would place such production on the basis of need, rather than subordinate it to the dictates of profit and loss. There is considerable consonance between this novel and some themes taken up by the proletarian novels of the 1930s.

The same can be said of *Looks and Smiles*, but for different reasons. Here we are back on the terrain of high unemployment, the conditions described by Bleasdale, with images of the 1980s which testify to the increasing sense of personal hopelessness of young working-class people in a very different context (no work), from that of *The Price of Coal*. Again, the writer stresses the male experience of unemployment. The narrative opens with representations of the energy and vitality of Mick and his friends, fresh from leaving school, and hopeful for the future. These hopes are soon dashed in the face of massive redundancies and lengthening dole queues. Mick's best friend is finally driven to join the army, leaving him to contemplate a future where 'All the days were the same on the dole'.[30] This pessimistic structure of feeling then becomes prevalent in the novel. Mick forms a relationship with Karen, and they take off on his motorbike across the country to visit her estranged father. Hines describes their motorway journey:

> A smoking van on the hard shoulder. Police cars lurking in lay-bys. A derelict coal mine. Slag heaps. A deserted village. Dead elm trees ... Blood on the road. A kestrel over a scorched bank. A slimy canal. New trading estates with FACTORY UNITS TO LET signs. Silent factories.

> Empty council houses . . . Polythene flapping on a barbed wire fence. Litter: in fields, in woods, in the streets. A convoy of army trucks. (pp. 168–9)

Personal despair is framed by public squalor, the metonymic collocation of these fragments signalling a general decay. The detritus of a market economy in crisis suggests that human life, when there is no hope, will become part of that same waste. The final reference to the army convoy strikes a distinct minatory tone; in the novel, the presence of authority, in the shape of the police, is pervasive, intimating a future police-state where control of the unemployed will become the overriding priority of the state. Such images acquire retrospective significance in relation to developments in the 1980s and the policing of the 1984–5 miners' strike.

Looks and Smiles ends:

> Next morning, Karen went back to work even though she had hardly slept. She daren't take any more time off as the staff had been repeatedly warned about absenteeism . . . Mick had to go into town too. He had to go to the Social Security Office to sign on the dole. His appointment was for ten-thirty; but he knew that he would have to arrive early to reach the counter by that time. The queues were longer every time he went. (p. 201)

The social and personal costs of Thatcherism are made quite plain. Mick is a long way from the freebooting, big-spending figure of Arthur Seaton, and the secure employment of the 1960s.

A much later novel, *The Heart of It* (1994), reflects on the 1984–5 miners' strike and its tragic aftermath. Cal Rickard, son of Communist and union militant Harry Rickard, is a film writer living in France, estranged from his working-class origins and his father's politics. His father is making a slow recovery from a debilitating stroke and Cal is compelled to return home for a family visit. Through conversations with family and friends, the reader learns of the events surrounding the strike (his father being a prominent activist) and witnesses the consequences of defeat for the mining community. As might be expected, we are a long way from the essentially confident narrative of *The Price of Coal*; yet the narrative is so structured as to remind us of the collective values and strong resistance still embedded in such communities, despite the havoc wreaked by unemployment and low-paid work. Cal finds himself attempting to retrieve his own past as he is reacquainted with school friends who tell of the strike, the police brutality and of the miners' struggle. Through these stories he begins to see in a different way both his father (not simply as the Stalinist ideologue he had perceived him to be) and, more importantly, his mother too, who found her own voice during the dispute and became prominent in the women's action groups. Cal observes: 'Things have changed around here, that's for sure. The people, the place. Everything's been ripped apart.' To this, Christine, his brother's wife, replies:

> It wasn't a total disaster, though, and a lot of people came out of it a lot stronger than when they went in. Especially the women. I mean, look at your mother. She was always a lovely woman, but totally dominated by your dad. She wasn't after the strike ended, though. They came out on equal terms.[31]

In a number of ways, then, the narrative is about Cal's mother, and other women like Christine, who, during the 1984–5 dispute, found an independence from patriarchal structures, and their own ways of struggling collectively against the forces of the state and capital. All this is contrasted with Cal's own present, working on Hollywood scripts, and being paid large sums of money for penning fantasy stories for the American culture industry:

> It was worth doing if the money was right. It was as simple as that. He couldn't afford the luxury of a social conscience, and anyway who wants to pay good money to see films about unmarried mothers throwing themselves off the balconies of high-rise flats? (p. 99)

Yet Cal increasingly feels compromised when faced with the realities of life in the mining communities, and thus a powerful subtext emerges in the narrative highlighting the contradiction between representation and reality, whether in relation to the strike (its media construction, as opposed to people's actual experiences) or the film projects Cal is involved with. Finally, Cal moves towards scripting something very different: an account of the strike itself. He begins to tape the testimonies of those directly involved, a narrative device in the novel itself which then enables the people to 'speak for themselves'. At the end of the novel Cal's father dies. But

A 'sense of loss': working-class writing from the 1980s

if this is symbolic of the death of a way of life, or of a type of work and politics (as figured in George Malone), hope and agency are encoded in the surviving values of those remaining in the community, and in the emergent radical structure of feeling articulated by the strong women characters in the text.

III Class and the cultural politics of language

The politics of language and the question of class preoccupies most of Tony Harrison's work. In much of Harrison's poetry he has been at pains to demonstrate how the relationship of language and class marks out ideological terrains which both silence and disenfranchise the working-class subject, imposing further constraints on the subordinated. Harrison has addressed this condition through the figure of his baker father in poems such as 'Marked with D'. We hear that 'he hungered for release from marked speech / that kept him down, the tongue that weighed like lead'.[32] One thing Harrison's poetry succeeds in doing is to bring into question the dominant ideology which posits a homogeneous culture, which is viewed as a kind of axis of equivalence suggesting parity. I want to look at this aspect of Harrison's verse before moving on to my main concern, his poem 'V'.

> The baker's man that no one will see rise
> and England made to feel like some dull oaf
> is smoke, enough to sting one person's eyes
> and ash (not unlike flour) from one small loaf
> (p. 155)

The structure of feeling expressed in 'Marked with D' is typical of Harrison's unfinished selection called 'The School of Eloquence'. Here 'England' has effectively silenced his father, the 'settled' language of what is in fact an overpowering and alienating tongue designed to keep him in his place – 'The baker's man that no one will see rise'. Language is both class struggle and class domination, as the poem 'National Trust' indicates:

> here at the booming shaft at Towanrouth,
> now National Trust, a place where they got tin,

> those gentlemen who silenced the men's oath
> and killed the language that they swore it in.
>
> The dumb go down in history and disappear
> and not one gentleman's been brought to book;
> *Mes den hep tavas a-gollas y dyr* (Cornish)
> 'the tongueless man gets his land took'
> (p. 121)

Harrison seems to be pointing to both linguistic and material appropriation by the powerful, something not recorded in the official history books. 'Working', through the story of Patience Kershaw, reminds us of the consequence of the Victorian values gaining ground in the 1980s, which were purported to express the essence of the national spirit.

> Among stooped getters, grimy, knacker-bare,
> head down thrusting a 3cwt corf
> turned your crown bald, your golden hair
> chaffed fluffy first and then scuffed off,
> chick's back, then eggshell, that sunless white.
> You've been underneath too long to stand the light.
> You're lost in this sonnet for the bourgeoisie.
> (p. 124)

The poem describes the labour of a fourteen-year-old girl in the mining industry, a victim of early industrial practice and Victorian values. Harrison is using his poetry to present a form of labour history. Culture – poetry – is appropriated to expose the barbarism of the ruling class, who cloaked their activities in discourses aligned to concepts of progress, modernization and 'values'. In rescuing the girl's suffering from historical oblivion, the poem dialogizes the social and cultural past (and present), suggesting that the values of this period were not universally beneficial but were, for some, quite deadly:

> Patience Kershaw, bald hurryer, fourteen,
> this wordshift and inwit's a load of crap
> for dumping on a slagheap, I mean
> *th'art nobbut summat as wants raking up.*

> I stare into the fire. Your skinned skull shines.
> I close my eyes. That makes a dark like mines.
>
> Wherever hardship held its tongue the job
> 's breaking the silence of a worked-out-gob.
>
> (p. 124)

Written during the miners' strike of 1984–5, Harrison's controversial poem 'V' contains an epigraph taken from Arthur Scargill: 'My father still reads the dictionary every day. He says your life depends on your power to master words.' John Lucas has described 'V' as a 'condition-of-England' address, giving voice to the irreconcilable tensions of two cultures and thus giving 'the lie to the government's pretence to speak for the nation and to that wider cultural orthodoxy which endlessly claims to be at once representative and authoritative'.[33] The 'V' of the title is an emblem of division (versus) and conflict, and Harrison wants it to symbolize division within both the class-mobile poet himself (the scholarship boy), and the nation. Though the poem hardly refers directly to the strike, the skinhead Leeds United supporter stands in for the victimized miners (not to mention other working-class youths), thus dramatizing the divisions endemic in English society. More than this, the 'skin' symbolizes that structure of feeling we have already referred to as a sense of loss.

The poem tells us:

> These Vs are all the versuses of life . . .
> class v class and bitter as before,
> the unending violence of US and THEM,
> personified in 1984
> by Coal Board MacGregor and the NUM,
>
> (p. 238)

The poet lists more conflicts signified by 'V': 'Hindu/Sikh, soul/body, heart v mind', and registers his personal despair at the graffiti sprayed upon his parents' grave by an angry United supporter in a Leeds cemetery. This leads, from an initial, bitter response, to a disquisition on the profound alienation and dispossession of working-class youth in Thatcher's Britain. In the voice of liberalism the poet tries to rationalize the skin's 'art-work', hoping it might symbolize 'deep aspirations', and thus construing it as a 'call to Britain and to all the nations / made in the name of love for peace's sake' (p. 241). After all, 'V' can represent more than conflict: the Churchillian overtones associated with the symbol connote victory and pride, a particularly strong moment of national unity. These mystifications get short shrift from the skin:

> Aspirations, cunt! Folk on t'fucking dole
> have got about as much scope to aspire
> above the shit they're dumped in, cunt, as coal
> aspires to be chucked on t'fucking fire.
>
> (p. 241)

The skin's uncompromising stance is a clear rejection of the poet's liberal platitudes. But he expresses the contradictions within his own position, too. BNP (British National Party) politics and its associated xenophobia lead him both to reject and at the same time to embrace a nation that offers him nothing; and the scapegoats for this condition, of course, are the 'PAKI GIT' and the 'NIGGER'. But in the end the working-class youth has no real identity at all:

> Ah'll tell yer then what really riles a bloke.
> It's reading on their graves the jobs they did –
> butcher, publican, baker. Me I'll croak
> doing t'same nowt ah do now as a kid.
>
> If mi mam's up there, don't want to meet 'er
> Listening to me list me dirty deeds,
> and 'ave to pipe up to St fucking Peter
> ah've been on t'dole all mi life in fucking Leeds!
>
> Then t'Alleluias stick in t'angels' gobs
> when dole-wallahs fuck off to the void
> what'll t'mason carve up for their jobs?
> The cunts who lieth 'ere wor unemployed?
>
> (p. 242)

Deprived of work, the skin is deprived of his own sense of self-worth. It seems that all the time Harrison uses the skin's mode of address to force us to contemplate public discourses of national belonging and citizenship; more than this, however, the poem's structure of feeling speaks of the crisis of the industrial working class.

In the graveyard, the stones tell the skin the very story of his history and culture, a culture where work and self-respect were and are closely associated. The work performed by past generations of working people, the skills they acquired, no matter how exploited they were in the process, are now actively withheld. This cannot be rationalized, or romanticized in poetry by the outside observer working with words. The skin asserts as much:

> Don't talk to me of fucking representing
> the class yer were born into any more.
> Yer going to get 'urt and start resenting
> it's not poetry we need in this class war.
> (p. 244)

The poet stands above a worked-out mine:

> Subsidence makes the obelisks all list.
> One leaning left's marked FUCK, one right's marked SHIT
> sprayed by some peeved supporter who was pissed.
> (p. 240)

The image here suggests that infrastructural collapse produces a corresponding decay at the cultural level. For Harrison, the skin is a semantic figure of ambivalence and, like himself, both inside and outside working-class culture. The miners' strike – the resonant subtext of the poem – represents not merely the reality of class conflict but, in defeat, the potential demise of a certain class formation and way of life. In many respects, then, the skin will have to inherit the crumbling industrial landscape once worked by George Malone and make of it what he can. A sense of loss, an accumulating experience of 'placeless-ness' (despite his nationalistic rhetoric of belonging), are the final motivating forces for the skin's anger (and the poet's, for that matter); symptomatic of that very structure of feeling I have been seeking to identify throughout this chapter.

For Williams, experience is mediated through the process of structure of feeling. While the writers discussed here produce a structure of feeling in their work which speaks of loss and crisis, there is also a sense of resistance and agency: the articulation of a practical consciousness resisting the platitudes, pressures and limits of the official ideology of a period. At the same time as a language, a way of understanding, is seen as breaking down, there emerges an intense effort to reinstate it. In the process meanings and values are articulated, contested or reaffirmed; forms and conventions within the writing are reproduced in significantly altered ways to express what represents a profound historical experience.

Overwhelmingly, this writing has shown a concern with a 'knowable community' of working-class people, and a structure of feeling explored in key moments and characters. *Boys from the Blackstuff* stands out in this context, and the figure of George Malone most memorably embodies that 'moment of danger' invoked by Walter Benjamin, as the political settlement and historic gains that George's generation had won come under threat. It could be argued that the overall strength of the drama lies in its refusal of defeat or nostalgia: George dies, no political resolution is offered, but the Boys know that they have to move on, that there is no turning back. Though this is echoed to some degree in both Hines and Harrison, pessimism dominates, which suggests that a 'structure of feeling' need not be radical, though still oppositional, or in Williams's terms, residual. Harrison uses the moment of the miners' strike to suggest not merely loss, but cultural degeneration; alienation stemming from a denial of identity which then finds degraded form in the taking on of a subcultural way of being. We cannot escape the sense of loss evident in any of these narratives, constituting the symptomatic moment of their production and made more strongly felt by the working-class backgrounds of the authors themselves. The real strengths of the narratives emerge in the way they give voice to such structures of feeling; the weaknesses lie in the overwhelmingly masculine trajectory of the stories.

With its relation to conventions and community, structure of feeling represents practical and social consciousness: signifies 'what is actually being lived', articulated in revolt or refusal (acceptance, too, of course) against officially sanctioned forms of the time. So structure of feeling occupies the space at the juncture of the 'language and the lived'; and its lack of a full articulation is the result of 'tension, disturbance, blockage'.[34] What emerge are changes within the language, produced when a straining for expression occurs in the field of the 'lived'. Language use is thus seen as intersubjective, both constitutive and constituting: linguistic structures produced in the flux of new understandings, politics, possibilities of change. And on this account, art constitutes an area of knowledge, a place of 'cognitive mapping'. Selected images, rhythms and experience offer identifiable structures and social content – providing 'evidence of forms and conventions [semantic figures] which can be related to the emergence of a new structure of feeling'.[35] Finally, then, 'structures of feeling' are social experiences *in solution*; and, though not *inherently* radical, can be oppositional to the social order, or 'official consciousness' of the time.

In conclusion, we might ask about the reception of the narratives discussed in this chapter. Here *Boys from the Blackstuff* offers some clear evidence with which to consider what we can call the orientation of the sign. Though critics have pointed up an underlying pessimism in the drama (and I concur, partly), John Tulloch identifies a failure to take into account the profound effect the series had on many of its working-class viewers (especially Liverpudlians) who, whilst registering the underlying despondency of Bleasdale's text, still drew strength from it: 'Although the series was very pessimistic towards the end . . . it's made me more resolved to say get off the floor and fight back.'[36] Another correspondent wrote:

> Never before have I seen my family, my friends and acquaintances, my class, the people I know and live among and love and often despair of, portrayed on the screen with such realism, sensitivity and affection: our hopes, our aspirations, our frailties and contradictions.[37]

Add to this the way aspects of the series were taken out of the text and on to the streets, with the Anfield crowd taking up Yosser's 'I can do that', and 'Giz a job', and the striking waterworkers' placards reading 'We are the boys from the wetstuff', and we find a complex interaction between text and audience.

Stuart Hall argues, in 'Notes on Deconstructing the Popular', that 'there is no whole, authentic, autonomous "popular" culture which lies outside the field of force of the relations of cultural power and domination'.³⁸ Popular culture, he suggests, is necessarily contaminated by capitalist social relations and the culture industry, so that if authenticity ever did exist, it existed in the distant past, prior to the emergence and dominance of mass cultural institutions in the late nineteenth century. So, Hall goes on, it is necessary for producers of popular culture to seek forms and activities with roots in the social and material conditions of classes, embodied in popular traditions and practices. Popular culture can then be seen as in constant tension with the dominant. Hall emphasizes a dialectic between resistance and containment. The key theoretical concept here is hegemony, signifying the continuous and necessarily uneven development and struggle by the dominant culture to organize and disorganize, or 'place' popular culture. It is possible to understand the place of *Boys from the Blackstuff* (and other cultural interventions, I suggest) within this problematic. Bracketed in the ideological formation of 'quality' television (hence apolitical, middle class) by the media institutions, its use of popular forms, parody and verbal idiom enabled it to break the integuments of this formation, intervening powerfully in public and social life, offering a voice to the working class at a key historical juncture, exploring a structure of feeling and experience 'in solution'. The very question of representation is essential here, both in its aesthetic/cultural sense (mobilized forms and conventions with which to represent) and – in terms of whose voice gets heard and whose experiences are articulated – in its broadly 'political' meaning too.

3
Figuring the dispossessed: the negative topographies of class

'It's a world I don't know Mister Parker . . . I wish I did but I don't'.[1]

The third episode of Alan Bleasdale's *Boys from the Blackstuff* deals with the effects of unemployment on marriage and the family. Chrissie and his wife, Angie, argue bitterly about the absence of money and food, the result of Chrissie's failure to find work. Chrissie's lack of self-esteem and his inability to provide suggest his 'failure' as a man. Angie appears at this point to be the stronger character facing up to their predicament with anger rather than the mixture of self-pity and sense of futility Chrissie has succumbed to. She is angry that having fulfilled in their early life together the role marked out for her as a mother – 'It was never much fun early on, how could it be . . . babies and sick . . . it's not like you imagine it to be, it's not like it is in the *Woman's Own*' – her horizons have been dramatically curtailed when she should have had more time and opportunity to '[g]o back to college. Job of my own. Out in the world.' She sees the ludicrousness and unfairness of it all, and demands that Chrissie 'fight back . . . fight back'. The exchange recalls those which take place in Walter Brierley's Depression novel, *Means Test Man*, where Jack Cook and his wife argue around the same subject – the absence of work, the shame and hardship this brings. And the same assumptions are in play: it is the natural role of the man to be the breadwinner. Angie is assertive, aiming her invective at her husband *and* state institutions. At the same time, however, she is demanding that Chrissie maintain the dominant position in the relationship. She wants him to fight back for her (and the kids) as well as himself. But for Chrissie, and the other Boys, the breadwinner role has been radically undermined, and Chrissie is acutely conscious of this.

Without work he feels he has 'no place' in society: 'I had a job . . . I laid the roads, girl, I laid the roads . . . lay-bys, motorways, country lanes.' Bleasdale dramatizes the consequences when an accepted way of being, or a 'common sense', falls into crisis. Primarily, Chrissie regards his role in both the public sphere and private relations as that of provider. Bleasdale seems to be suggesting, in the face of historical change, that this construction needs finally to be rethought.

The 'emasculation' of Chrissie leaves us to consider the role of working-class men in a 'work-less' environment: or at least in a labour market increasingly altered by processes of de-industrialization. The ideology which marked women out for domesticity and men for the workplace is still operating in Bleasdale's narrative, but is showing signs of collapse. The representation of Angie remains ambiguous in all this, and the overall masculine edge to the series ensures that she (and other working-class women in the series) retain a subordinate role, despite her independent and forceful spirit. But, in the end, the only way Chrissie can maintain his dominant position, it seems, is symbolically seen in the final shot of the episode where, in a cathartic moment, he attempts to resolve these contradictions. The scene is set in the backyard where the family keep chickens, rabbits and geese. Money and food are exhausted and, driven by despair and anger, Chrissie slaughters most of the animals. The scene can be read as Chrissie's attempt to reassert his power and status, signified by the appropriately 'phallic' shotgun. Symbolically, by providing food, Chrissie contrives to remasculinize himself. Moreover, at a wider level, this scene acts as a way of resolving the deeper contradictions stemming from the socio-economic conditions which the episode dramatizes. From this perspective, the scene represents an ideological resolution to stark material conditions – the lack of basic necessities – and this can be related to a more fundamental problematic in the series which flags up a crisis of any other substantial form of collective or political action. Even so, a return to the essentially individualist role of breadwinner still seems closed off for Chrissie, and he ends up weeping and helpless in the arms of his wife. The camera pans away for a high long-shot of the back yard, with Chrissie and Angie helplessly 'encaged' by the four walls surrounding them. Whether or not this scene properly constitutes the cathartic moment, then, is uncertain, for it is unlikely that the audience experiences any form of purgation, as a closure to the crisis is refused. This idea of entrapment within altering social landscapes, and the existential dilemmas triggered by it, will be central to the concerns of this chapter.

I Mapping the landscape: the negative topographies of class

My focus here will be on texts which map urban and industrial – or, rather, post-industrial – landscapes, in the context of representations of the changing relations of working-class life in the 1980s. I will concentrate chiefly on the writing of Scottish novelist James Kelman, though as a precursor to this I want to examine some other writing which attempts to understand the processes of social and economic restructuring referred to as deindustrialization. As I indicate in the opening comments of this chapter, representations of the male proletarian protagonist will be a special focus here. The spatial displacements of class became a distinctive feature of the period, as working-class communities, often based around traditional industries of coal, steel and the shipyards and docks, were closed down in rapid succession.

Edward Soja's discussion of the geopolitics of social space informs this argument. He calls attention to the need 'to see more clearly the long-hidden instrumentality of human geographies, in particular the encompassing and encaging spatializations of social life that have been associated with the historic development of capitalism'.[2] Soja highlights the historico-geographical coordinates and determinants considered neglected by social theorists, yet which remain crucial in the shaping of class power and inequalities. David Harvey forwards a similar argument: 'the control over spatial organization and authority over the use of space becomes [a] crucial means for the reproduction of social power relations. The state, or some other social grouping . . . can thus often hide their power to shape social reproduction behind the seeming neutrality of their power to organize space.'[3] Money power reconstructs social space and disrupts once fairly stable environments. Within this context, and in relation to individual and collective experience, important questions of social consciousness and cultural identity become pressing. Constant capital renewal disrupts the present and, in so doing, can erase any sense of the past: the dynamics of restructuring and rationalization in the pursuit of profit ensure that all that is solid melts into air.

This was Tom Nairn's point, discussed very briefly in chapter 2. Doreen Massey, some ten years on, re-theorizes Nairn's argument in a broader geopolitical frame. The global reach of late capitalism, she argues, has produced new and more flexible forms of accumulation and surplus extraction with the internationalization of production. As new technology, and the information industry, open up new fields of investment in the First World, the Third World experiences industrialization. This leads, she asserts, to new forms of inequality, within a global hierarchy of power.[4] An outcome of this is the radical transformation of familiar terrain: the kind of 'creative destruction' defined by Schumpeter. Massey suggests that 'each geographical space in the world is being realigned in relation to new global realities . . . their boundaries dissolve as they are increasingly crossed by everything from investment flows, to cultural influences, to satellite TV networks'.[5] Massey emphasizes the dialectic between the local and the global, and points to the exacerbation of time–space compression now characterizing late capitalism.

Time–space compression suggests the shrinkage of space through time, and the confluence of diverse yet separated communities, more often than not in some form of competition with each other, creating a condition of both fragmentation and homogenization. These developments, intensified during the past twenty years, have had, according to David Harvey, 'a disorientating and disrupting impact upon political-economic practices, the balance of class power, as well as upon cultural and social life'.[6] Such changes, working on a global scale, inform Fredric Jameson's account of postmodernity. Part of Jameson's analysis and response to this is a call for 'cognitive mapping', which might enable subjects to make sense of their individual and collective lives in the world of late capitalism, with its spatial disruption constituting, Jameson argues, the depthless terrain of the postmodern life-world, and an accompanying waning of historical memory, or affect. Thus Jameson envisages the postmodern world as 'peculiarly without transcendence and without perspective . . . and indeed without plot in any traditional sense'.[7]

These arguments are born out to some degree in Patrick Wright's selection of essays *A Journey Through the Ruins*, in which he explores parts of London's East End. He charts the demise of post-war planning and the welfare state, usurped by the 1980s free-market development masquerading under the joint signs of enterprise and renewal, and in the process transforming 'architecture [into] property', and redundant factories into yuppies' designer homes. Wright documents the decanting of an older working class from areas like the Isle of Dogs, and the transmutation of this territory into Docklands. He visits residents of the neglected and run-down nineteen-storey tower blocks of Holly Street Estate, describing how the 'modern chasm dweller, [t]hese people of the new abyss',[8] attempt to organize their lives despite being 'victims of a council that can't manage its own resources, [and] a national government that has enjoyed making symbolic capital out of the disorder of Labour authorities, while at the same time forcing through policy changes designed to reduce council housing to a residual welfare net'.[9] As the social democratic visions of progress fail to deliver for so many within the inner cities, they are left to the devices of the 'market', and their own determination to survive (or, if possible, move to greener pastures). Meanwhile, the environment, openly prey to property sharks for disposal or gentrification, becomes alien to people who have lived in it all their lives, but who now 'get lost sometimes' in the new geography of Docklands.

Peter Dunn and Lorraine Leeson remark how the marketing of Docklands in the 1980s by multinational corporate interests painted the area as a 'virgin site' ripe, as the language suggests, for 'penetration' and development. The metaphor implies conquest and availability; that there has been simply nothing there prior to this. Thus history is effectively erased, locals 'washed out' so as to create 'a blank canvas upon which we can paint the future'.[10] Docklands became all about borders and exclusions, as luxury housing had to be protected from the remnants of modernity. Dock walls were retained, surveillance equipment and gates erected. If this was not enough, 'strategic tree-planting was also used to mask the unsightly. Finally, if all else failed, the Development Corporation provided money for the refurbishment of council properties',[11] but only for those properties that seemed likely to spoil the view from luxury apartments. This is the context of Wright's mapping of the 'ruins'. He gives the place a past within the present, even as its future is being decided elsewhere, and by those with vested interests.

Similar changes occurred outside the capital, as sites once occupied with production are transformed into lifestyle locations or consumerist spectacles. Thus in the north-east of England, around the city of Newcastle, we are told that

> in places like Elswick and Meadow Well, industrial work is becoming a folk memory, something that Grandad did. Many families are now entering a third decade of giro dependency, while the almost sacred sites of work on the river bank are being transformed into mariner villages and informational technology offices. This produces more than a few geographical juxtapositions. Walker looks down on the high-class housing and private yachts of St Peter's basin; Elswick and Benwell have visually witnessed the bulldozing of Armstrong's and the building of a business park; North Shields sees the decline of an industrial waterfront being replaced by upmarket housing. It is no surprise that this disintegration of the old landscape and the economic and social order which it supported is accompanied by trauma.[12]

This setting is reminiscent of the one I will be examining later in Pat Barker's novel *The Century's Daughter*. There, it constitutes the framing landscape in which the main protagonist, Liza, spends her dying days and against which she narrates a past life informed by a more communal structure of feeling, a historically specific one embedded in family, neighbourhood and work practices. It is one that has gone, leading, in recent times, to a fragmentation of class consciousness and culture, and a profound remaking of the British working class. The demise of this habitus finds articulation in a powerful image from Irvine Welsh's *Trainspotting* (1993), a novel concerned with mapping ruins also.

> We go fir a pish in the auld Central Station at the Fit ay the Walk, now a barren, desolate, hangar, which is soon tae be demolished to be replaced by a supermarket and swimming centre. Somehow that makes us sad, even though ah wis eywis too young tae mind ay trains ever being there.
> —Some size ay a station this wis. Get a train tae anywhair fae here, at oane time, or so they sais, ah sais, watching my steaming pish splash oantae the cauld stane.
> —If it still hud fuckin trains, ah'd be oan one oot ay this fuckin dive, Begbie said. It wis uncharacteristic for him tae talk in that way. He tended tae romanticise the place.

At this point an old drunk approaches Begbie: this is the haunt of down-and-outs. 'Whay yis up tae lads? Trainspotting, eh? He sais, laughing uncontrollably at his own fuckin wit.'[13] The 'auld drunkard' is Begbie's father and, as Bell points out in his comments on the novel, 'the whole episode dramatizes the collapse of the social fabric'.[14] The scene emblematizes the post-industrial: the end of production in the shape of the 'desolate hangar' about to be refashioned into a site of consumption (a supermarket), and the demise of the industrial worker, symbolized in the decrepit figure of Begbie's father. What we have here is a terminus point. The narrative is, however, devoid of the elegiac, regretful tones found in *Boys from the Blackstuff* (or in Barker's work, as we shall see) because this seems now a settled fact. Renton, Sick-Boy, Spud and Swanny glory in dependency (one of the reasons for the later film's controversy), as a response to the shallowness of consumer culture, the emptiness of a dole-life in the industrial wasteland of Scotland. What is predicated then is a state of homelessness, the emergence of a vacant space, filled with the imaginary landscapes invoked by heroin. In turn, this act constitutes a kind of negation of the negation, seemingly the only viable response to prevailing circumstances. Renton's world is a postmodern location where, as he snarls, everything's 'shite' and nothing matters. The later filmic adaptation maintains the manic pace and the powerful vernacular dialogue of the novel, producing a kind of heightened realism (often verging on the surreal) which has the effect of revealing the danger and degradation of junk culture at the same time as exposing it as oddly and exhilaratingly 'heroic' – a perspective which in fact is not the dominant structure of feeling of the novel. While having no particular 'authoritative' centre, the novel articulates a number of narrative strands around themes of class loyalty, subcultural disaffection and the generational divide separating a working-class industrial world based on mass production from the destruction of this landscape in the 1980s, which leaves working-class youth with little to look forward to but long-term unemployment or short-term work-schemes. Thus, heroin provides the existential escape route from the despair of drug-saturated estates and the denuded industrial terrain of Edinburgh. Yet it is more than 'escape', it is 'choice'; the giving-over of self to drug hedonism, rather than economic exploitation (when work itself is available). Identity, then, might be seen very strictly as a *performative* act, a typically postmodern take on subjectivity, though carrying with it, in this context, the less positive connotations postmodern theorists generally ascribe to it. Thus *Trainspotting* constitutes a quite different 'escaper' narrative of working-class life, and a very different view of *agency*, from others we have examined, say, from the 1960s. Renton is no Arthur Seaton or the Boy in Colin MacInnes's *Absolute Beginners*, and he is not Billy Elliot. If optimism and resistance (as well as anger, at least in Sillitoe's case) found articulation in the earlier novels and films of the working class, Welsh's narrative presents us with characters set apart from a society and a culture in a state of stasis.

Christopher Meredith's *Shifts* (1988) also takes up the theme of de-industrialization. It is set in a south Wales valley town in the late 1970s, and tells of the closing-down of the steelworks, and the ramifications of this for both the town and the people living there. Thus *Shifts* is concerned with the effect of de-industrialization on working-class lives, and centres on the characters of Jack, a wanderer returned, Keith, a stalwart of the town and the steelworks, and Keith's wife, Judith.

What is striking about the novel is the overwhelming sense of inevitability infusing the narrative. The closing of the steelworks is an indisputable fact, and the men have no control over events. Despite some of the angry remarks of the men regarding this outcome (particularly the older generation, with memories of other times and whole lives invested in the industry), they remain powerless, disclosing a fatalism which, if anything, expresses a profound alienation from the whole process of work and production itself. The solidarity and collective agency expressed in the 1930s proletarian fiction of Lewis Jones are a passing memory here. In the whole novel there is barely a mention of the works' trade union, and only sardonic remarks about socialism. Collectivism finds expression in the men's banter, a black humour compensating for the impending loss. The novel's structure and symbolism reinforce this sense of closure. Thus the narrative begins and ends with the character 'O' clocking off: the timeclock constituting a potent symbol of how the men's lives are tied to the rhythms of industrial labour, the dull compulsion of the economic. The *shifts* of the title then becomes significant: on one level referring to how life is shaped by work patterns; metaphorically, signifying the changes about to be wrought on the community. The meaning of Ben's outburst during a work break brings these two things together:

When hot steel passed on the strip out of the mill its roar filled the little room. 'Almost like the old days, with the mill running like this,' Norman said.

'What?' Ben was upset, but not too upset to alter his pose. 'They'm on'y rolling one shift mind, days regular five days a bastard week, three shifts a day it used to be. Three shifts a fucking day seven days a week.' Unhappy with this, he elaborated his theme. 'Twenty-four hours a day. Six till two, two till ten, ten till ballacking six. Continuous rolling. End of a shift you 'ouldn' know whether you was coming or bastard going.'[15]

The shifts are reduced, setting a new pattern for the men's lives, but one which only signifies their increasing redundancy. In a curious inversion – and despite the fact that its days are numbered – *agency* is given over to the steel mill itself, an emphasis foregrounded in the metaphorical constructions used to describe work processes, something very reminiscent of D. H. Lawrence's writing on industrialism. The mill has a life of its own, which is figured in 'bodily' signs. Thus we hear that the roughing mills, 'drew out the slabs [of hot metal] into long *tongues* of steel'(p. 23; emphasis mine); 'By the time the slabs reached the finishing-mill stands they were inch-thick, long tongues like the one he had seen on the crane, only red-hot on the rolls'(p. 29); and 'It was the guts of the place and the strip carrying the hot steel on rolling days was like the skin, the bit people saw from the mill floor on the other side of the strip' (p. 137). The workers here seem removed from the actual processes the mill performs, a condition corresponding to the concept of alienation Marx described. And in a dialectical twist, their own *sociolect* is infused in turn by the labour process:

> 'Them doors do open up with them chains and the slabs do drop out. These rolls where they do drop out is called the delivery table, just like in the maternity ward . . .' Jack remembered his father using the term 'tapping off' when a neighbour's wife was about to give birth . . . a metaphor taken from the open hearth furnaces, where the metal was actually molten, not just soft hot as it was in this department. (p. 23)

It is notable that in this description the doors are opening by themselves (no one works the chains), and childbirth is couched in the language of a different kind of labour. Hence we see objective structures (the mill) acquiring subjective qualities, while the subjects (the men, the wider community) appear determined (down to the very language they use) by objective structures. The space of community here, together with the work which has sustained it, rather than nourishing or nurturing, constitutes something of an 'encaging spatialization' itself. At the same time we see the contradictory condition of labour for the working class: at once the source of identity and livelihood, but also (under certain determinate conditions) alienating and imprisoning.

Clearly not a novel of *resistance*, then, but one which speaks of a generalized defeat. The malaise is reflected in personal relations (Keith and Judith's failing marriage) and bodily comportment (Keith's premature middle-aged spread and poor love-making). Even Jack, the 'escaper' returned, who starts an affair with Judith, fails fully to live up to the footloose Arthur Seaton type he appears to reference in the narrative. Jack straddles this working-class community, both inside and outside its structures of feeling, in part accruing to himself the exotic outsider status, attracting Judith, Kath and, less successfully, Connie. Yet what emerges is that his conquests are not his own: Judith pities him, Kath uses him for her own pleasure, Connie rejects him – agency, again, becomes illusory. Jack ends the novel by leaving, with only a vague sense of what he might do next.

The only person who seems to gain something in the end, Meredith suggests, is Keith. The sense of ending which echoes throughout the narrative is stalled or, in some subtle sense, re-accentuated through Keith's engagement with local history. Keith's researches do not constitute a nostalgic looking-back – though Jack accuses him of this: 'You're bloody morbid you are, butt . . . Obsessed with the past. . . Tradition. Balls' (p. 208) – but are an attempt to map out the community's history, which a film crew, arriving on the mill's last working day, wants only to record and reify as 'archives' (p. 203). As I will argue in some detail in my discussion of Pat Barker, the structure of feeling of 'nostalgic memory', or radical remembering, turns on a view of history as presence and continuity bound up with inevitable change and re-construction. Thought of this way, the notion resembles Fredric Jameson's idea of cognitive mapping. This seems to constitute Keith's view, as he witnesses the final closing of the mill, whose history he has traced back to its original nineteenth-century founder, Samuel Moonlow. As the last slab leaves the mill, he thinks:

Odourless, invisible history would blow them all apart and they would hurtle away from each other through space and never really understand what had shifted them. Except blowing apart was the wrong idea because it was a continuing process, evolving and breaking slowly and then occasionally twitching like this. And it included everything. (p. 211)

What Keith sees and accepts, though, is fate: the historical determinism which lies at the heart of this insight reiterates the theme of powerlessness, denying agency once more. The men, and those before them, are the playthings of indomitable forces. But an understanding of those forces compels Keith to continue his search for the past so as to make sense of the present, and he recalls the words of an old nineteenth-century election handbill he has found: '*Dinistr y Deml* – the Destruction of the Temple . . . *Diwedd y Byd* – the End of the World' (p. 155). The Welsh words help him grapple with these historical processes, and with the passing of the last hot slab he realizes that what he has been experiencing is 'Dinistr y deml, though not, of course, diwedd y byd' (p. 211). Keith will survive and find another way to go on.

These particular structures of feeling powerfully express the experiences of de-industrialization, the upheavals characterizing a historic moment of transformation in working-class lives and industrial and urban communities. They are evident in James Kelman's working-class writing, though there are significant differences too, and it is to Kelman's work that I will now turn.

II   On the edge: voicing the politics of resistance

Two distinct yet inseparable concerns form the substance of James Kelman's fiction: representations of the (male) working class, and the nature and condition of urban life. Glasgow is the scene and setting for most of Kelman's imaginative writing, and the fate and predicament of the working-class man is invariably the subject matter of his sometimes tortuous narratives. Kelman consciously articulates this specific cultural identity to explore and redefine the historical changes that have taken place in working-class life and experience in recent times. Depicting what I will call urban 'class geographies', Kelman's stories pursue themes of alienation and dispossession, and reconstruct the everyday life of work and the despondency of long-term unemployment. His writing articulates extremes of personal or existential anxiety, with characters often at the mercy of conditions seemingly beyond their control. Speaking of his own writing, Kelman highlights the importance of *representation*, maintaining that historically mainstream literature has produced only caricatures of the working class.[16] In a sense, then, Kelman is searching for the 'authentic' voice of the (Scottish) proletariat, infusing and introducing the power and energy of the demotic into his narratives. I would suggest that his work witnesses a new kind of working-class writing, focusing on the dilemma of the male proletarian seen often to be negotiating with the painful consequences of economic and political 'exile'.

It is tempting, though not easy, to try to fit Kelman into a lineage of working-class writing, the cultural formation discussed in earlier chapters. The nearest comparison, taken from the 1930s, would be with Lewis Grassic Gibbon, not so much for the Scottish connection as for their shared preoccupation with literary style and expression. But Kelman does follow in a tradition of writers – which found particular expression in the inter-war years – who focus on Glasgow, and the realities of Glasgow life. In Kelman's exclusive concern with inner-city and urban industrial life we might detect the anti-Kailyard sentiments of *A Scots Quair*, those narratives depicting Scotland as some rural idyll; or some of the energy and humanity found in James Barkes's *Major Operation* (it must be said, however, without 'those novels' overt politics). One would search Kelman's writing in vain, though, for other 'epic' figures of 1930s working-class writing: the 'heroic' Communist or working-class autodidact with a Marxist analysis to relieve the workers' ills. Here no one is fighting in particular for any 'cause'; the struggle is merely to get by. Thus Kelman articulates the often oppressive and stifling nature of material conditions, addressing the experiences of those pushed to the margins of society, denying us the luxury of ignoring their existence. In his writing, the city itself emerges as the locus of unequal social relationships and functions of bureaucratic power. In the short story, 'By the Burn', the protagonist, desperate to arrive at a job interview on time, has to negotiate a patch of wasteland close to the tower-blocks where he lives. But he is late, and it has started raining, and the land is churned up: 'the fucking bogging mud man a swamp, an actual swamp, it was a fucking joke.'[17] The narrative goes on: 'High time they extended the path along this way for the poor cunts living up the flats, the fucking council, it was out of order the way they didn't bother' (p. 240). The schemes were fine until 'you wanted to go some place' (p. 242). The desolate landscape (full of bad memories, avoidable disasters, personal despair) is a recurring image in Kelman's work, giving it a distinctly 'scenic', or spatial, structure of feeling in which the urban is fragmented, or divided between declining and thriving areas. Often the figure of the vagrant, or the isolated unemployed man wandering the streets, maps these fragments and tenuously draws them together.

These thematic concerns determine the very form and structure of the short story. Kelman's practice, at times, is to reduce the short story to a virtual 'snapshot' of metropolitan life, a fleeting glance; the stories range from fifty pages to a few lines. The experiences of the working-class figures come across then as all too short, or, conversely, painfully drawn out, and lost in 'empty time' (as in the experience of joblessness). The writing subverts many of the accepted modalities of literary representation and language. The vernacular predominates and is spiked with (so-called) obscenities, which sit brashly with the more conventionally stylized literary modes Kelman incorporates in his writing. The social and the aesthetic come into dialectical tension, suggesting how the real can be simply a product of discourse. This recognizably modernist strategy foregrounds textuality itself, although Kelman's use of language identifies a particular class discourse and consciousness grounded in social experience. Thus a curious hybrid form emerges, combining a modernist register with literary naturalism, or realism. But it is the 'voice' in Kelman's writing which enables him to contest notions of what literature should be, reclaiming the discourse from bourgeois (metropolitan) ownership. Consistent use of the word 'fuck' is a class strategy, and a mode of writing enabling the real and the concrete to be objectified, allowing 'the present day to burst in, linguistically'.[18]

The city represents for Kelman the concrete, and contradictory, social space of late modernity, a site of encounter between self and other. Urban experience is often registered as one of shock, a structure of feeling to be found in the story entitled 'MORE COMPLAINTS FROM THE AMERICAN CORRESPONDENT', from the collection *Greyhound for Breakfast*.[19] The story is only a few lines long:

> Jesus Christ man this tramping from city to city – terrible. No pavements man just these back gardens like you got to walk right down by the edge of the road man and them big fucking doberman pinchers they're coming charging straight at you. Then the ghettos for christ sake you got all them mothers lining the streets man they're tugging at your sleeves, hey you, gies a bite of your cheeseburger. Murder polis. (p. 113)

Then, in 'THIS MAN FOR FUCK SAKE':

> This man for fuck sake it was terrible seeing him walk down the edge of the pavement. If he'd wanted litter we would've given it him. The trouble is we didn't know it at the time. So all we could do was watch his progress and infer. And even under normal circumstances this is never satisfactory: it has to be readily understood the types of difficulty we laboured under. Then that rolling manoeuvre he performed while nearing the points of reference. It all looked to be going so fucking straightforward. How can you blame us? You can't, you can't fucking blame us. (p. 116)

The writing emphasizes this sense of shock, of sudden encounters, flashes of the unexpected or the unbearable. The use of language is compact and succinct, almost poetically self-contained, and interpretation is thwarted, it seems, by brevity or ellipsis. There is no simple way of distinguishing a point of view, whether authorial or characterological. The use of the definite article 'the' in the first example suggests the particular, the specific: not AN AMERICAN CORRESPONDENT, which might then imply a journalistic discourse, the man on the spot, someone doing their job. Instead, THE implies a generalized, totalizing world-view – a judgement, in fact. This in turn suggests the privileged gaze of the imperialist subject; and the shock of deprivation is laced with intimations of contempt. The intensity of the moment crystallizes a specific condition, of urban decline or poverty. 'Tramping from city to city', the narrator identifies a clutch of negative signifiers which represent, metonymically, aspects of the ghetto, or the Third World barrio. The hostile gaze of the other, 'tugging at your sleeve', demands attention and more – food. But here metonymy is turned ironically on the American correspondent (a tourist perhaps, or maybe a journalist), and fast food (a cheeseburger) stands to represent the world's only self-proclaimed superpower.

In the second narrative, the pronoun 'we' offers a different inflection. The observed (one of those 'marginal' figures who fill Kelman's stories) walks 'on the edge of the pavement'; the observers watch, constrained by the 'types of difficulty we laboured under' (p. 116). The rhetoric absorbs and expresses the intensity of this single experience, within a wider frame of the city, or metropolis, inscribing extremity in a mode of writing concerned with interrogating themes of identity and non-identity: a negotiation between the self and other(s). This representation could be seen to embody the way modern life has degraded, or perverted, the human subject. If the second narrative projects a more sympathetic stance towards the Other (though, arguably, the notion of 'observing' carries with it the risk of objectification) the former dramatizes a deeper alienation – a sense of outrage and shock. As Habermas has reminded us, this sense of shock – 'those forward gropings and shocking encounters' – is among the most intense experiences of late modernity.[20]

In 1983, commenting on working-class writing, Ken Worpole argued that:

> As deindustrialization and the movement of capital disrupt settled industrial communities, we shall need to make the break from the traditional working-class novel with its emphasis on the continuity of the diurnal family life. Displacement, fragmentation, cosmopolitanism, the life of the streets rather than in the homes . . . are likely to be the new conditions of experience for the next generation of working class people.[21]

As we have seen, industrial decline accelerated rapidly in the early part of the 1980s, producing the very breakdown Worpole identifies. Kelman's stories articulate this condition through the figure of the down-and-out, the man on the dole, or through representations of urban and industrial dereliction. So we hear, matter-of-factly, 'I'm just skint. People are skint these days you know.' Or: 'It's a fucking dump of a city this, every cunt's skint.' In another story from *Greyhound for Breakfast,* we hear:

> He had bypassed his own street and kept on towards the Cross. The traffic was heavy; lines of buses at the terminus. People who still had jobs . . . He arrived at the pier. It was derelict. He stood by the railway peering through the spikes. The ferry boat went from here to Partick. (pp. 215–16)

Later we are told that

> the docks was a creepy place but, deserted and fucking derelict. And this pier, how you could see the actual particles of coaldust lapping in on the surface of the water, on the steps for fuck sake, if you wanted to commit suicide you'd choose a better place, you wouldn't want to choke. (p. 229)

Here the 'scenic', or spatial, aspect of Kelman's narrative again dominates. It still, however, registers a concept of the historical, tracing the decline of an older mode of production, and centring its residue (in a human and material sense) in the protagonist's thoughts: the river Clyde with 'its rubbish lapping on the sides . . . you couldn't see into it . . . so cloudy, so fucking mawkit' (pp. 216, 227); the dead docks, the unemployment and 'every cunt's skint'.

The transient or displaced, then, comes to symbolize a specific historical condition which in turn articulates some of the new post-industrial experiences of working-class life. The unemployed man, or urban vagrant, traverses a decentred post-industrial landscape; and the rootless individual constitutes the diaspora of the un- or under-employed seeking work. But the nature of work has altered, too. Not Sillitoe's factory, or Lewis Jones's mine; not the camaraderie of the shop-floor or the solidarity of the pit-face; and not the wider consolations or certainties of community. There is instead the diaspora workforce of the story 'Renee': the migrant Portuguese women, the displaced Yorkshireman and Scot, the girls from the 'south-east tip of England', crystallized in the city and in the service industry.

The city is the place where these figures come together, but at the say-so of history. The diasporic workforce live in hostels or, in Jock's case, home is the warehouse floor where he secretly sleeps. These figures service the fantasy of a post-production world. From a political perspective, these representations are shorn of any of the old forms of solidarity which have become part of the mythography expressed in some of the working-class writing we have discussed. This mythography is gestured towards, only to be denied, in a story from *The Burn*. An ageing industrial militant tells the young protagonist of the story, 'A Situation', that 'with me mind you there's aye the wish that a young fellow like yourself could one day take up the cudgels where me and the muckers left off. But these battles have finished, just like the days they happened in are finished' (p. 46). No false sentiment here, though we might infer from the militant's dialogue that there is a need to remember, and not to foreclose on this experience too readily. 'Renee', though in a subtly understated form, highlights the importance of articulating the still exploitative conditions of working-class life, where the daily deprivations imposed by economic necessity thwart (as in the case of Jock and Renee) the most elementary forms of pleasure. Work is still seen here as primary, still forcing constraints upon the human subject and social relations, its presence or absence fully, and often finally, the determining factor.

Nevertheless, the stories speak of discontinuity, a historical condition consonant with the experiences of working-class life over generations. The 1980s, with their pattern of decline and uneven development, went a long way to breaking the mould in the west of a traditional industrial capitalism. As well as the destruction of jobs and communities, we see the transformation of that frightening, but clearly defined, object of nineteenth-century development – the city. As Kristen Ross has pointed out, in late modernity the city is often a ghost of its former incarnation. She suggests that with 'the emergence of global space, the city, the cradle of accumulation, the locus of wealth, the subject of history, the centre of historical space, shatters'. This fragmentation, the city's 'barrio-ization', is, she argues, 'no less true of Paris than in the Third World'.[22]

Thus, for Kelman, public space is often coded as some kind of dead-end: the corner café, the cinema are places where his characters kill time, filling the minutes and hours with the cheap commodities from the bottom end of the market-place. Figures sit alone and alienated in cafés, desperate for 'a bit of breathing space instead of all this crowding in on a person, stuffy rooms and all that smoke engulfing you, making you feel, making you feel' (*The Burn*, p. 92). At the same time as he suggests that there is more than there seems to be to ordinary, everyday existence – it is richer, or more complex – he points to something stifling and deadening about this reality. If Kelman's work can be accused of being repetitive, it is because he is also responding to the endless repetition of commodity production and exchange, which is lived as 'empty time' through which we catch only glimpses of alternative possibilities.

The modernist consciousness 'has a strong tendency to encapsulate all experience within the city'.[23] Raymond Williams proposed that the history of modernism emerged from the experiences of exile and emigration. The movement and displacement of modern artists to foreign countries and capital cities produced an intensified focus on the very nature of language and form,[24] because the cityscape presses upon the modern consciousness as the site of change, transience and as a patchwork of meaning. As it shatters under the movement of history, the city of late modernism, however, presents its own internal forms of exile and dispossession. This is suggested powerfully in Kelman's first novel, *The Busconductor Hines*.

In this narrative we see the figure of Rab gradually going under. Living in the 'District of D', Hines describes himself and his family as 'comprising husband wife and wean whose astounding circumstances are oddly normal'.[25] The rhetoric – the 'District of D' – recalls the nomination of some anonymous eastern European housing scheme, but also an urban setting which might be found in any city, anywhere in Europe. The oxymoronic linguistic construction implies irony or, rather, contradiction. Considering the 'astonishing circumstances' in which they live (a no-bedroom flat, in an area due for demolition) the phrase might even inscribe a victory in achieving some kind of normality. No matter where you live, if you are working class there's always a good chance you might live like this; and as in most of Kelman's work there is the implied (or explicit) presence of the state or of bureaucratic power – those anonymous men in grey suits, figured, for example, in a brief story from *Greyhound for Breakfast*, 'Governor of the Situation':

> I hate this part of the city – the stench, violence, decay, death; the things you usually discern in such like places. I don't mind admitting I despise the poor with an intensity that surprises my superiors. But they concede to me on most matters. I am the acknowledged governor of the situation. I'm in my early thirties. Hardly an ounce of spare flesh hangs on me – I'm always on the go – nervous energy. (p. 90)

The divided city is exposed to the processes of domination. Hines is acutely conscious of this, but feels unable to respond sufficiently. There is a strong sense of powerlessness inscribed in the novel, a terrible alienation which dominates Hines's existence both at work and in the home. Only occasionally, in the dynamic energy of the vernacular, the demotic, do we get a sense of resistance, a possible transcendence, and the emergence of a historical consciousness which denies any 'waning of affect'. In *The Busconductor Hines* Rab is trying to educate his young son, provide him with the knowledge of the way things work:

> son they were robbing you blind with their kings and their queens and the rest of the shite the chiefs and so on making it to the top in their entrepeneurial mejisteh son they were stealing the bread out of your mouth and if they couldnt reach it you were opening the mouth wider son the eyelids shut that you didnt offend son that you didnt see son in case you actually saw son that you actually do, because one thing you didnt want was to do son so the eyelids shut you put forward the mouth with head lowered while the slight stoop or curtsey and forefinger to eyebrow the sign of the dross, we do beg ye kindly sir we do beg ye kindly, for a remaindered crust of the bread we baked thank'ee kindly y'r 'onour an' only 'ope as we might bake 'em more sweetly for 'ee t' nex' time 'appen y'r 'onour as'll do us t' privilege o' robbin' again sir please sir kick us one up the arse sir thanks very much ya bunch of imbecilic fucking bastarn imbeciles. (pp. 91–2)

A number of narrative strands collide here: the subtext of Hines's outburst refers not only to the historical domination of Scotland by colonial forces to the south, but also to the expropriation of the poor by the rich, or of the workers by the idle. Rab's language grapples here for agency at the same time as that desire is undercut; the discourse depicts the workers' exploitation, whilst announcing their own complicity with it (the tone here is not that far removed from the tone to be heard in parts of Robert Tressell's *The Ragged Trousered Philanthropists*). Yet the movement from the private thoughts and feelings of Hines, which are so clearly intertwined with objective conditions, suggests a deconstruction of the divide between the public and the private, the personal and the political, denying modernist solipsism and naturalism's deterministic closure.

The Busconductor Hines produces a range of literary and linguistic registers, from almost pure naturalism (the matter-of-fact description of making a pot of mince stew, for instance), to the subjective and modernist representation of Hines's inner consciousness. Kelman's novels differ markedly from the snapshot quality of the short stories. In the novel, the conditions Rab speaks of sustain a debate and polemic around issues and experiences of everyday working-class life in Glasgow. A major achievement in the novel is the way Kelman succeeds in breaking down the narrative distance between the voice of the narrator/author and that of the protagonist/character. This points to the desire for authenticity, releasing the demotic voice; and one way Kelman sustains this is by rejecting speech markers, and thus fusing the spoken and the written (a feature of Grassic Gibbon's *A Scots Quair*), to produce the voice of the streets. The writing projects a proletarian consciousness struggling to understand the condition of modernity, which has driven a wedge between essence and appearance, fact and value, and where the modern citizen 'knows he is at the mercy of a vast machinery of officialdom whose functioning is directed by authorities that remain nebulous to the executive organs let alone the people they deal with'.[26] In the construction and control of social space, and the alienation therein, the fragmented city Kelman describes and where Hines lives is, like many post-war European cities, in decline or transition. And there seems to be no way out.

If we gain access to the nature of the city through Kelman's characters then we can see these characters as on the periphery, looking in, experiencing what Ross calls 'the new "world city" of postmodernism'.[27] We also get the sense of the city as both decentred and controlled, fragmented and 'planified'; but if the modern city resembles Foucault's 'container', with all the negative undertones of that description, Kelman's narrative still strives to express a utopian impulse, a narrative desire for transcendence and a need to get beyond reification:

> And the white just makes everything opaque. And most cunts go about like this, heads chokablock with the primary rubbish that what they realises from input has been shovelled into them. And being so choking on the rubbish they cannot, they can never, never even hope, to realize the black, that depth, from there into transparency. No chance, not a fucking iota, not a solitary fucking hope.
>
> And then you have got to do something because the cause. The things being seen, no longer whitewashed. It can take a while. It can rumble about for ages, in different forms even, but the result will be fine; it will be fine if allowed to come to pass. It rumbles around gathering force, then bubbling up and spewing out in terms of whatever the fuck it

doesnt matter, it doesnt matter; it does not matter, fuck them all, just straight in, straight in to clear it all out. (*The Busconductor Hines*, p. 105)

This is Hines as he shifts between the poles of anger and despair, activity and inertia, agency and subjection. The passage articulates a traditional motif in working-class writing, suggesting, despite the manifold impediments, the need to see beyond the surface, and to comprehend a deeper reality, and it seems appropriate in relation to Kelman's work to use the spatial metaphor. Hines's subjective, and often circular, musings yield to a more direct and quasi-political (perhaps quasi-anarchistic) discourse.

The tension between naturalism and the estranged diction of a more modernist register or, in formal terms, a slide between the metonymic and metaphoric poles of poetics, has important functions. The naturalistic register defines the nature of deprivation, and the pressures and constraints that determine everyday life. This project is characteristic of working-class writing, as we have seen, hence naturalism's popularity as a mode of representation. However, Hines's more subjectivist mode is not a retreat from the social, but represents a poetics responsive to the metaphysical desire to transcend such conditions, whilst still pointing beyond them to a reality where oppression begins. The narrative transcends the empirical at the same time as it exposes its inequities. Art and the social cannot be separated, but the strictly political, that older language, or grammar, of class struggle and its modes of representation, remains absent.

This absence is most clearly registered in the novel in the issue of the strike. Hines faces reprimand for failing to turn up for a morning shift. This involves a trip to head office, a journey he is expected to undertake in his own time, not the bus company's. He refuses – he is not being paid for it, and his leisure time is his own – and an argument results, during which he is threatened with instant dismissal. The shop-steward and then the union intervene on Hines's behalf; a vote is taken at the bus depot, which unanimously endorses strike action should Hines be fired.

We might imagine that all is set here for a 1930s-style victory for the workers over oppressive management. The outcome is quite different. The narrative presents a critical view of the strike, and of the officials handling it. The union is seen not as an organization prepared to contest with management on behalf of the workers, but as a body designed simply to mediate and defuse conflict. Antagonism is emptied out of the confrontation by the very nature of the relationship. The broadly democratic process is seen at work in the canteen (the voting for strike action, the airing of different views, despite the shop-stewards' repeated call for 'order') in favourable contrast to the union hierarchization processes and the depot's macho management techniques. But all the time Kelman, through Hines, is questioning the whole process, exposing its limits and contradictions, pushing up the ante. Cairns Craig has argued that this episode relates to an overriding sense of political pessimism which infuses Kelman's writing.[28] For Craig, Kelman speaks above all of working-class depoliticization and communal fragmentation; the hopes of solidarity and emancipation are explicitly denied in Kelman's stories. Instead, we have the atomized and dispossessed condition of the urban working-class, a product of de-industrialization processes and community dissolution. This accounts for Kelman's intense focus on life on the margins, the diaspora workforce, the desperate and the displaced. I have suggested this myself, and would not wholly disagree with Craig's judgement, but I would also argue that the bleakness predicated of some of Kelman's narratives does not represent the whole story. In relation to the strike scene there seem to be other, important things happening which relate to the nature of dominant representations of the working class. For one thing, Hines's response is a principled stance not based simply on an 'economism' which the middle class see largely as the bottom line of working-class politics. Kelman's approach is related to his aim to explore, and mine, working-class culture more 'truthfully'. For the middle class, the proletarian is driven primarily by 'appetite', and introspection is not considered one of their vices. The complexity of thought and feeling we see in Rab's character has often been considered only the preserve of the Mrs Dalloways of this world. Kelman's 'politics of representation' also contrasts with some earlier working-class writing, where the proletarian might be seen as little more than a worker, or a potential cog in the wheels of revolution (and passively led by the Party). The complex representation of Hines forestalls any simple identification with him as a working-class man or, more to the point, undermines the stereotypes of working-class men which have gained currency (this might be especially the case in relation to dominant representations of the male, working-class Glaswegian hard man). At another level the episode problematizes accepted, and in many ways deeply compromised, political (and class) strategies, and thus questions the efficacy of the prevalent post-war ideology of Labourism.

The final image is of Hines, back on the buses, discussing life with Reilly. It is curious that he should return to a job which so alienates and frustrates him. They speak of work, touch on religion, discuss Saturday's match – they joke and harangue each other. 'Hines shifted his position, he wiped the condensation from the back of the window and looked out' (p. 237). This image reiterates a preoccupying theme of the narrative as a whole, and relates, if more prosaically, to the earlier passage ('And the white just makes everything opaque'). It signifies the need for clarity, to look beneath the surface, and the implication – a kind of utopian gesture – that there might be the possibility of something better. If Hines's moments of despair are symptomatic of a lack of any possible political alternative or agency, any chance that he might be able to change the conditions of his existence single-handedly, then we are left to consider that perhaps only a collective response will do. Perhaps that is Hines's conclusion too, hence his return to work, realizing that his existential dilemma, related so fundamentally to the everyday world of labour, requires a collective resolution. This is partly Pat Doyle's dilemma in Kelman's later novel, *A Disaffection*, one which in the end Doyle fails to resolve.

In *A Disaffection*, Pat Doyle struggles with the existential crisis of the loss of his working-class identity, a consequence this time of his own upward mobility. His petit-bourgeois status as a teacher alienates him (he believes) from his past. The novel constructs an opposition between Pat's role as a 'tool of a dictatorship government', and the lives of his brother Gavin and his family, economically insecure but emotionally rich. This opposition is 'sealed' in place geographically – Gavin located on an outer-city housing scheme, Pat ensconced within a wealthier part of the city itself. There may be a divide here between the periphery and centre, but it is established within a wider hierarchal structure of colonization and capital: 'I hate Greatbritain. It was fine before all these selfish and greedy aristocratic capitalist mankindhating landowners started dividing things up between them and saying where ye could walk and where ye couldni.'[29] The control and commodification of space rile Pat and, worse still, he recognizes his own duplicity as an agent of the imperialist state he so despises. He sees himself as

> [a] guy who is all too aware of the malevolent nature of his influence. He is a tool of a dictatorship government. A fellow who receives a greater than average wage for the business of fencing in the children of the oppressed poor. (p. 67)

Again, this sunders Pat from his working-class roots, and his alienation comes into tension with his own often articulated, and frustrated, air of superiority to those he sees merely as the 'poor auld flagellants' (p. 329).

In *A Disaffection* the city is divided by wealth, and Pat seems to be trying to negotiate the distance separating his relatively secure petit-bourgeois lifestyle from that of his still working-class family and friends. Through Pat we see the (post)modern city as it is – relative wealth co-existing with hardship or need, a kind of Third World within the confines of the First World. This structural opposition between Pat and his older brother Gavin is reinforced by money, something to which Pat's lonely deliberations repeatedly return. This theme echoes Marx's argument that money works to dissolve all bonds (not based on exchange) with others.[30] Again and again in Kelman's work money, in some determining form or other, is the bottom line. It signifies estrangement or lack of empathy or simply hardship. 'It's the economic and after that again the economic.'

> SALE! BIG REDUCTIONS!! The last man in the queue looked at him [Pat] as if to say something. He was dressed in a fawn trenchcoat and tweedy bunnet . . . with a really thin face . . . The shoes were cheap efforts . . . No good . . . No good at all. He [Pat] pursed his lips, indicating his dissatisfaction with the quality to the rest of the queue, but they appeared not to be bothering about his opinions. How come they were going to buy such shite. Because they were skint. Because they had no fucking dough. People would buy anything if it was cheap. (p. 208)

This static picture of human life embodies the reification of commodity fetishism. Pat's movement in and out of the queue contrasts with the silence and 'immobility' of the 'poor auld flagellants'. We understand that Pat does not have to make do with 'shite', and money is again the arbiter of the good life. At the same time this alienates him from those with whom he would identify. He is forced to rehearse the unhappy consciousness, or bad faith, of the declassed intellectual, becoming an example of Sartre's 'objective traitor' who, as Fredric Jameson has put it in a different context, 'is forever suspended between the classes, yet unable to disengage from class realities and functions, and from class guilt'.[31]

Pat rages at the world but can do little to change it. His philosophizing merely rehearses Marx's dictum that 'the philosophers have only interpreted the world in different ways, the point is to change it', but if the agents of that change – the working class – are now for Pat simply passive consumers, then maybe nothing will alter. The profundity of Pat's disaffection emerges in a disintegration, or conflation, of language itself, exemplified in his use of the term 'capitalistobliquesocialisticexploitative', where distinct political discourses are collapsed and become indistinguishable. This might be seen as signifying the 'end of history' for Pat; the dialectic frozen into a bizarre mutation where political choice or affiliation appears superfluous. When later he utters in anger, 'how come he wasnt blowing it up', the irony, and the contradictions, intensify as we realize – as is surely clear – that it is impossible to destroy something you cannot in the first place properly name. A crisis of agency is bound to a crisis of identity: throughout the narrative the personal pronouns used by Pat include 'I', 'yous', and 'they', but hardly ever 'we' or 'us'. The collective social identity which might mobilize agency becomes impossible to inscribe.

The working-class writing of the 1930s could name the 'beast', and offer images of resistance to it. Though Pat registers aspects of oppression, his arguments, in the end, appear circular and collapse back into themselves. We are back to Marx's critique of the philosophers for, as Pat says, 'All I seem to do is talk' (p. 321). Even mere words at times fail him, or betray his confusion, and in Pat we catch a glimpse of the postmodern intellectual who is fully aware of the all-pervasive nature of power, and is thus sufficiently cowed to state that little can be done to overthrow it. From a position of power (Pat is a teacher) we are told that power is all there is.

It is significant that the last third of the novel should involve Pat's 're-entry' into the more communal environment of his brother's family. At times it is tempting to infer from Kelman's narratives that any real values can be found only in the heart of working-class culture and community, and it is here that Kelman's writing denies the overall pessimism predicated of it by Craig (though it might be possible to accuse it of idealization). In these later pages of the novel the working-class voice articulates versions of localized class history, class memory and politics, and a materialistic desire to share, signified by the central placing of food and drink.

> They were friends, this trio of neighbours; they shared their grub and they shared their drink. They got on fine together. They were friends. And they were not making him feel excluded; that was one thing, they were not making him feel awkward. (p. 268)

Even so, in the flat with Gavin and two of his friends, Pat's frustration again surfaces. Here Kelman brings to the fore questions of communication and culture, as Pat inwardly rages at what he sees as the banalities of the conversation, expressing a Heideggerian contempt for what he perceives as 'small talk'. These unemployed men should be talking of more relevant issues:

> How much fucking wage do you earn? Are you getting exploited badly or just ordinarily so? Is your rate for the job fixed by person or persons unknown? Is your union as corrupt as mine? Did your leaders sell ye out the last time as usual? (p. 280)

The irony is that the men have been talking of such matters, but Pat has not really been listening (he misses the point of their conversations, much as he misses the only goal scored at the football match he goes to watch, for old times' sake). Exploitation, politics, class are all part of the conversation. This is also evident in Gavin's critical stance towards Pat, when he learns he is quitting his job. His anger lies in Pat's throwing away work when 'more than half of Scotland's no got a job' (p. 225). These are the realities which the narrative works to expose and which official ideology contrives to deny, and Gavin knows well enough that the cause of unemployment is structural and the fault of an irrational economic system, and not the manifestation of individual failure, as official discourses might represent it.

The model generated here – the closeness of the 'nuclear family' – could be regarded as a fairly conservative move. But Kelman's is not the normative nuclear family. Social and economic change has precluded such constructions. Nicola is the breadwinner, Gavin a house-husband, at home minding the kids. In *The Burn*, too, the working-class woman becomes a central figure, strong and supportive in both an emotional and economic sense, in contrast to a significantly diminished, dispossessed and troubled man.

Discussing James Joyce's *Ulysses*, Raymond Williams notes a paradox:

> through its patterns of loss and frustration, there is not only search but discovery: of an ordinary language, heard more clearly than anywhere in the realist novel before it; a positive flow of that wider human speech which had been screened and strained by the prevailing conventions: conventions of separation and reduction of the actual history.[32]

We have seen that Kelman's treatment of urban working-class life is inseparable from his concern with language and the demotic. Assailing the conventions associated with polite traditions of literary language and representation – the dominant conventions of metropolitan literary culture – he produces a form and idiom that struggle to give voice to the voiceless. This use of language means that Kelman's writing acquires a radically dialogic character, although the prime antagonist – the voice of bourgeois hegemony – remains a kind of absent cause. When it emerges more clearly in *A Disaffection*, it is ruthlessly parodied. When Pat is seen romanticizing his dilemma, comparing himself to 'high' liberal intellectuals like Hegel and Hölderlin, and entering the realm of pure contemplation or high-bourgeois discourse, the move represents a mimicking of bourgeois critical practices which contribute to the hegemonic values in society. Kelman is quick to mobilize the narrative in a critique of liberal cant. When Pat becomes annoyed at an unthinking racist remark by Gavin, a liberal discourse is brought into dialogic relation with a materialistic discourse in diagnosing the roots of racism:

> Fine. Fine. I don't have any doubts. My doubts ceased a long time ago. I am fine. I am an instrument of all that is fine and far-sighted. I receive almost twice as much of the provender of survival as do my brother and

sister-in-law and nephew and niece rolled into one neat bundle. And we are all to be at one, yes, at peace, reconciled, fully. Says who? Says me. I say it. I say to my big brother, don't for fuck sake do what you are doing but listen to me as an equal and let us talk to each other, and in that talking we shall be finding the way ahead.

What a pile of fucking shite. What a pile of absolute gibbers! The very idea that such forms of conflict can be resolved! This is straightforward bourgeois intellectual wank. These liberal fucking excesses taken to the very limits of fucking hyping hypocritical tollie. (p. 306)

This is a critique of liberal 'tollie', of 'bourgeois intellectual wank'. In the end, however, the ostensible discourse on racism collapses into a rumination on Pat's own position, on whether or not it is appropriate for Pat to judge Gavin's behaviour at all. The implication is that the gap is too great to be reconciled by reasoned liberal discourse which, as this passage unfolds, proceeds to implode.

Kelman's writing also discloses a tension, as I suggested earlier, between the mobilized discourse of anti-imperialism and the discourse of class struggle – between oppression derived from colonialism and oppression derived from class relations. This is again related to the 'spatial' imagination at work in the writing, emerging in the tracing of colonialism's commodification of space, and capital's disruptive, de-investment strategies. Nationalist struggle and class exploitation are combined concerns. The workings of multinationals are linked to cheap consumer goods for the working class in the metropolitan areas, at the expense of work for those same people:

> Nah . . . I used to be involved in making shoes – the shoe industry – but then they shut down the factory and transferred all the stuff out to Taiwan or maybe Thailand I'm not sure but it was Tai-something, one of these places where the same job gets done by six-year-old weans with the added bonus of only having to pay them a flat rate of three lollipops every second century. (p. 333)

Strictly speaking, this is fantasy on Pat's part, a performance which has no actual basis in the reality of Pat's life and is thus problematic. The language expresses a consciousness of the spatial determinations and boundaries of capital, and offers an insight into the workings of the contemporary global system, yet it is curiously undermined by its essentially 'fictive' status. A more 'authentic' discourse (the introduction of the 'real' worker whose place Pat takes) is not available, and the effect of this – aside from rendering Pat a decidedly unreliable narrator – is to see him once again alienated from the language he speaks, which fails to correspond to his lived experience. Yet the language does speak of a specific historic experience, which is the absence of that Marxist discourse of the 1930s which confidently spoke of exploitation and remedies to it. Once again the question is raised as to what discourse might provide sufficient force to emancipate the workers; and, as we have noted, this is often quite literally an absence in Kelman's writing, a mode of response he refuses to write.

Many of the concerns analysed here come together in Kelman's Booker Prize-winning *How Late It Was, How Late* (1994). *How Late*, describes, mostly through interior monologue and stream of consciousness, the world from the standpoint of Sammy Samuels, whom we might see as a 'typical' Kelman proletarian protagonist. Sammy has endured periods of unemployment and stretches inside, and is currently on the dole. After a beating from the police, Sammy ends up blind, and the narrative is then given over to an exploration of how he deals with his encounters with the medical profession, the police and other state bureaucracies, and with navigating the city itself – a city which is an increasingly alien place to him. This is figured early in the narrative in a telling encounter Sammy has with, possibly, tourists or, as Sammy imagines, more likely, foreign representatives of the business community, with investment opportunities in mind. The vernacular landscape Sammy occupies is about to be cut from under his feet by money interests.

> Maybe they were tourists, they might have been tourists; strangers to the city for some big fucking business event. And here they were courtesy of the town council promotions office being guided around by some beautiful female publicity officer with the smart tailored suit and scarlet lips with this wee quiet smile, seeing him there, but obliged no to hide things . . . it was probably part of the deal otherwise they werenay gony invest their hardwon fortunes.[33]

Sammy is badly hung-over, though not yet blind, and is attempting to sort out his dishevelled state as they approach him. Sammy sees them seeing him, and he represents here the unrepresentable: the seamy side of town to be made over, given a new look (much like the transition from the Isle of Dogs to Docklands). As they gaze upon him they in turn, for Sammy, turn into the 'sodjers' who will soon beat him up and leave him blind. The two groups, then, become inseparable: those who police the people and those who govern or 'own' them folding into a single, hegemonic image.

In the course of the novel Sammy comes to symbolize the disinherited working-class subject marooned in a social landscape now utterly strange to him (metaphorized, of course, through his sight loss). Disaffiliated from the class habitus and community, he opts for isolation: he refuses the help of Ally, who offers to represent him in court in his case against the police; he loses his partner, Helen; he can no longer connect with Charlie Barr, a political activist, with whom the police suspect Sammy of associating. These are symptomatic moments: the structure of feeling which here encodes a kind of exile from others is particularly resonant with regard to Charlie Barr, signifying again that a political answer to working-class anguish is 'barred off' – 'Ye couldnay trust nay cunt but . . . One guy he could trust . . . nah he couldnay . . . That was it about life man . . . Not a solitary single bastard that ye could tell yer tale of woe to' (p. 251). Any gesture of solidarity dissolves; at the same time, however, Sammy's blindness leads him to new insights and experiences which reveal to him the deeply iniquitous nature of the social world and its institutions. His encounter with the doctor, when he goes to be assessed for disability benefit, foregrounds the dynamic of class and cultural power in a revealing way:

> Are you saying I'm no really blind?
> In respect to the visual stimuli presented you appeared unable to respond.
> So ye're no saying I'm blind?
> It isn't for me to say.
> Aye but you're a doctor.
> Yes.
> So ye can give me an opinion?
> Anyone can give you an opinion.
> Aye but to do with medical things.
> Mister Samuels, I have people waiting to see me.
> Christ's sake!
> I find your language offensive.
> Do ye. Ah well fuck ye then. Fuck ye! (p. 225)

There is a clear opposition constructed here between Sammy's straight talking and the doctor's evasiveness. As Geoff Gilbert indicates, what the language highlights in this exchange is 'a contest of opposed positions', where 'the anger which issues in Sammy's swearing is a recognition of this relation, and swearing functions to clarify it . . . Here Sammy Samuels refuses to accommodate himself to the language of institutions.'[34] It is one of those brief utopian moments in Kelman's writing when the agency of the dispossessed is reinstated or affirmed.

I argued earlier that Kelman's use of swearing in his fictions constitutes modes of resistance which, it could be suggested, encode within themselves gestures of *negation* (negating the negation, in fact, a partly utopian impulse); discursive acts of violation, but also a kind of class strategy for privileging silenced voices. In the sense quoted earlier, this use of language represents a mode of expression which allows 'the present day to burst in, linguistically'. Yet as the controversy around 'bad language' following his Booker victory signifies, such acts of transgression must be resituated in their rightful place. Thus, for one reviewer, Sammy is 'just a drunken Scotsman railing against bureaucracy', and Kelman himself was likened by Simon Jenkins to 'an illiterate savage'.[35] Opposing Kelman's story, in an act of class negation itself, Jenkins's response reveals how identities depend on the exclusion of the Other, or the abject – or at best a recuperation of it – and highlights Stuart Hall's belief that identities are often 'constructed within the play of power and exclusion . . . the result of the overdetermined process of closure'.[36] Sammy (Kelman) is beyond the pale; a class antagonist not fit to be seen, or heard, in public. This is Jenkins's point – his class fantasy and nightmare, that Bakhtinian image of the grotesque invading his social and psychological space. But perhaps Kelman had been prepared for such responses to his representations of working-class life all along, placing them prophetically in the mouth of the doctor when he tells Sammy, 'I find your language offensive.' To which the only response must be: 'Fuck ye, then. Fuck ye!'

Kelman's tracing of the city, especially in the short stories, represents the de-industrialized world of the Thatcher era, revealing new forms of dispossession and alienation and the resulting transformations of people's lives. This 'cartographic impulse'[37] is a literary and artistic response to spatial change, the desire to map the territory, identify markers and work over the 'real', a response to the relation of power and powerlessness. In mobilizing that exceptional moment of identification or estrangement, or tracking the isolated figure through the altered landscape, Kelman allows us to gain access to 'the spatial contradictions of the present', and in doing so he 'allows history to emerge'.[38] The writing discloses a curious dialectic of the sentimental and the aggressive, as it reflects, sometimes broods, upon the status of community, a charged word for any consideration of working-class life. Despite the predominance of bleak images in his work, Kelman's writing tenuously explores possible spaces for collective and individual agency, spaces which derive, in Edward Said's terms, 'historically . . . from the deprivations of the present'.[39] Engaging in his writing with the themes of community and class, Kelman at the same time places them temporarily — to echo the final words of *How Late it Was, How Late* — 'out of sight'.

4
Recovered perspectives: women and working-class writing

The main focus of this chapter falls on what one critic has labelled the 'feminization of British working-class fiction'.[1] It was pointed out in the introduction how, in a number of studies, female academics have re-posed the question of class to expose what we might term the 'hidden' significances of gender in class and of course class in gender. Clearly, representations of the working class always have been gendered: discussions of earlier writing has made this apparent already. Some dominant forms of writing the working class privilege the male experience, while other modes of representation figure the working-class woman as the quintessential Other: 'eulogized in the figure of "our Mam", or pathologized as bad and insensitive mothers, or laden with sexuality and dirt . . . these women are constituted as exotic and repulsive Others when observed from a middle-class perspective.'[2] In working-class writing by men, despite often sympathetic portrayals of women, it is from the perspective of the male working-class subject that the narrative is organized; female identity is subjected to male desire and fantasy, or their agency subordinated to the protective male embrace. The former emphasis is evident in a novel like *Saturday Night and Sunday Morning* (and is vigorously reiterated in the film adaptation), the latter manifest in some 1930s' writing which figured the working-class woman as the embodiment of abjectness or shame – Jane in *Means Test Man*; the 'slatternly women' in *Love on the Dole* (this is not 'essentialized', however, but the *result* of shaming socio-economic conditions) – though even here there were exceptions, in the writing of Lewis Jones and Lewis Grassic Gibbon and, of course, Ellen Wilkinson. As a new wave of revisiting the working class from a broadly feminist position took shape in the 1980s, a challenging new perspective on the working class emerged. This is reflected in fiction by women writers like Pat Barker, Livi Michael and Agnes Owens, in the early novel of Jeanette Winterson, *Oranges are Not the Only Fruit* (1985), as well as in the stark, naturalistic drama of Andrea Dunbar, most notably in *Rita, Sue and Bob Too* (1985). Owens's writing takes as its subject matter similar concerns to those of Kelman: the difficulties of finding work and making ends meet in a post-Thatcherite, post-industrial Scotland.[3] These same harsh material conditions find searing expression in Dunbar's 1980s' plays, described as New Brutalism. Aspects of this writing hark back to the 'kitchen-sink' dramas of the 1950s and 1960s, echoing at times Shelagh Delaney's *A Taste of Honey*, though they are far more uncompromising in their depiction of social breakdown and personal despair. Thus *The Arbor*, *Shirley* and *Rita, Sue and Bob Too* – presented at the Royal Court theatre in 1980, 1986 and 1987 respectively – explore the strains poverty places on family life, articulating a powerful structure of feeling in which the relations and connections between generations of working-class people seem to be breaking down inexorably under these pressures.

Livi Michael's novel *Under a Thin Moon* (1992) takes as its subject the social and economic fallout of the 1980s, too, and focuses on poor working-class women: those people mainstream culture would prefer to define as the underclass, a response that encodes not only an ideological strategy to vilify and thus neutralize the reality of their exclusion and exploitation, but one which signifies the re-emergence of an old class anxiety, referred to in writing about the poor in chapter 1, related to notions of the 'abyss' or the 'mob' – sections of society considered beyond the reach of civilized norms. The location is a run-down north-of-England housing estate and the novel traces the lives of four young working-class women, Wanda, Coral, Laurie and Valerie.

A sense of powerlessness pervades the narrative, and the women are seen to be constrained not just by the ideological and material structures of patriarchy, but also by the hierarchies of class relations, dialogically inflected in the thoughts of Wanda as she struggles to make ends meet. Michael achieves this by mobilizing very clearly that phenomenon Bakhtin described – in his analysis of Dostoevsky's work – as 'inner-voice discourse'. Discussing the Underground Man, Bakhtin points out the acute dialogization of the hero's consciousness, so that his 'speech has already begun to cringe and break under the influence of the anticipated words of another, with whom the hero, from the very first step, enters into the most intense internal polemic'.[4] We witness this very structure in the case of Wanda. Her own 'inner-voice discourse' is tormented by the voice of the dominant as it intrudes to deny the real conditions of her life:

> No-one is helpless, says the voice in her head. There's always a way out. If you've got it in you, you make it in the end.
> You have to work for what you get, says another voice. You never get anywhere without work.
> If you don't work you deserve everything you get, says another voice. The weakest must go to the wall.
> Wanda gets up, suddenly determined to get rid of the voices.[5]

These voices echo the Social Darwinist creed of New Right Conservatism, oblivious to the profound structural causes which prevent Wanda from escaping the poverty cycle. In school Valerie must face the ideological reproduction of class difference, a knowledge of herself as Other. She 'listens to the teacher going on about the habits of the working classes, their employment and their unemployment, where they shop and where they spend', and she is reduced to a statistic, able to read books full of 'information on the working classes, where they live, how they live and most of all what they buy'. This, she recognizes, only obliterates the real people: 'It is an unreal feeling, like she doesn't exist at all' (p. 106). This is the type of objectification, or dehumanization, Edward Said has described:

> [t]he object of such knowledge is inherently vulnerable to scrutiny; this object is a 'fact' which, if it develops, changes or otherwise transforms itself . . . is nevertheless fundamentally, even ontologically stable. To have such knowledge of such a thing is to dominate it, to have authority over it. And authority here means for 'us' to deny authority to 'it' . . . since we know it and it exists, in a sense, *as* we know it.[6]

This *othering* produces a dialectic which marginalizes through processes of reification and objectification, while at the same time centring the subject in the very act of classification. To reinforce Said's formulation, we can turn again to Bakhtin. For Bakhtin, in opposition to the essentially dialogic nature of language and communication stood monologic tendencies; what he called centripetal, or centralizing, powers which frame or determine the existence of centrifugal, or marginalized, forces within a supposed unitary language or social order.[7] As an act of closure (describing, therefore controlling), it constitutes a powerful hegemonic process which, in Michael's narrative, her characters have little agency to resist.

Hence, there is a remorselessness about *Under a Thin Moon* in its representations of the alienation and dispossession of working-class women in the shadow of socio-economic and urban blight. As with forms of literary naturalism, the narrative shuns any moralistic discourse or liberal rationalizations to account for the women's plight. One review of the book stated that it represented a 'distressing economic parable' which 'succeeds in its relentless assault on its subject matter', adding, quite correctly, that it is one of the few 'English novels to tackle issues such as money, class and power head-on' (printed on the back cover of the 1994 Minerva edition). It is urgently concerned with how class and gender domination are reproduced; how we come to internalize class hierarchy in the schoolroom, or gender roles from the representations of domesticity or femininity in glossy magazines. The lives of Wanda and the other women are constant counters to the carefully crafted ads, the glib promises of pop-songs, or the rhetorics of consumer ideology. The narrative presents these images and discourses in painful, and darkly ironic, contrast with the reality of these women's lives.

> . . . a huge billboard on the side of a shop advertising perfume. There is a woman on it. Her head is thrown back like she is making love and her long blonde hair fills one half of the picture like silk . . .
> She stands several moments in the thin soaking drizzle before she knows what it is. The picture reminds Wanda of the image of herself she once had, the blonde hair, green eyes, neat features, all remind Wanda of herself. (p. 116)

And, repeatedly, money stands as the final arbiter of the good life, or the measure of social relations of power:

> You need money to look like that, she thinks. Then she thinks, you need money to be seen like that. She begins to walk away from the poster thinking of all the images of beauty she has seen . . . all of them really

images of money ... Being poor is like being ill all your life, she thinks. You are always struggling to fill the gap between what you are supposed to be and what you are, and always failing. (p. 165)

She understands that the ideology of femininity is 'writing' her, and seems powerless against it (though recognizing its invidious nature, a step towards self-determination), and through the lineaments of both class and gender, the novel traces those ideological dimensions which construct desire and identity.

How to be a good mother, how to be a 'good woman' are recurrent themes. In this landscape, characterized by forms of dispossession and poverty, it is almost impossible to be either. Daily life takes on a nightmarish quality – the struggle with uncaring state bureaucracies, or waiting for welfare cheques that don't turn up, always penniless yet realizing that spending money 'is a social occupation. Without it you don't belong in the world' (p. 25). Another woman, Laurie, takes up shoplifting; she intends to make a career out of it until she is caught. And in the end Wanda kills herself. Resistance is represented only ambiguously, in the figure of Valerie's alcoholic mother, rebelling against the endless unfulfilment of her life, the desires deferred and oppressions endured over too long a time. In the end, a cocktail of drink and drugs becomes a last defiant gesture with which to confront the norms of patriarchy and an unequal society. Her drunken rants are a rage against a wider world, and Valerie comes to see that 'she is too loud for them, too noticeable. They want to wipe her out' (p. 212). Valerie's mother is a victim of a disintegrating welfare capitalism, and the younger generation are the recipients of this inheritance. There is an overpowering sense of disenfranchisement both from the class community and from society as a whole.

Overall, the narrative trajectory of *Under a Thin Moon* is marked by incomplete thoughts or circular movements. Michael presents a community 'unknowable' in the extreme, a structure of feeling where intersubjective relations have yielded to individual anomie, a contrast to some of the more upbeat and defiant writing I examine below. Towards the end of the narrative, though, the act of writing itself is foregrounded, a move which seems to suggest a strategy to combat the silencing effects of a totally administered world. We have seen Coral move from being Wanda's child (and victim of her physical abuse) to insecure adult, recovering from a broken relationship, afraid to go out alone, unsure of her own identity; but she has come to recognize one thing: 'Everything comes back to money.' Coral tells herself stories, 'to make space for herself'. She tells stories to remind herself she is still alive, but,

> are her stories any different?
> why is she always the victim?
> Coral thinks, I am writing their stories for them.
> That is the meaning of power, she thinks. (p. 229)

She wonders if she has any other stories to tell; stories that might make a difference. 'There is silence in the kitchen in spite of all the noise outside. Coral knows she must begin to type. She must write something, even if it makes no sense' (p. 230). We are asked to see this act of agency as the first defiant gesture in recovering her self. By articulating her experiences, she tries to make connections with others. Even so, this kind of recovery through self-expression is frustrated by the absence of any act of collective identification, and alienation and a sense of 'separatedness' dominate.

Finally, Jeanette Winterson's novel is worthy of mention here, too, in the context of these newly emerging voices. *Oranges are Not the Only Fruit* is not usually regarded as working-class writing: critics are silent on its representations of class experience, favouring instead the novel's concern with sexuality. But the text has many of the qualities and features of the British post-war working-class novel, and subtly recodes and reaccentuates many of the themes and emphases of the classic 'escaper' narrative we have discussed earlier, offering a new perspective that is not only that of a girl/young woman (as we have seen, it has traditionally been men who occupy the position of escaper), but which has the added dimension of sexuality, in a community dominated and shaped by working-class women.

As with the novel and drama, so cinema, too – with such films as *Letter to Brezhnev* (1985), *Blonde Fist* (1990) and *Business as Usual* (1987) – produced representations of northern working-class women as tough, sexy and self-confident (though it can be argued that British soap-operas have been doing this for some considerable time – television has never really marginalized working-class life, merely contained it in safe and saleable packages). At the same time academic feminism began interrogating the intersection of gender issues with concerns of both race and class, recognizing, in Kaplan's formulation, that social hierarchy and female subjectivity represent a 'Pandora's box' for all feminist theory. For Kaplan, feminism had failed to pay sufficient theoretical attention to other forms of social determination. This suggests that a politics of difference concerned simply with celebrating women's essential difference and autonomy from men, couched in a radical critique of patriarchy, quite often ignores the constitutive dimension of class relations.[8] The writing focused upon here attempts to check this tendency, and one key strand of this work turns on the trope of 'recovery' in the articulation of female experience.

I Memory texts and the narrating of working-class experience

My central focus here is the early fiction of Pat Barker. In *A Literature of Their Own*, Elaine Showalter observes that 'there is a female voice that has rarely spoken for itself in the English novel – the voice of the shopgirl and the charwoman, the housewife and the barmaid',[9] and Barker's writing goes some way towards filling this silence. The novels I choose were all published in the 1980s: *Union Street* (1982), *Blow Your House Down* (1984) and *The Century's Daughter* (1986). These three texts provide examples of an often-returned-to thematic emphasis in Barker's writing around issues of memory, gender and class, while the construction of working-class identities (especially working-class women) and working-class communities found there offer – by way of her concern with a gendered class experience – a significant reworking of images and representations of working-class life embedded in a range of cultural forms and expression. Above all, Barker uses the novel form to represent those individuals and groups hitherto 'hidden from history'. Thus *The Century's Daughter* articulates a broad historical sweep, ranging from the turn of the century to 1980s' Britain, seen through the eyes, and the memory, of the novel's main protagonist, Liza Jarrett. Taking in the First World War, the inter-war Depression and the post-war emergence of the welfare state, the reader is offered stories of the development and disruption of working-class lives and communities in north-east England, the novel ending with a bleak view of a post-industrial landscape transformed and denuded by a decade and more of

Conservative government. *Blow Your House Down* and *Union Street* both represent a community of working-class women dealing with disruptive forces impacting on their lives, whether in the shape of economic change or of male violence and threat. A central emphasis in the writing, despite some of the harrowing experiences delineated by Barker, is a feeling of renewal – of both an individual and a collective kind. It is this sense of 'reconstitution', in the face of events that initiate moments of radical discontinuity, which provides instances of hope, despite the stark and unforgiving existential and historical conditions Barker speaks of in her work. Through the lineaments of gender and class the experiences of generations of working-class women and their communities come to light, and their defeats and victories are assiduously recounted. I would suggest that it is possible to view this writing as contesting some of those settled representations of working-class women extant in a variety of discourses within British culture, signalling an intervention in a long history of cultural – and especially literary – production that has all but ignored the lives and experiences of working-class women, even when such cultural production was produced by members of the working class itself or those sympathetic to it. An important and emergent structure of feeling evident in much of Barker's writing, one which enables it to confront and problematize a number of assumptions articulated at these various levels of theoretical debate, political practice and artistic representation, is an insistence on how gendered experience is inevitably informed and shaped by the objective determinants of class position. Her approach to this dynamic offers important insights on the 'lived experience' of class; other aspects of the writing remain open to the dangers associated with any turn towards memory or 'nostalgia', which I will examine later. Moreover, her writing is significant in another important respect. I concentrate on the three novels referred to above, not simply because they provide excellent material through which to come to terms with key areas of her writing, but also because they mark an important contribution to debates in the 1980s concerning the 'condition of the English working class'. Any analysis of Barker's writing during this period, then, must pay attention to the context of the wider conditions of production in which it emerged: the historical changes which occurred in Britain in the 1980s, which radically transformed the working-class communities and working-class lives Barker writes about.

This focus is part of an expressive feeling of loss, evident in many texts of the time, though recoded in various ways in Barker's novels. The novels offer a view of the past through the eyes of working-class women, present in its making. Thus a major narrative concern in Barker's work is memory and remembering – what I will call 'nostalgic memory'. 'Nostalgic memory' represents a symbolic act of recovery: of neglected experience, forgotten voices, silenced groups. However, the concept of nostalgia carries with it a number of negative connotations. Hostile critiques surround discussions of nostalgia, encoding it as a sentimental response to the fear of change, a reaction which distorts the past in a search for, or assertion of, some lost golden age. Nostalgia is, moreover, associated with conservative forces, whether in the shape of some of the political rhetoric of the Right on such issues as family values, or of those commodified spectacles of history that constitute the heritage industry. Nostalgia, then, is a sign of misrepresentation or a symptom of alienation and, as a structure of feeling, is an ineffective force for understanding ourselves or for historical interpretation. 'Nostalgic memory', however, can be a response to a range of complex needs and desires, and its articulation can construct a variety of values and ideals to contest dominant ideological positions.

We need to ask to what a particular example of 'nostalgic memory' is a response. There are forms of 'nostalgic memory', I would suggest, which can be *enabling*. Stuart Tannock, in his discussion of nostalgia as a structure of feeling, suggests we should try to understand its underlying problematic as one of continuity and rupture. Aware of the drawbacks of nostalgia, Tannock nevertheless insists that 'it does not necessarily entail retreat; it can equally function as retrieval'.[10] 'Nostalgic memory' can imply historical recovery, a radical remembering. This process can be more than a simple excavation for lost souls: it can act as a rhetorical practice – indeed, a utopian impulse – providing 'resources and supports for community and identity building projects in the present'.[11] Such action involves 'a return to the past to read [and to write] a historical continuity of struggle, identity and community . . . comb[ing] the past for every sense of possibility and destiny it might contain'. This means 'digging around central structures to find the breathing spaces of the margins, spinning up old sources into tales of gargantuan epic – a resource and strategy . . . for all subaltern cultural and social groups. Nostalgia here works to retrieve the past for support in building the future.'[12]

In Barker's writing on working-class life there is clear evidence of this tendency. Narrative is a socially symbolic act of speaking an absent presence. She has stated herself that memory is crucial to her writing project. 'Memory is my subject', she has claimed, writing history/fiction as a desire for recovery, seeking 'absence as presence'.[13] 'Nostalgic memory', then, constitutes a key theme in her work, both in terms of content and formal structure: for instance, in the use of flashbacks and recollection, narrative devices especially evident in *The Century's Daughter*. And her concern with the past is there again in her First World War trilogy (*Regeneration, The Eye in The Door, The Ghost Road*), which offers, among other things, an example of 'history from below' – Billy Prior, the main character, is a working-class recruit elevated to officer class – and the work provides Barker with further spaces to explore issues of gender, class and memory. This overall narrative concern analysable in Barker's kind of 'nostalgic memory' links 'now' with 'then', enabling and facilitating an understanding of history and identity in the present as partly a product of the past. To understand the past is to illuminate the present and imply a future, suggestive of Gramsci's insistence on the necessity to 'know thyself . . . as a product of the historical process to date which has deposited in you an infinity of traces without leaving an inventory'.[14]

In *Social Memory*, Fentress and Wickham explore memory as a social phenomenon that encodes personal and collective identity, and conscious and unconscious political desire. Memory and nostalgia are elided in some of the accounts discussed by these writers, though nostalgia is given a different gloss to that found in postmodern accounts. Thus, nostalgia is also 'social memory': potentially the expression, in various forms, of a 'collective experience . . . identify[ing] a group, giving it a sense of its past and defining its aspirations for the future'.[15] Social memory can become a 'source of knowledge', manifesting itself not as a 'passive' phenomenon but rather as a 'performative' act. For historical consciousness to be felt in any significant sense, subjects must feel – as E. P. Thompson might have stressed – that they have been involved and active in making history. Subaltern stories must elaborate a definable class memory outside the paradigm, or episteme, of a hegemonic national memory; one which, Fentress and Wickham suggest, is always 'articulated or created by the bourgeoisie, or for the bourgeoisie *first*'.[16] Such discourse works to define a national community, enabling the bourgeoisie to legitimize its 'structures of political and economic dominance, by which the elite justifies itself as an elite'.[17] In the construction of memory/history there is no disinterested party, and hegemony assures that 'alternative memories are to be regarded as irrelevant, inaccurate and even illegitimate'.[18] Thus the political importance of class memory, particularly in times of rapid change, cannot be underestimated.

As a chronicler of working-class life, Barker necessarily engages with a stock of images of the British working class, images which, as we have suggested, have been overwhelmingly masculinized. Gina Wisker sees the position provided for working-class women in the working-class novel of the 1950s and 1960s as that of the

> fag-smoking, maternal, frying-pan wielding Mam, or the floosie tarted up in her high-heels and lipstick, ripe for a bit of a fling. Women figure as sexual objects on the route to male sexual liberation and assertion of a world dominated by materialism and small-town, grimy gasworks machismo.[19]

Another version, of course, is the one put forward by Richard Hoggart – the reassuring figure of 'our mam'. This view is significant in relation to another important attempt in the 1980s to deal with issues of class and gender, found in Carolyn Steedman's *Landscape for a Good Woman* (1986). This book recalls a working-class mother and a working-class childhood (both her own), and relates them to what she calls the explanatory paradigms of our culture: those modes of explaining individual lives, whether psychoanalytic, economic or cultural. As Barker disrupts established representations of working-class women in fiction, Steedman challenges theoretical constructions of female subjectivity that deny the importance of class or offer simplistic accounts of its effects, in particular ones ignoring the important dimension of the private sphere in conceptualizing the indignities and injustices of class. Her anger is with influential British post-war cultural critics, who reproduce the working class as 'passive', bearing only 'the elementary simplicity of class consciousness and little more'.[20] Steedman rejects this reductive approach, one which denies both men and women of the working class an inner and psychological complexity, and is particularly critical of Richard Hoggart's influential post-war account of working-class lives which produces 'a background of uniformity and passivity in which pain, loss, love, anxiety and desire are washed over with a patina of stolid, emotional sameness'.[21] She thus traces the lives lost to the dominant explanatory modes of mainstream culture, presenting a kind of history writing intent on recovery, reproducing her mother's working-class life and commenting on the processes of her own 'flight' (to academia and embourgeoisement).

Identifying 'an extraordinary attribution of sameness to generations of lives', she argues that the

> Heaviness of time lies on the pages of *The Uses of Literacy*. The streets are all the same; nothing changes. Writing about the structure of a child's life, Seabrook notes that as recently as thirty years ago (that is in the 1950s, the time of my own childhood) the week was measured out by each day's function – wash-day, market-day, the day for ironing – and the day itself by 'cradling and comforting' ritual.[22]

It is this homogenizing 'ritual', and representations of working-class mothers (and the home) as unified and non-contradictory, that Steedman rejects. Instead of this she wants to 'open the door of one of the terraced houses in a mill town in the 1920s, show ... my mother and her longing ... see the child of my imagination sitting by an empty grate, reading a tale that tells her a goose-girl can marry a king'.[23]

It soon becomes clear in Steedman's account that her own mother was nothing like the mythical figure of 'our mam'. For a start, she worked almost all of her adult life. Nor was she the loving mother, selfless to the end. She did not particularly want her children. She rejected the traditional community of her childhood and youth and its Left politics and class consciousness, and moved south, becoming an unashamed working-class Tory. Steedman's memories of this mother contradict both Hoggart's and Seabrook's accounts. Where the male constructions she critiques offered stability and warmth, Steedman recalls uncertainty and distance. In place of self-sacrifice, Steedman's mother disclosed an insistent desire for material things which was never assuaged. Her politics were the politics of envy, and she was not afraid of articulating them. She resented what she felt was withheld from her in life, desiring a 'New Look skirt, a timbered country cottage, to marry a prince'.[24] And Steedman identifies a father who was not there, himself a marginalized voice within the much wider public sphere of class relations and social hierarchy.

Foregrounding *difference*, Steedman traces these lives lost to the dominant explanatory modes of mainstream culture. The book proposes to interrogate and challenge those narrative devices and conventions through which the lives of working people have become defined and understood. She reveals, in episodic rather than causal or linear fashion, the deprivations of the welfare state, the historical shifts of people shaped by the industrial revolution, the large and small humiliations of class division and inequality that can mean more to people in the end than the carefully acquired knowledge of surplus value and of capitalist exploitation. She reveals a private life shaped by social and economic forces, and pieces together a story – her own, her mother's – which constitutes a cultural memory that contradicts or questions dominant meanings.

Her notion of writing the self – her autobiographical 'I' – of articulating one's place in the processes of history (or, in Steedman's case, articulating the place, and consciousness, of her mother) constitutes a key trope in Pat Barker's writing. The event of writing her mother's life (and part of her own) disrupts the stereotypical language of sameness smothering the lives of the working class. This process of demystification reaccentuates ideological accounts in recent history, and the working-class subjectivities found there. Steedman's hope is to propel the narrative 'beyond the point of anecdote and into history'.[25] Yet she produces in this account a distant 'voice in the wilderness', a contrary structure of feeling – as we shall see – to the one found in Barker's narratives, where the voices of individual women, and their past and present lives, constitute the collective voice of a community.

These different attempts at writing working-class experience in some way depend upon, or explore ideas around, memory. The structure of feeling of 'nostalgic memory' turns on this tension, then, between recovery as reification of subjectivity and history, or recovery as process: an insistence on presence and continuity bound up with inevitable change and reconstruction. Annette Kuhn has defined this practice succinctly: 'memory work offers a route to a critical consciousness that embraces the heart as well as the intellect; one that resonates in feeling and thinking ways, across the individual and the collective, the personal and the political'.[26] Barker treads this border at times precariously, invoking voices from past and present, recoding images of working-class women in fiction and representing them and their lives in a more complex manner than either the cultural historians or the novelists before her. Overall, she largely succeeds in this project: it is only in her most ambitious novel of the 1980s, *The Century's Daughter*, that she falters, moving dangerously close to reproducing some of the older mythographies of working-class identity she endeavours to contest.

II Working-class fiction: locating the female voice

Lyn Pykett suggests that Barker's writing offers representations of 'struggle, of familial and class conflict, of individuals who are in perpetual danger of being obliterated by oppressive surroundings and economic conditions – in fact by history itself'.[27] Realism is the mode favoured by Barker though not, it must be added, the kind of 'classic realism' that has been associated with the nineteenth-century novel. No hierarchy of discourses is detectable in her narratives; instead, Barker closes the gap between enoncé and enunciation, eroding the distance between 'outside' observer and observed (evidenced in a far more sustained way in Kelman's work, as we saw in the previous chapter). In Barker's writing this results in a kind of oral history which, as Peter Hitchcock points out, enables the narrator to 'move in and out of the language of the sign community'.[28] Realism has received criticism as a literary form in recent times, although I would argue that Barker's narrative technique eschews some of the ideological strategies associated with the bourgeois realist text. The narrative of *Union Street*, for instance, is strictly non-linear; in fact, it is possible to read the novel as a series of short stories. Furthermore, in all of Barker's writing there is a persistent effort to create a collective experience and consciousness, rather than the individualistic one associated with the novel of middle-class life. We are presented with a community in these novels and this sense of community is sharpened by her use of dialogue and dialect. It is, then, an issue of 'voice' and of 'presence' which concerns us here. In these two fairly simple examples, first from *Union Street* and then from *Blow Your House Down*, we hear, even in a piece of omniscient narration, the *voice* of the characters.

> Getting out of the car was a right performance. She felt people watching her and that made her worse. Half her body was useless, dragged along by the rest. She had to cradle her dead hand in her living hand, and then how the hell could she manage a stick?[29]

> You do a lot of walking in this job. More than you might think. In fact, when I get to the end of a busy Saturday night, it's me feet that ache. There, that surprised you, didn't it?[30]

Union Street, quite simply, documents the thoughts and experiences of seven working-class women, whose ages range from seven to seventy and, whilst recording individual lives, intertwines these past and present experiences so that the story becomes, in the end, a community's. Omniscient narration is rarely intrusive here, and this method characterizes Barker's general approach. In the first extract the narrator does not comment from 'outside' on the elderly Alice Bell's struggle with infirmity, but instead Alice Bell's own voice expresses her own personal trials. In *Blow Your House Down*, the sudden switch from third- to first-person narration, enables the prostitute Brenda to address the reader directly. Even more telling is the way Barker opens the sentence with the pronoun 'you', rather than 'I'. If only fleetingly, this strategy draws the reader into a form of intimacy with Brenda, and thus imposes the act of identification with her, even if only one of refusal.

In Bakhtinian terms the narratives are seen to refuse the pitfalls of monologism, a characteristic predicated of classic realism. Dialogism is framed within and also articulates the often oppressive and exploitative social relations of working-class women both in the home and at work. The narrative encodes a variety of struggles against patriarchy, capital and the state. Bureaucracy is figured in the inclusive, but anonymous, 'they', who invariably represent some form of authority: establishment figures like the police or schoolmaster, bosses or violent husbands who must be denied. The ageing Alice Bell in *Union Street* struggles to die as she wishes, determined to 'hang on to her house, to save up for her funeral', defying the 'posh voices, the questions, the eyes everywhere' (p. 233) of prying social workers. Alice's story is that of a woman desperately trying to retain some dignity and independence, deprived of the older solidarities and support of the working-class community of her youth and early adulthood.

> Her home. They were taking it away from her. The dirt and disorder, the signs of malnutrition and neglect which to them were reasons for putting her away were, to her, independence. She had fought to keep for herself the conditions of a human life.
>
> She was calm again. What she wanted was simple. She wanted to die with dignity. She wanted to die in her own home. And if that was no longer possible, she would go away. She would not be here waiting for them when they came. (p. 260)

Determined to cling to those aspects of her life which constitute her sense of self, Alice identifies those who would put it under threat. The welfare aspect of the welfare state is seen as little more than a form of social engineering. Alice's condition is generalized across gender and generation: 'the memories threatened to overwhelm her. These fragments. Were they the debris of her own or other lives? She had been so many women in her time' (p. 263). Alice's 'fragmented' recollections might be images of a fragmenting community, as her thoughts turn to others in an intersubjective act of communality.

An 'Us and Them' structure of feeling is frequently evoked, what Hitchcock has called a 'sociology of the poor',[31] and which he argues is a simplified response that nevertheless has a real history to link up with. Within this opposition Alice acknowledges her own solidarities: with the women of her own generation (Iris King); with the miners, striking against a Conservative government ('They'll see the old people don't suffer'); and, across the generational divide, with the girl, Kelly Brown. Their coming together occurs in the local park, a public space in which the private terrors of the girl and the old woman are voiced. Kelly's story in *Union Street* has revolved around her experience of sexual brutality and rape, a shocking experience which had led her to suspect everyone. Thus, for Kelly, 'they' becomes the universal figure of 'Man', whom she has to resist to survive. Both women are alienated, by being invisible (Alice) and manipulable (Kelly). In each other they recognize mutual pain and a kind of sisterhood which transcends age and is grounded in identifications of gender, class and community. For both, survival is the main priority:

> 'There must be another way,' . . .
> 'There's no other way. They're trying to take everything away from me. Everything.' She smiled. 'Well this way they can't,' . . .
> In spite of the smile she was still crying. Kelly reached out and touched her hand.
> 'I won't tell anybody,' she said.
> She looked down at their hands: the old woman's cracked and shiny from a lifetime of scrubbing floors, her own grubby, with scabs on two of the knuckles. (p. 68)

Kelly identifies the material effects of class and gender as they mark the body, which becomes a social construct determined by an individual and collective existence: one scarred by labour, the other by a harsh social environment and by personal despair. There is also a subtle comparison in this scene, between the close identifications Kelly makes and the narrative inscribes, and the anonymous response of state bureaucracies whose function is to 'hide' Alice's ageing body from view (as it happens, in what Alice still thinks of as the workhouse, though it has long been converted into an institution for the elderly and/or senile). Barker often foregrounds social relations in this 'intimate' manner. In *The Century's Daughter*, the child Liza accompanies her mother to her cleaning job at the 'big house'.

> Her mum rocked from side to side as she scrubbed, trying to ease the pain in her leg. Under the sacking apron her belly sagged.
> She [Liza] moved round the room, stroking the cushions, feeling the silk catch a flap of skin where a blister had burst . . . She thought, *This is where they live, the Wynyards, this is where they eat and sleep and talk and laugh*, and she remembered her father's hands, scarred with iron dust.[32]

The silk cushion and the flap of skin: encoded in this description is the starkness of class inequality, which Liza internalizes, and which continue to inform her activity and shape her world view deep into adult life. In *Union Street*, Kelly has recognized similar traces of labour and hardship in Alice's hands, though Alice is comforted by Kelly's presence. A sense of mutuality is developed which calls for a recognition of commonalty and kind. Thus,

> at first [Alice] was afraid, the child had come so suddenly. Then – not afraid. They sat beside each other; they talked. The girl held out her hand. The withered hand and the strong young hand met and joined. There was silence. Then it was time for them both to go. (p. 265)

Renewal is suggested: the coming together of young and old, the past and the present, to resist the faceless forces which threaten their lives. Barker's writing encodes the mutual determinancies of gender and class in a constellation of conditions: domestic drudgery, childbirth, sexism or the extraction of surplus value. The last condition emerges through detailed representations of factory work, where the rare sight of women at the workplace contrasts with the more familiar practice of bourgeois writers to omit the work process from their fiction altogether. The earlier extract from *The Century's Daughter* is a representation of one form of work, in effect, a live-out servant's labour. In *Union Street* we are presented with factory work:

> The noise was horrific as usual. There was no possibility of conversation. Even the supervisor's orders had to be yelled at the top of her voice and repeated many times before anyone heard. At intervals, there were snatches of music. It was being played continuously but only the odd phrase triumphed over the roar of the machines. Some of the women moved their mouths silently, singing or talking to themselves: it was hard to tell. Others merely looked blank. After a while not only speech but thought became impossible.
> The first sponge cake reached Jo. She began the sequence of motions that she would perform hundreds of times that day. It took little effort once you were used to it and, provided the cakes continued to arrive in a steady stream, it could be done almost automatically. (pp. 84–5)

Then, in the chicken factory in *Blow Your House Down*:

> The noise started up and a procession of headless chickens advanced into the room. At the gutting table the green-clad women took the birds

down, wiped blood from their necks and, pushing their hands into the vent as far as the wrist, pulled out piles of steaming gut.
'Messy job that,' Annie screamed above the noise. 'This is better.'
'This' was basically shoving chickens' legs up their arses, only it wasn't as easy as that because the chickens were chilled, sometimes near frozen and you had to really force the legs inside . . . By the time the first tea-break came her hands were frozen, but the rest of her, inside the nylon and plastic uniform, streamed with sweat. (pp. 34–5)

Intrinsic to the work process, the workers are nevertheless 'silenced' by the machinery. They are forced to struggle not only for speech but for thought itself. Their actions become as functional or 'automatic' as the machinery around them; they constitute a mere appendage of the machine, and only the dull compulsion of economic necessity drives the women on. In *Blow Your House Down*, the event of Brenda turning from work in the chicken factory to the dangers and humiliations of prostitution is over-determined by factors beyond factory-labour – by the absence of childcare for single mothers, by the continual absence of enough money to pay mounting bills. Thus Barker can offer representations of another type of work, when the selling of one's labour (in the sex industry) has consequences too terrible to contemplate, as the subtext of *Blow Your House Down*, with its clear allusions to the 'Yorkshire Ripper', implies.

Barker's historical narratives, her efforts at acknowledging working-class women, find their fullest expression in *The Century's Daughter*, a kind of 'gargantuan epic' in itself. It is this novel, I would argue, which engages most comprehensively with the political imperatives of the present by excavating the past. Written in the mid-1980s, when much of the heavy industry characteristic of the north-east had succumbed to the Thatcherite onslaught of shutdowns and redundancies, and when communities were threatening to disintegrate under the pressure of these developments, the novel constitutes a 'condition-of-England' narrative through which, as Lyn Pykett says, 'the social and economic crises of the eighties are seen through the perspective of other twentieth-century crises, most notably the 1930s'.[33] This perspective is mobilized through the figure of Liza Jarrett, whose birth at the turn of midnight on 1 January 1900 gives the book its title. It is Liza's unfolding memory of her long life – her reliving of that life as she nears death in her ravaged working-class community – that leads the reader through a history of social relations from the turn of the century to the present.

It can be argued that memory and history are interdependent, and that there are specific conjunctures when the ideological pressures working within the latter seem intent upon destroying the former. In considering Barker's mobilization of memory within the context of the 1980s, and the perceived break-up of the working class under the pressures of economic change and ideological attack from the Right, it is possible to read *The Century's Daughter* as an intervention within this complex discursive matrix. Liza's recollections are rooted firmly in the concrete and, as the narrative unfolds, she abstracts from these images and events a wider collective history, which undermines the strict linearity of official discourse or the teleological master-narratives of orthodoxy. In both *Union Street* and *The Century's Daughter* a profound concern with 'nostalgic memory' propels the narratives, providing a sense of continuity in the midst of rapid change. Thus Peter Hitchcock can argue that, in *The Century's Daughter*, history is measured

> in the births and deaths of working-class women, in the labour of their labour, in the material bonds of birth and upbringing. This is a very different form of history from the measured empiricism of surplus value and union men. It is not that those histories are inseparable, but that the evaluative criteria of the latter has tended to obscure or obviate the experience of the former.[34]

This is another important point to make in relation to British labour history. Barker interrogates the official history of public events (the First World War, the 1930s), which are dialogized through Liza's personal memories. She also reaccentuates a labour history which contents itself only with the history of class struggle as 'surplus value and union *men*', thus recovering experience through the production of a gendered class memory. If we accept this, then we acknowledge that feminist texts in the form of stories, novels and autobiographical writing have frequently attempted to capture a sense of a common, or representative, experience. A feminist politics not rooted in the postmodern theory of difference also aspires to construct a collective identity and structure of feeling: in Bakhtinian terms, perhaps, to orientate discourse not only in contestation with dominant meanings and constructions, but in possible identification with those that are common and shared. For Richard Johnson and other writers of *Making Memories*, the imaginative production of 'popular' memory in this sense, then, remains a 'vital source, helping us to understand the nature, historicity and changeability of current conditions'.[35] We might even refer to it as a kind of cognitive mapping.

Liza's recall becomes as much a product of a revolt against the pressures of a Thatcherite present as an exploration of the past. Recall, however, requires an 'aide-mémoire'. This is symbolized by Liza's metal box, secluded beneath her bed and containing objects collected from the past which, metonymically, represent 'links in a chain of women stretching back through centuries into the wombs of women whose names they didn't know' (p. 211). For Liza, personal reminiscence always carries with it the wider public and collective resonance which gives meaning to her life so that, 'it startled him [Stephen, Liza's social worker] to realize that Liza had more faith in the future at eighty-four than he had at twenty-nine. He looked around at the people he worked with here and on the Claggs Lane Estate, and it seemed to him that he was witnessing the creation of a people without hope' (p. 219). Liza derives her optimism from memories of a more organic community, despite the atomization of individuals and communities which produces a sense of despair in Stephen.

In an extract quoted earlier, we witnessed Liza at the Wynyard mansion becoming dimly aware of class relations. The experience of 'otherness' (as a woman, as working class) dialogizes and ruptures the continuum of history, produces a disjuncture in which simplistic ideas of progress founder. Liza's life is a struggle for the 'crude and material things' without which no narrative could ever be told. The newspaper cutting she keeps, and reveals to Stephen, narrates her 'historic' birth at the turn of the century, and holds for her contradictory memories: pleasure at the brief notoriety, mixed with the consciousness that she was probably a burden on her hard-pressed family. She recalls her mother's professed pride over the event but adds, 'it was me she wasn't keen on. I was the seventh, and she'd lost four. Three of them in one week. Took more than a bit of paper to make *her* jump. Especially over a girl' (p. 8). The stark realities of her existence are identified, moving from childhood and the First World War, to the 1930s, then the Blitz, and finally to the community redevelopers of the post-war period, with their own brand of demolition. The working-class experience of modernity, we see, is one of gain and loss: indeed, modernity is an 'incomplete project'.[36] This brings us to the present, and the desolation of de-industrialization and the work patterns deeply embedded in the community the novel describes. This scene then takes on a painfully elegaic quality (not a dissimilar structure of feeling to that explored by Bleasdale in *Boys from the Blackstuff*) as Stephen and Liza (who has accepted a visit to his home) journey through the industrial desolation of late modernity.

> High barbed-wire fences enclosed work yards that would never work again. The wires throbbed and hummed as the wind blew through them. Bits of cloth and polythene clung to the barbs and snapped ...
> She walked a few steps, holding on to the side of the car. In her mind's eye she saw this place as it had been. Tall chimneys, kilns and furnaces loomed up through the brown smoke of a winter afternoon. Trains rattled, hammers banged, furnaces roared, and always, day and night, columns of flame rose up to the sky.
> 'There's nothing left,' she said, and, although she'd known that it must be so, her voice was raw with loss ...
> The wind keened across the brown land, and it seemed to Liza that it lamented vanished communities, scattered families, extinguished fires. Mourned the men who'd crowded to the ferry boat, at each and every change of shift, the boots striking sparks on the cobbles as they ran. (p. 216)

The extract constitutes a description of a lost way of working and living, the dislocation of a culture which Liza can perceive all too clearly here, and which then articulates a dominant structure of feeling in the novel. Yet the very articulation – the 'remembering' – of this experience represents an effort to reinstate its validity and value, its intrinsic place within community and history.

The novel is constructed through flashbacks, where the past is used to illuminate the present, or simply recorded to give voice to marginalized experience. Hence memories of the First World War do not point up male heroics, or nationalistic fervour, but the mindless slaughter – 'an entire neighbourhood' – and the dangerous labour of working class-women in the munitions factories. Flag-waving euphoria is diluted by reference to the factory-owner Wynyard's war-profiteering as, after 1918, they 'moved out ... to a bigger house in the country' (p. 64). And Liza's memory of giving birth to her son, Tom, sees her

> absorbed in her long labour and yet not divided from the life of the street around her. The tramping of feet of men who had work to go to, the squatting on haunches of men who had none, the skitter of stone over the pavement as children played hopscotch, the hanging-out of washing . . . women with open-pored, harassed faces chasing a little bacon round the frying-pan asking, *will it be enough* . . . All these things and more revolved around the periphery of her vision, and she felt as her labour went on that she was giving birth to them all. (p. 142)

Some of these things Liza can actually hear – the tramping of feet – others she imagines or 'feels': the men on their haunches, the women fretting over bits of bacon. This structure of feeling, I believe, Barker explicitly wants us to contrast with the present, and the perceived dissolution of community and culture. Out of it emerges a class-specific feminist consciousness: flagging up the exploitation of women's labour in childbirth, in the kitchen and at work. Much later, when Liza remembers a visit to Tom's grave (he was killed in the Second World War) the realist narrative gives way to a dream sequence where she meets up with Lena Lowe, whose son has also died in the war. She recounts the dream to Stephen:

> She come to see me in that mucky old mackintosh she used to wear. And she had something in her hands, something very bright, and I couldn't understand what it was, because I knew they were jewels, and yet they seemed to be alive. Sapphires, rubies, diamonds: but brighter. And they were all moving about, and making this little squeaking noise, as if they were singing. (p. 214)

A stream-of-consciousness technique offers an examination of the unconscious, or of a preconscious state, the workings of the individual psyche. It also elaborates fantasy and desire, transgressing linguistic norms to disclose an emancipatory poetics of the semiotic rather than the symbolic order.[37] Such writing might express unfulfilled desire, hopes, dreams, an emergent structure of feeling in solution, one striving to break through. A common bond exists, though not based on an idealized or sentimentalized experience of 'hard times', and Liza underlines this, telling Stephen that the pressures working-class women were exposed to in the 1930s meant that 'they were worn out by the time they were thirty'. The common activity of women in the thirties depicted here fills the gap alongside the 'canonical' images of men in this period – 'heroic' miners, the decent breadwinner or the down-at-heel unemployed man. And though her memories are dominated by the experiences of sacrifice and survival, Liza still believes that the structures of the post-war welfare state have taken something away, as well as offered something to the working class:

> Because that's where they went wrong you know. It was all *money*. You'd have thought we had nowt else to offer. But we *did*. We had a way of life, a way of treating people . . . You got stuck in seven days a week and bloody did it, because you knew if you didn't you wouldn't survive and neither would she. We had all that. We had pride. We were poor, but we were *proud*. (p. 218)

Here, Liza articulates a historical condition which in other discourses and representations has become slightly caricatured over time. In this context her words come dangerously close to sentimental comment, pastiche or nostalgia, close to Fredric Jameson's conceptualization of historical thought in the postmodern age, and an example of the potential dangers of 'nostalgic memory' I highlighted earlier. A sense of loss might lead to an insistence on a lost golden age, which appears to contradict Liza's earlier assertions about the hardships of past times. Yet this is a symptomatic moment in the narrative as a whole, evoking the full charge of memory in its social and political dimensions, interacting dialogically with the 1980s and the Thatcherite assault. But it is a moment which threatens to repeat some of the mythologizing closures we have predicated of, for instance, male writers on the working class and the working-class community. Liza evokes a communal past, and the possibilities this may have held for a different future, in contrast and contestation with a blighted present, and rejects Stephen's contention that this structure of feeling has all but died. She tells him that there are 'still people who will do a good turn for anybody. There's thousands like that' (p. 219). Celebrating, or invoking, this past, in a mode of representation that has taken on the form of caricature and pastiche (one is reminded of *Monty Python* sketches) threatens to disperse the real, the historical referent, into simulacra, however.

Stephen expresses little hope for the future of the local people. As a social worker, he is at the sharp end of community relations (or lack of them), performing what he gradually comes to regard as a 'containing job', finding ways to occupy unemployed youths (the same youths whose violence leads to Liza's death) with trivial tasks to fill the vacuum left by the flight of capital. In the end, the relationship between Stephen and Liza suggests some sense of the healing of the rift with Stephen and his own past. Lyn Pykett notes that, 'Liza's death is directly linked to Stephen's resumption of life following the death of his father, and both deaths play a part in Stephen's painful recognition of the links of the chain which binds him to his familial and communal past.'[38] This generational 'link-up' is again foregrounded; we saw it with Kelly and Alice Bell in *Union Street*. Towards the end of *The Century's Daughter*, Stephen has a dream.

> He knew the cowled figure of Liza, and yet the hands that came out of the folds of the cloak were male. Blindly he held out his hands. Then, just as their fingers touched, just as Stephen felt the shape and weight of the box [Liza's memory box] he woke and lay in darkness, sweating, because he had remembered whose hands they were. Somehow, in the labyrinth of the dream, his father and Liza were one. (p. 272)

The dream language again enables the expression of utopian desire and transcendence. There is arguably a double healing suggested here: as Liza and Walter come together, the rift with his father is erased and the distance he feels from his past is diminished. Through Liza he begins to understand some of the community's deeper resiliences and its more valuable continuities, which are linked to a history that the forces of the present are trying brutally to erase.

Barker's writing can be compared with that of writers like Toni Morrison, concerned as it is with giving those written out of bourgeois history's triumphal procession a participating voice. Using Patrick Wright's formulations, where he elaborates on the value and possibility of a 'vernacular history', we can see in the figures of Liza and Alice Bell an active memory evoking history as more than

> public instilled illusion and ideology but also everyday historical consciousness – of stories, memory and vernacular interpretation

which differ (sometimes in fully conscious opposition) from that superior 'History' which, while it has always spoken with easily assumed authority, is distinguished not just by its laurels but also by the difficulty it experiences in achieving its glorious national 'truth'.[39]

There is a danger of sentimentality, or idealization, in Barker's writing, where the narrative reverts to the type of reactionary nostalgia to which the concept of 'nostalgic memory' is always vulnerable. At these points in the writing it is possible to regard Barker's texts as seeking an 'integrated' working-class community that never fully existed, ignoring, in the process of doing this, the alienations and exploitation inevitably associated with so much of working-class experience. Thus, in lamenting the disappearance of a type of working-class life, the characters in her novels might be seen to be articulating, not an 'enabling' nostalgia, but one which speaks only of loss and regret. At times, in *The Century's Daughter*, Liza expresses just this structure of feeling. Yet I would insist that this is only a tendency in Barker's work, one that hints at the limitations of nostalgia as a structure of feeling, while going beyond those limits in productive and illuminating ways. Seeking presence in absence and history in myth, Barker situates her female characters' experiences within the broader framework of community and class. Thus, in *The Century's Daughter*, the act of remembering comes to be seen as a radical act in itself, a struggle for individual and collective identity in a time when historical thought is articulated as pastiche or mere period 'style', and when any deep sense of working-class community, under the relentless pressure of social change and political force, comes under threat. In doing this, Barker's writing from the 1980s constitutes the most sustained attempt to write working-class women into the novel.

5
Mapping difference and identity: race, class and the politics of belonging

There is a scene in Salman Rushdie's *The Satanic Verses* (1989), where we witness the outlandish appearance of Saladin and Gibreel from a cool English sky, a descent announcing the insurgency of the post-colonial subject into the monologic enclaves of empire. This is the return of the repressed and Gibreel rejoices at the prospect: 'These powerless English! – Did they not think that their history would return to haunt them? – "The native is an oppressed person whose permanent dream is to become the persecutor" (Fanon).'[1] The Indian actor Gibreel, equipped with a successful film career of imitating gods, is well suited for imitating the little gods of empire, which he undertakes at the home of the Englishwoman Rosa Diamond. Ensconced in the rural idyll of southern England, Rosa feels history in the reassurance of repetition, of things changing but somehow remaining the same: 'repetition had become a comfort in her antiquity' (p. 130). But the fantastic appearance of the two Indians shatters a hegemonic national history, one characterized by its ideological selectivity and symptomatic silences, as much as by its celebrated 'events', exposed as it is to the accusing gaze of its historically despised Other. The national narrative is displaced and the continuum of history exploded to signify a disjuncture, in turn, symbolized at a personal and ontological level by the 'cracks and absences' Rosa suddenly feels within herself.

Gibreel dons the clothes of Rosa's dead husband, an ex-colonial landowner. Indeed, Gibreel becomes the post-colonial mimic-man. 'The menace of mimicry', Homi Bhabha explains, 'is its double vision which in disclosing the ambivalence of colonial discourse also erupts its authority.'[2] Bhabha argues that colonial authority is always threatened, and potentially subverted, by the presence of the 'imitating' native. Rushdie's narrative seemingly confirms this, only in reverse this time; the Other is now firmly ensconced in the metropolis. There is something clearly subversive at the sight of Gibreel, Indian filmstar from the teeming backstreets of Bombay, attired thus. The migrant hybrid, decked out in Sir Henry Diamond's 'maroon smoking-jacket and jodhpurs . . . smelling faintly of mothballs', signifies Bhabha's 'ambivalence', though in fact reversing the binary roles set out for Gibreel in the eyes of the metropolis years ago. Undermined here are the comfortable (and comforting) binaries constructed by imperial regimes, enacted in the actions of armies and administrators, and inscribed in the writings of Macaulay and his ilk – and still breathing deep in Rushdie's Thatcherite England. The demarcation lines of the nation-state, the borders which strive to define a homogeneous national identity without reference to the constitutive presence of the Other, present no barrier to Gibreel, and thus the colonizer is brought to book. Here Rushdie attempts to deconstruct a powerful ideology: the mythical concept of the nation as imagined community so often used, much like religion, to political ends in delineating a common identity. As Bhabha, referring to the significance of Gibreel, puts it, 'The post-colonial space is now "supplementary" to the metropolitan centre; it stands in a subaltern, adjunct relation that doesn't aggrandize the *presence* of the west but redraws its frontiers in the menacing agonistic boundary of cultural difference that never quite adds up, always less than one nation and double.'[3] In other words, then, it appears that the terms 'oppressor' and 'oppressed' are compromised in this act of cultural translation or transgression. There remains no essence to which a subject can cling or return, either as individual or as member of a nation state. Narrating the nation constitutes a central problematic in these discourses, and it is my aim in this chapter to explore the relationship of race and class within the wider context of identity politics.

I Erasing borders in the writing of race and nation

It has been argued that in the period following the Second World War English society was transformed by its earlier imperial encounters. A flow of immigration to the imperial centres, initiated by respective British governments to favour the aims and needs of British capital, led to what some commentators have described as 'colonialism in reverse . . . a new sense of what it means to be English'.[4] In this context, then, the 'margins' meet the 'centre' and at a symbolic level the very boundaries of the nation-state become blurred and 'under erasure'. Rushdie's writing engages powerfully with this process, which sees an irretrievable change in the 'purity' of the English language and of 'Englishness'. Of course, this 'purity' was largely mythical anyway, fractured and written over by the deep tensions and historical contradictions of class relations. Fixing a hegemonic version of what it is to be English/British is a long established ideological manoeuvre of the dominant order determined to maintain the status quo. Rushdie's comment that 'English, no longer an English language, now grows from many roots; and those whom it once colonized are carving out large territories within the language for themselves'[5] can be applied to a number of writers already discussed in this book, as much as to Rushdie's own post-colonial context, and it articulates an important and emergent structure of feeling. But the idea of English being some monologic tongue, one reaching out to colonize and control distant people and places, is in many respects a mystification also, ignoring the fissures of class and power so deeply embedded in language and culture, a condition explored succinctly in the work of James Kelman and Tony Harrison.

While this chapter turns on an investigation of the dialectic of race and class, it is concerned also with the notions of identity and 'belonging', especially relevant in the context of the nation-state. A renewed emphasis in the 1980s on questions of identity, articulated by both Left and Right, drew into sharp focus during this period issues of nationality and of citizenship. Increasingly, an orientation towards identity politics established itself as the new 'common sense' in political and social theory, with a stress on the need to extend entitlements beyond 'economic, political and social rights . . . to the cultural, with the assumption that in some way we may speak of the cultural rights of citizenship'.[6] Emerging out of these developments – as discussed in the introduction – was the politics of 'new social movements', with its centre in ideas of cultural difference, in turn developing theory and practice with a primary focus on formations of race/ethnicity, gender and sexuality. While this has had the necessary effect of privileging long-silenced, or marginalized, voices, it has also had the (perhaps) unintended consequence of dislodging former concerns with class. The politics of identity – the cultural politics of difference – became a ground of heightened contestation, particularly in the United States, but increasingly in Britain. It has been summed up by Cornel West in the following way:

> Distinctive features of the new cultural politics of difference are to trash the monolithic and homogeneous in the name of diversity, multiplicity and heterogeneity; to reject the abstract, general and universal in light of the concrete, specific and particular, and to historicize, contextualize and pluralize by highlighting the contingent, provisional, variable, tentative, shifting, and changing.[7]

The oppositions articulated here have a very clear hierarchy of their own, suggesting that any discourse or practice inclined towards universalist ideas in particular must be abandoned in favour of plurality, contingency, the heterogeneous. The developing tendency to celebrate 'difference' will have contradictory results, however, when applied to our understandings of class, and to associated issues around economic and political inequality. In this view, identity is constituted exclusively in the realm of culture, so that class as economic/political category becomes dislodged. Economic justice yields the way to a stress on cultural recognition (these things need not be incompatible). A concentration on the cultural figured strongly in discussions of class in the late 1950s and 1960s; there, however, the approach was designed to reinstate, if in the end contradictorily, the significance of the working class as a real presence, its culture and structures of feeling explored and examined in part as a way of understanding the possibilities for wider political change. In this later juncture, the whole issue of class gradually becomes, in the words of one commentator, the 'forgotten identity of identity politics'.[8]

In the 1980s, the discursive mobilizations of Thatcherism employed their own brand of identity politics, with a focus on the nation and ideas of Englishness, which revolved powerfully around senses of belonging. These articulations were characterized by a rhetoric imbued with a 'common-sense', populist patriotism. Thatcherism renewed the rhetoric of the nation through which to operate a politics of purported national interest – 'there is no alternative' – but, from its inception, one which most clearly represented the interests of a specific group or class. Accompanying radical shifts in economic management was a language of renewed moral greatness, with a decisive emphasis on the national 'character', rooted in the past. The specificity of this past invoked the mythology of Victorian values, military conquest, the days of empire. Such discourses make up what Eric Hobsbawm has termed the invention of tradition. Tradition is seen here as:

> a set of practices, normally governed by overtly or tacitly accepted rules and of a ritual or symbolic nature, which seek to inculcate certain values and norms of behaviour by repetition, which automatically implies a continuity with the past. In fact, where possible, they normally attempt to establish continuity with a suitably historic past.[9]

These monologic utterances represent a cultural and political hegemony which facilitates the articulation of a selective past for the construction of an acceptable present. In Bakhtinian terms centripetal forces engage in silencing centrifugal interventions and tendencies, and under the rubric of a national identity the realities of a series of oppressions determined by race, class and gender positions can be extinguished, redefined or defused. The construction of a nation-state, however, and the official interpellation of 'We British', in both Rushdie's and Bhabha's views, represents a radically fragile identity, although it remains one around which people are still mobilized. According to Stuart Hall, this was one of the achievements of New Right ideology in the 1980s: Thatcherism cut across divides and conflicting interests, including class interests, by deploying, amongst other things, 'the discourse of "nation" and "people" against "class" and "unions" '.[10] The discourse of difference, in this context, is employed in quite different ways to those adumbrated by theorists of the politics of difference referred to earlier.

Thatcherism extolled the virtues and values of a national identity, but also decisively expelled those who did not embrace the official version. Those Others then came under the sign of alien cultures or the enemy within. The rhetoric of 'English culture' has particular ramifications for black British. In the moral and cultural absolutism of Thatcherite discourse, the liberal view of a multicultural idyll had no real place. Thatcher's own use of 'race' is expressed in an infamous statement she made leading up to the 1979 election:

> [P]eople are really rather afraid that this country might be swamped by people of a different culture. The British character has done so much for democracy, for law, and done so much throughout the world that if there is any fear that it might be swamped, then people are going to be rather hostile to those coming in. We are a British nation with British characteristics. Every country can take some minorities, and in many ways they add to the richness and variety of this country. But the moment the minority threatens to become a big one, people get frightened.[11]

Thatcher is explicit here about her desire to protect the ethnic identity of 'Britishness', which, I would argue, in Thatcherite terms most often implies 'Englishness'.

The assertion – or reassertion – of the nation and national identity is constituted largely within the domain of culture. Enoch Powell, in the 1960s, elided race, nation and culture in a discourse which emphasized 'rootedness', and which implied that any radical racial mix – the result of immigration policies – was fundamentally wrong, at best misguided.[12] During the 1980s, thinkers on the Right associated with the conservative journal *The Salisbury Review* firmly grounded national identity within an organicist view of British culture, implying a deep and intuitive – thus 'natural' – sense of belonging. Roger Scruton rejects outright class as a sociological concept or historical agent and privileges a national unconsciousness as the 'genuine agent in history. Language, custom, associations and traditions of political order – in short all those forces which generate nations.'[13] Here class, race and gender antagonisms or differences are subsumed under an undifferentiated national culture and heritage. This homogenization of culture focuses attention on the Other as the alien presence, or enemy within.

> There is no way of understanding British and English history that does not take seriously the sentiments of patriotism that go with a continuity of institutions, shared experiences, language, customs, kinship . . . English patriotism . . . has as its centre a feeling for persons of one's own kind.[14]

This rhetoric is loaded against all those who do not share the language and meanings which constitute what it is to be British (or is it English?). The imagined community invoked here is predicated upon a sense of continuity and tradition (essentially *changeless*), and patriotism is an intuitive response based on blood. This national culture is then to be defended against a West Indian community that 'is *structurally* likely to be at odds with English civilization'; or Asians who, though better disciplined, disclose a '*profound* difference in culture', so that 'they are most unlikely to wish to identify themselves with the traditions and loyalties of the host nation'.[15] This is Cambridge professor John Casey speaking. As 'host' suggests 'parasite', Casey is forced to conclude that 'the only radical policy that would stand a chance of success [and maintain the integrity of the national culture] is repatriation'.[16]

The ethnic purity of 'Englishness' has to be defended against alien hordes. The coherence assumed in this construct of English culture is grounded in an Us and Them ideology, a form of 'common sense' which condemns outsiders. It constitutes the kind of essentialist discourse rigorously attacked by proponents of the politics of difference. Like all ideology, such discourses attempt to organize people's behaviour, their perceptions of themselves and others. Such thinking can acquire many registers in the social formation and need not necessarily be associated solely with ideas of race or nation. Thus in the miners' strike of 1984–5, striking miners were contrasted with those who did not withdraw their labour and who were thus, in Thatcher's words, 'working for Britain'.[17] The Greenham Common women, protesting against nuclear armament, are defined as deviants, operating outside the bounds of acceptable practice and social norms. The inner-city uprisings in England during 1981, and later in 1985, were presented in the media, and in official political discourse, as a race problem, and black youths particularly targeted as criminal and outside the law. Or, more specifically, they were seen as outside English law and custom. Very little notice was given in the mainstream media to the interracial nature of the clashes, and to the official statistics which revealed more white arrests during the uprising than black.[18] We can conclude that the construction of the nation, and a national identity, dependent on specific historical coordinates, remains a vital ideological tool for the dominant order. Through the wielding of power – and through a matrix of representations, 'grounded' assumptions which become a form of common sense, and institutional mobilizations – the production of 'necessary' fictional selves as organically part of the wider national order and distinctive culture offers a mode of identification with the state which has often transcended (and still transcends) other modes of collective identification such as class consciousness.

Conversely, Paul Gilroy has argued that the very concept 'race' remains malleable, working to 'bind the processes by which ethico-political hegemony is . . . produced'.[19] If class antagonisms in Britain are lived through the prism of race and racial ideologies, specific cultural practices by blacks which resist these conditions become a form of class struggle despite their ostensibly prioritized anti-racist discourse. This is not simply to reduce anti-racism to class struggle. Gilroy stresses the impact of a diasporic culture and a sense of community in struggle against centripetal forces. He sees community as 'central to the view of class struggle'. This is so because 'it links distinct cultural and political traditions – which have a territorial dimension – to collective action and consciousness and operates within the relations of economic patterns, political authority and uses of space.'[20] What Gilroy does not address, however, is how the disruption of space – as I argued in chapter 2 – disorganizes those communal places in which oppositional strategies might form.

In *There Ain't No Black in the Union Jack* (1987), Gilroy analyses what he terms 'expressive culture'. He views some forms of black popular music as cultural practices which challenge the structures of capital, the ideological discourses of racism and the endemic Eurocentrism of British culture. He specifies reggae music, highlighting its potential to invoke a positive response and identification among disaffected white working-class youths now distanced from the rhetoric of empire and race supremacy. Thus struggles against the state/nation bureaucracies and the experience of mass unemployment lead to a form of class struggle, not at the point of production, but within the 'space' of community. He argues elsewhere that such developments 'indicate the relatively precarious nature of the youngsters' commitment to race and nation'.[21] Through such struggles class is constituted politically, as a response to material conditions which increasingly deny real forms of freedom and equality.

Furthermore, Kobena Mercer has argued that film – or what he calls 'image-making' – has become an important area of cultural contestation in Britain, especially during the 1980s. He suggests that this contestation is 'over what it means to be British today; contestation over what Britishness itself means as a national or cultural identity'.[22] He highlights how recent black film-making discloses consistent thematic concern with contradictory experiences in the formation of black British identity, taking as examples such films as *Handsworth Songs*, *Passions of Remembrance* and *Playing Away*. Black film-making in the 1980s, by pursuing what Stuart Hall has described as the 'politics of representation', not only critiques traditional conceptions of Britishness, which have depended on the subordination of other ethnic identities, but calls the very concept of a coherent national identity into question 'by asserting instead . . . a culture of differences'.[23] Thus *Handsworth Songs* attempts to challenge dominant representations of British blacks as 'natural', or inherent, law-breakers. Representations here are given a new and counter-hegemonic inflection; formal strategies – placing the camera with the 'mob', for instance – construct the police as the antagonistic force, countering widespread and officially mediated images of black violence. A 'dialogic recoding'[24] is enacted, rejecting those 'white' codes which stereotype the black individual.

Black film-makers contributed significantly to the revival of the British film industry in the 1980s, but this revival was also accompanied (perhaps in more definitive ways) by the marketing of a particular image of the nation and, more importantly, of the national past. These images and constructions were often quite consonant with the Thatcherite project itself (whether consciously or not); and can equally be seen as part of the general 'heritagization' of the national past in the form of the commodification of history in safe and saleable packages. These productions have been termed the heritage film.[25] The films discussed above can be seen as counters to such constructions. However, here I want to look at the work of Hanif Kureishi, examining in particular *My Beautiful Laundrette* (1985) and, to a lesser degree, *Sammy and Rosie Get Laid* (1986). Rejecting the nostalgia mode of heritage films, where a national past is constructed around a specific 'pastoral identity and authentic [upper-class] culture', Kureishi's two films present national identities which are 'shifting, fluid and heterogeneous'.[26]

As one critic has described them, these films attempt to 'cross barriers',[27] healing the divisions of class, race and sexuality, and recoding the pervasive stereotypes of a culture infected by the myths of the New Right. Though Kureishi could not be described, by any stretch of the imagination, as a working-class writer, it seems to me that these two films – but *My Beautiful Laundrette* in particular – are concerned in important ways with the dialectic of race and class, even if, in the end, this concern is displaced. At the same time, both texts are seminal in the way they approach and begin to articulate the emergent politics of difference and the imperative, developed increasingly within postcolonial theory, of *hybridity*, a concept which, I would suggest, throws up as many problems in relation to identity as it seeks to resolve.

The notion of hybridity in *My Beautiful Laundrette* surfaces in relation to both form and content. Focused on the lives of 'ordinary people', a conventional thematic of British social realism, the content and concern is extended so that the groups described above take up a central positioning in the narrative. Formally, also, the two films show a marked difference to the conventional social realist text, which is often marked by what John Hill calls a 'realism of the surface'.[28] As 'state-of-the-nation' films – commentaries on the fallout of Thatcherism – both *My Beautiful Laundrette* and *Sammy and Rosie Get Laid* embrace the conventions associated with this style of realist narrative, but depart from them too, for instance in the use of pastiche and symbolism (the laundrette being the most obvious symbolic device, something I will discuss later). According to Hill, this tendency is itself a product of the historic moment, reflecting a need to show the increasing complexity and contradictory nature of society, thus 'pushing the boundaries of realism outwards in order to give expression to those "realities" which a realism "of the surface" might not otherwise be equipped to provide.'[29]

The polemical nature of the two films is transparent. *My Beautiful Laundrette* challenges the Thatcherite construct of entrepreneurialism, reworking some of these ideas and giving the concept a specific class and racial dimension. *Sammy and Rosie Get Laid* is an altogether bleaker production, set against a backdrop of urban riots, quasi-military policing and property scams by which the city (London) is being crudely parcelled up and sold to the highest bidder. Both films are highly critical of Thatcherism. At the same time, they articulate a critique of the nation in its post-colonial phase and, more pertinently for us, problematizing notions of identity by focusing on the contradictory relations and determinations of race and class, both seen as products of history.[30]

Kureishi has argued that racism goes hand in hand with class inequality.[31] This is a rather contentious statement, suggesting as it does that racism is chiefly associated with working-class structures of feeling and attitudes. However, it is true that the relative powerlessness and inequalities experienced by a white working-class man or woman – whether that inequality is the result of the disparity of economic capital, symbolic capital or cultural capital[32] – are often displaced into antagonistic relationships with 'immigrants'. Kureishi is suggesting, then, that class inequalities reinforce and perpetuate racism. Class antagonisms are lived through the prism of race, fuelled not only by material impoverishments and disappointments, but also by an ideology of nation and national identity mobilized around the historical legacy of an imperialist past.

In *My Beautiful Laundrette* Kureishi seems to suggest that identity, whether for the white working-class Johnny, or the struggling black entrepreneur Omar, is the product of a particular history and a particular culture which they share, but from different ends of the spectrum. We see in the construction of working-class characters, like Johnny, Genghis and Moose, an active consciousness written over and scored with the traces of an imperialist past which constitutes their identities in the present. As the narrative develops, this condition, at least for Johnny, becomes history as a nightmare from which we feel he is trying to awake.

Dispossession stands as a key subtext of *My Beautiful Laundrette*, with a paradoxical relationship to the white working-class figures Kureishi depicts. Despite the emphasis on British Asian experience in the film, race is a subordinate issue to a more subtle exploration of the workings of class inequalities and the power relations within them. At one point in the film, the Asian businessman Nasser – who has hired the unemployed white Johnny to evict a black poet from a property he wants to re-let – tells the white youth, 'There is no question of race in the new enterprise culture.' This scene replicates an earlier one, which opens up the film. Here it is Salim, with the aid of black and Asian heavies, evicting Johnny and Genghis from their squat. The connotations are fairly clear: there is no place for Johnny and Genghis in the entrepreneurial environment created by Thatcherism and capitalized upon by Salim and Nasser. The city then becomes ghettoized and anonymous. There are no clear establishing shots which denote the location specifically as London, though we know that it is: instead, we are shown social space given over to, and expropriated by, those with the power to speculate and accumulate. Thus we move between the lavishly appointed apartments and homes of the Asian middle class, and the confined and constricted locations of the dispossessed and the poor. The laundrette constitutes the liminal space, or *place*, somewhere in-between; the symbolic dimension which helps propel the film, as Hill points out, away from 'traditional' realism.

The shifting-between is, of course, a central thematic as well as structural feature of the narrative. It is the existential dilemma faced by most of the main characters, and draws out questions of identity in terms of race, class and sexual orientation. In this context we can examine the representation of two important figures: Nasser, and Omar's Papa. Post-war immigrants from Pakistan and destined, by birth and immigrant status, to play the truly subaltern role in the 'host' nation, both men still perceive advantages to be had within British life and culture. In the new world of Thatcherite entrepreneurialism, Nasser has clearly benefited most. He has acquired a business empire in his small corner of the capital. He and the local Pakistani community 'keep the country in the black'. Nasser and Salim accumulate wealth and power by, unsurprisingly, exploiting others, whether they are black or white. Social hierarchies (based on the subordination of blacks through their immigrant status) are overturned in the film, and we are reminded of Fanon's argument that the colonized/subaltern perpetually yearns to take the place of the colonizer. In fact, Omar articulates this view when he angrily tells Johnny, 'I'm not going to be beaten down by this country. When we were at school, you and your lot kicked me all around the place. And what are you doing now? Washing my floor, and that's how I like it.' Nasser is perhaps less 'race' conscious. Business comes first, above all else. He tells Johnny: 'I'm a professional businessman, not a professional Pakistani.' He is more likely to screw people for profit than historical come-uppance.

Papa has a wholly subaltern position within the constructed class and racial hierarchies of the film, though we feel that prior to leaving his own country he was a figure of some limited distinction and respect. It is helpful to contrast the two brothers, Nasser and Papa, in this way because we can then highlight an emergent and dominant structure of feeling which Thatcherism explicitly endorsed. Papa, as a figure of the 'old' Left, had envisaged that a leftish political culture which he had perhaps once identified with the British state would offer him and his family a culture of opportunity, but he had not reckoned with the legacy of colonialism (fed in the 1970s by Powellism and later by Thatcherite rhetoric) and the power of the colonial myth. His disillusionment is symbolized by his turning to drink. He wants Omar educated – 'We must have knowledge . . . to see clearly what is being done to who in this country', he tells Johnny – but at the same time recognizes that 'this damn country has done us in'. This is a remark that has resonances beyond the current historical conjuncture and post-colonial racism, and that refers to a long history of colonial domination. After all, in many ways – with his very English quips, such as 'old man' – Papa is very much a 'mimic-man' himself, although the condition is far from parodic or empowering.

It is not too fanciful to see Papa as an Indian Independence figure imbued with the leftish values of the struggle, values which had also characterized the Attlee administration of 1945, which oversaw decolonization. Thatcherism's specific crusade was to eradicate both the reality and the memory of this formation from the nation's consciousness, replacing them with the more atavistic images of Empire or Victorian values. The 'death' of socialism is thus echoed in Papa's lament, that 'the working class are such a disappointment to me'.

This brings us to the film's representations of the white working class. It is perhaps easy to write these figures off as members of the growing 'underclass', thus somehow outside the class formation and social relations, a more degraded example of Marx's notion of the lumpenproletariat. This is not really the solution, however, and it is more appropriate to read these figures (Genghis, Moose and Johnny) as victims of economics and history. Whenever we see the youths, after their breaking with Johnny, they are invariably represented within a milieu of 'decline', or they come to symbolize some form of dispossession. We see them first in the squat, later in the empty, grey streets. The imagery suggests entrapment, contradicting their own assumptions of territorial rights. In fact they have nowhere to go and they accept – so we assume from their aggressive 'Englishness' and race hatred – a past that is both mythical and all too real. The irony is that the imaginary community they so want to inhabit, and which they would glory in, has left them to rot.

Earlier in the chapter I argued that the New Right employed a certain rhetorical address in its discursive interpellation of an exclusive 'we'. I also suggested that such an ideological strategy partly resolved the contradictions of race, class or gender in its construction of national identity. The noise generated by patriotism and xenophobia still contains, in all senses, the silences of the powerless and dispossessed. The jingoistic noises made by Genghis and his friends fill the gaps left by the reality of their own dispossession at an economic level. It becomes paradoxical, then, that in the Thatcherite purview, Nasser as the successful (but Pakistani!) entrepreneur will be most favoured. Thatcher, after all, had applauded the Asian and Indian shopkeepers as the nation's new 'meritocrats'.[33] Thus Genghis and the others – not professional businessmen but, it seems, professional Englishmen – are written off by Thatcherism – and, contemptuously, by Salim – as little more than 'scroungers'. Class relationships, for the likes of Genghis, are indeed lived through the prism of race. The reality of Thatcher's comment on 'alien cultures' is that it does not apply to the nostrums of difference, or the Other, but to the subject as agent of economic performance.

What, then, are we to make of Kureishi's representations of the white working-class figures? Are they members of the bulldog breed and prime fodder for the BNP, or merely individuals marginalized by the new priorities of late capitalism? For in the end, despite their menacing presence, they come over as quite pitiful characters (Salim's beating aside), experiencing themselves through tired symbols of a selective historical past, and victims of false consciousness indeed. Despite their fervour to 'belong' there is something quite rootless about them, as their somewhat aimless wanderings imply. Genghis pleads with Johnny, 'Don't cut yourself off from your own people, everyone's got to belong'; but Johnny's reply is 'I want to forget all them things'. The irony here is in Genghis invoking a national identity which seems to have no place for him. The capitalists, Salim and Nasser, have good reason to reject the nationalist mythography, conscious of their real relations to working-class youth. Salim runs down Moose, so deep is his contempt for the white working-class youths who terrorize him because of his colour, and who occupy an economically subaltern position in the class relationships written into the film. The hierarchies of race and class are very much in tension here and they have to be resolved finally in the essentially allegorical relationship between Omar and Johnny.

The development of that relationship is concerned with the crossing of barriers and the breaking of taboos. The process transgresses historical and cultural identities of colonizer and colonized and, especially in Johnny's case, those hardened class-stereotypes that forbid the working-class man (especially of the skinhead/punk variety) to harbour homo-erotic desires; thus the ambiguous symbolism of the launderette, a place where the stains (of the past) can be washed away, and where the lines of racial, sexual and class antagonism can be ironed out. This is the place in-between, a utopian impulse of reconciliation and difference. As a business venture the launderette also reaccentuates the ideological markings of entrepreneurialism. In the rhetoric of Thatcherism, entrepreneurialism signified individual success, but seen through the lens of *My Beautiful Laundrette*, it is recoded to articulate not simply personal and business success but a more communal good. Admittedly this effect is undercut by Omar's more overt desire to make money, to 'make a go' of things, but I would argue that this attitude is undercut, too, by the sense of 'renewal' associated with the laundrette's reopening and refurbishment. It is a rather idealistic and overly symbolic resolution, but one that seems appropriate for the particular difficulties of the historic moment.

However, *Sammy and Rosie Get Laid* drops all hint of recoded entrepreneurialism and offers a leading character (Rosie) who, in her role of beleaguered social-worker, is attempting to prop up a society now seen in steep decline. It seems to me that the key to understanding this film lies in the use of the city itself. The opening shots are of urban rioting, following the killing by armed police of a black woman. The scenes are both realistic and heavily stylized, continuing the formal hybridism that combines the social-realism genre and elements of art cinema. Nevertheless, they are also firmly grounded in history: these 'shots' have been preceded by the voice of Thatcher, part of her victory address after the 1987 election campaign: 'We've got a big job to do in the inner cities . . . no one must slack.' This, of course, was the cue for Canary Wharf.

It is primarily the use of the city, in both films, which performs the counter-discourse to the heritage films I mentioned earlier. Particularly in this second film, Kureishi constructs the city as a setting for hybridity and difference; a polymorphous perversity which he asks us to acknowledge and which contrasts with the 'Brideshead' image and class inflection, and the stifling middle-class Englishness of suburbia embodied in the film in the character of Alice. Arguably, then, in *Sammy and Rosie Get Laid* the city is used to dissolve concepts of national identity – Sammy says at one point, 'We are not British, we are Londoners' – and the engagement with class issues takes the construction of 'the people' versus 'the power bloc'. We are offered a stand-off between two opposed cultures: a repressive one, represented by Raffi and by the British establishment and its state apparatuses, and an open and more liberal formation which includes the figures of Sammy and Rosie, but also Danny and the two lesbians. Sammy sees in the city 'a mass of fascination', whilst for Rosie life on the street represents 'an affirmation of the human spirit'. Yet we should also note that Sammy and Rosie are both economically secure – they can afford their romanticization of the city. These comments should be read into the images of uprising as 'the people' attempt to reclaim the streets. The city, then, is not where chaos waits but a setting of potential fermentation produced by a dialectic of degeneration and regeneration.

However, a sense of displacement is a characteristic emphasis in the film, as the social is seen to be reconstituted and shaped by power and money, and some of the thematic concerns here are clearly consonant with discussions of de-industrialization and urban refashioning in the previous chapter. Danny, who represents the dispossessed blacks, tells Raffi: 'No one knows the shit the black people have to go through . . . We have a kind of domestic colonialism to deal with here, because they never allow us to run our own communities.' Danny and a group of others – a kind of new-age travellers' band, a range of individuals who occupy the margins of the social – inhabit a piece of wasteland which is being eyed greedily by property sharks. The bulldozers move in and we are asked to question what kind of England can be sold so easily to the highest bidder. As the travellers move on, their defiance suggests a possible counter-hegemony – some future utopia emerging out of a dystopic present. But like any utopia (when the term is not used in its strict sense of 'no-place') it would have to define itself against some 'other', some degenerate 'now' it becomes vital to transcend, some oppressive space in need of transformation. In the most abstract sense this can be read as Thatcherite Britain and, more concretely, as the representatives of the state and of business who uproot and dispossess people. Yet beyond that image of the defiant 'people' vacating the wasteland looms a clutch of high-rise flats, stark and immobile. There are no characters in the film who speak for this constituency: the voices of the white working-class Londoners who occupy the film's margins (those margins explored so effectively in Kelman's work) are never heard. A narrative concerned with the condition of 'ordinary' people thus discloses a particular 'silence' or absence of representation from this position; a silence, or omission, not as pronounced in *My Beautiful Laundrette* (but there, all the same). Those evicted from the land at least have the consolation of a limited and constrained mobility, the possibility of inhabiting a new place; those inhabiting the high-rise do not, and must endure whatever monstrosity property-money decides to erect in their midst.

Thus, I would suggest, *Sammy and Rosie Get Laid* is a much more problematic film than *My Beautiful Laundrette*. *Laundrette* succeeded by knitting together the themes of race and class within a much wider concern with national identity, and the dynamics of history which constitute us all. The film reminds us of Rushdie's insistence that we are 'irradiated with history . . . radioactive with history and politics'.[34] The 'third-space' produced in *My Beautiful Laundrette* offers a location where the 'dead hand' of the past, increasingly mobilized in the present by the forces of reaction, can be transcended. Kureishi himself has stated that 'it is the British, the white British, who have to learn that being British isn't what it was.'[35] This is a tall order indeed, particularly in the mid-1980s when this was written. As Gramsci knew, when the old refuses to die the new cannot be born.

When, in *My Beautiful Laundrette*, Omar's Papa states that 'the working class have been such a disappointment to me', we are in the presence of a particular historic juncture, one in which the working class is perceived to be eclipsed as a historical force. Papa, the modernist intellectual Leftist and anti-imperialist, passes judgement on the failed hopes of socialism. In the film, the working class are figured as not much more than aggressive little-Englanders, right-wing and reactionary, to be pitied at best, despised at worst. Their Englishness is predicated on a dated and redundant colonial myth of racial superiority, shaping their world view, binding them to the past and blinding them to the new and emergent multicultural social space they inhabit. Within such narrative devices the film produces an allegorical representation which – through a concern with transgressive identities, lived through liminal spaces – encodes the fragmentation of culture and the social in an embryonic postmodern landscape of multiple selves. But this emergent structure of feeling – the logic of *difference* enunciated in this imagined community – is built on a necessary exclusion of class altogether. I will consider this further by looking at other writing which takes the migrant experience, in particular, as the central structure of feeling of the work.

II Hybridity and belonging in the construction of self and community

The concept of hybridity referred to earlier is significant here. The concept, developed by writers concerned with elaborating the politics of difference within the context of post-colonialism, is defined by Homi Bhabha in this sense:

> the theoretical recognition of the split-space of enunciation may open the way to conceptualizing an *inter*national culture, based not on the exoticism of multiculturalism or the *diversity* of cultures, but on the inscription and articulation of culture's *hybridity* ... And by exploring the Third Space we may elude the politics of polarity and emerge as the others of ourselves.[36]

The self here is always *becoming*, but also forever *deferred*. It represents an anti-essentialist position which posits a decentred, fluid subjectivity, at the same time privileging the migrant experience of diaspora, where the condition of border crossings signifies an ever more characteristic event in the real world, as well as performing as an active metaphor for understanding global transformations and shifts and postmodern subjectivity. We referred to the idea of the diasporic workforce figured in some of the narrative modes in James Kelman's work: groups of individuals dispersed from their homelands, seeking work, and represented in the writing as existentially uprooted and economically exploited or dispossessed. Diaspora, in the context of the politics of difference, places the emphasis more on the celebration of this type of rootlessness, suggesting that agency and resistance to the dominant now rests at the margins, always threatening the centre with its double vision. At the same time, the notion of hybridity, and associated terms such as transnationality and creolization, are utilized to bring into question any sense of a homogenized, essentialist culture.

> We are drawn beyond the ideas of nation, nationalism and national cultures, into a post-colonial set of realities, and a mode of critical thinking which is forced to rewrite the very grammar and language of modern thought in directing attention beyond the patriarchal boundaries of Eurocentric concerns and its presumptive, 'universalism'.[37]

Hybridity emerges as the place in-between (the laundrette), and the politics of particularity replaces 'universalism' (nationalism, yes, but class identities also) in what constitutes a form of agency that is, according to one commentator, 'post-working-class, where locality, culture and political autonomy are essential replacements for class identity'.[38] Class belongs to an older understanding of the social, a modernist moment eclipsed by the eclecticism of the postmodern. Identity politics – though drawing class into the triptych that is race-gender-class – privileges an approach which, it has been argued, prioritizes 'the frenzied and constant refashioning of the Self, through which one merely consumes oneself under the illusion of consuming the world', which constitutes 'a specific mode of postmodern alienation which Bhabha mistakenly calls "hybridity", "contingency", "postcoloniality" '.[39] While there is no denying (or eluding) the radical changes produced by globalization, these changes have not necessarily erased the pressing problems of the past, merely added to them. This is not to imply either that there are no potential gains from the processes currently operating at a global level – Marxists, for instance, have long insisted on the inevitable global reach of capitalism and thus the emergence of its dialectical opposite, a global proletariat. But the stress on displacement which these theories identify, and generally approve, are conditions which the majority of migrants, or 'displaced' persons, experience as lack, disempowerment, vulnerability. And this emphasis, with the inevitable associations of powerlessness, poverty and inequality, returns us again to the question of class. It raises, also, the related question of 'belonging'.

The question of belonging, enunciated in *My Beautiful Laundrette*, is the central theme of a more recent work, Meera Syal's *Anita and Me* (1996). This is quite specifically a novel about race and class. In many ways *Anita and Me* is a recognizably working-class novel, but it is one in which setting, character and plot are recoded through a different, alternative, perspective: working-class life and community seen through the eyes of nine-year-old Meena, the daughter of the only Asian family in the tiny West Midlands working-class village of Tollington. Tollington is a village in the throes of decline: its mine has been closed, its school is being relocated and its identity gradually being breached as the wider urban conurbation of Wolverhampton encroaches upon it, signified through the building of a new housing estate nearby and the extension of the motorway to run within shouting distance of the village. The novel, through the figure of Meena, rehearses the familiar narrative strategy of the shift from innocence to experience; a rites-of-passage construct, articulated from within the diaspora structure of feeling. Meena's parents left India for England in the hope of a better life; their memories and attachments to their homeland initially are not Meena's, and she makes this evident in the narration. Feeling neither Indian nor English, Meena stands somewhere in-between. This is the novel's central trope, and we see Meena attempting to navigate between these two worlds. On listening to one of her Papa's frequent renditions of a traditional Indian folk-song, we hear:

> Papa's singing always unleashed these emotions which were unfamiliar and instinctive at the same time, in a language I could not recognize but felt I could speak, in my sleep, in my dreams, evocative of a country I had never visited but which sounded like the only home I had ever known. The songs made me realize that there was a corner of me that would be forever not England.[40]

Meena is then both inside and outside the English culture she aspires to be part of, embodied in her rebellious role-model, young

Anita Rutter. While her parents feed her traditional, freshly cooked Indian dishes, she wants fish-fingers and chips; instead of playing willingly with her Indian cousins when they visit, she yearns to be out with the other 'Tollington wenches'. Mimicry is the process through which she imagines and *images* her access to 'Englishness', and in the process, it has been suggested, Meena's 'in-betweenness' becomes a 'Third Space', a synthesis of the two cultures of which she is part.[41] This location, the narrative seems to imply, offers a privileged insight into the fate of Tollington and its inhabitants.

Within the village, Meena and her family are both accepted and exceptional. Their migrant status renders them exoticized Others. Initially, Meena erases these differences by 'becoming' Anita, forming a friendship with her which leads to Meena power-sharing in their gang. This quest for belonging is tenuous, however: it stands in tension with her growing understanding of her Indian self, intensified with the arrival of her grandmother from the sub-continent:

> It was all falling into place now, why I felt this continual compulsion to fabricate, this ever-present desire to be someone else . . . Before Nanima arrived, this urge to reinvent myself, I could now see, was driven purely by shame, the shame I felt when we did India at school. (p. 211)

Constructed through colonial discourse, Meena's real self has been eclipsed. Moreover, as the narrative develops we become aware of an aggressive racism developing, emanating from the gang of local white youths who are themselves effectively marginalized by the wider developments impinging on the community, disrupting place and space. When Meena's friend Sam Lowbridge, interrupting a local church charity event designed to raise money for Africa, yells out of the crowd: 'Yow don't do nothing but talk . . . and give everything away to some darkies we've never met . . . This is our patch. Not some wogs' hangout' (p. 193), it becomes clearer to Meena that she can never be a 'Tollington wench'; and when Sam and Anita form a sexual relationship afterwards, this sense is confirmed.

Up to this point, Meena's consciousness has been articulated *dialogically*, entering into an (often antagonistic) relation with what is constructed as the essentially monologic and residual structure of feeling characterizing Tollington. As Bromley has argued, the village's inhabitants are largely stereotyped, so that 'all the voices are filtered through the mimicry and simulation of the narrator; the white British characters have no voice of their own'.[42] As a narrative device, this enables the gaze of the Other to be returned. Yet representations of the working-class characters, as seen through Meena's eyes, range from the patronizing to the pathological. Elderly husbands are invalided with mysterious illnesses which render them infantilized and helpless; local women are 'tarts with hearts', or – as is the case with Anita's mother, Deirdre – 'white trash'. There are suggestions of incest and child abuse. They are seen as racist out of ignorance, or racist with intent. Their dreams are shown to be hopelessly unrealistic (Anita fantasizes of a flat in London, a pony of her own), their hopes banal, their futures mired. Locked in the 'negative emplacement' that is Tollington, their agency is denied or takes the form of race hate. As Sam angrily tells Meena, 'Yow've always been the best wench in Tollington . . . But yow was never gonna look at me, yow wont be stayin will ya? You can move on, how come? How come I can't' (p. 314).

Thus Meena coming to understand who she is is predicated, also, on who she is not. Though the hybridity written into Meena's identity suggests the erosion of strict binary oppositions (black/white; Indian/English), by the novel's close, these oppositions re-emerge. This is figured through a transition which takes Meena out of the working-class community – seen as destroyed and destructive – into the 'ideal' petit-bourgeois suburban location which better signifies the individual self, and which corresponds to the class location which her parents' cultural capital bestows upon them – her father seemingly an accountant clerk, her mother a teacher – but from which the dominant culture has so far exiled them. This, too, is a working-class 'escaper' narrative, then; here, however, Meena does not escape from the class into which she was born, but from one into which her parents' immigrant status has pitched her/them. The novel's close rehearses the classic liberal individualist pose, as Meena tells us, 'the place in which I belonged was wherever I stood and there was nothing stopping me simply moving forward and claiming each resting place as home' (p. 303). Migrant agency, in the end, is not in any significant sense different from bourgeois individualism; coded through an ideological perspective which parallels the dominant culture's way of seeing, it remains essentially consensual.

Finally, I want to turn now to other writing, outside 'mainstream' publishing, which has sought to define a diaspora structure of feeling, but within the wider and *associative* context of class. Here it is instructive to draw on a source of writing produced in recent years within local writing and publishing groups. One powerful strand of criticism aimed at the politics of difference is linked, paradoxically enough, to its perceived class habitus. Aijaz Ahmad is suspicious of the migrant, post-colonial intellectuals who, stationed in the metropolis and enjoying privileged lifestyles, then articulate their own cultural hybridity as the norm, the generalized experience and structure of feeling, expressing the migrant location as such. But

> in the dialectic of belonging and not belonging a new agency may be formed but not unless it is recognized that, as Ahmad argues, post-coloniality is seen as also a 'matter of class'. A politics of identity which stresses a third space, new ethnicities and the performative and transgressive but which denies the complex intersections of colonialism, 'race', class, ethnicity and generation runs the risk of over-emphasizing the power of individual agency.[43]

We might argue that if a new agency is shaped in *Anita and Me*, for instance, through an emphasis on the post-colonial subjectivity of Meena (forever the performative self), then it is indeed predicated on a type of classlessness, or a class belonging that will not speak its name. The imagined community to which Meena projects herself is comfortably classless. Friedman, too, suggests that these positions derive essentially from an intellectual elite, taking advantage of their cultural location to articulate a view that is 'outside/above', and which means therefore that

> class becomes crucial in understanding just what is going on. Briefly, hybrids and hybridization theorists are products of a group that self-identifies and/or identifies the world in such terms, not as a result of ethnographic understanding, but as an act of self-definition – indeed, of self-essentializing – which becomes a definition for others via the forces of socialization inherent in the structures of power that such groups occupy: intellectuals close to the media; the media intelligentsia itself; in a certain sense, all those who can afford a cosmopolitan identity.[44]

A position and argument that rejects class is seen, then, as a developed perspective derived precisely from class position. In fact, one might argue, following Raymond Williams's critique of another position on cultural identity written some time ago, what is represented here is the position of 'enlightened minority, degraded mass'. If this is the case – and Friedman's argument is persuasive – then let us examine texts which speak 'from below'.

Local publishing projects in Britain, developing since the mid-1970s, have enabled local people to write and record their own experiences in a context outside mainstream commercial publishing. As an alternative cultural formation, the Federation of Worker Writers and Community Publishers encourages people to become the producers of writing rather than simply consumers of representations offered through conventional publishing and other media; with the 'aim to create a living, non-competitive popular history and literature. By the people, for the people.'[45] In a number of respects, the aim is to *democratize* literature (and, in the process, question exactly what literature is, or is meant to be); writing is produced and consumed within and for communities, from specific regional bases, by a process that is collective, shared and supportive. Work takes the form of anthologies or separate projects, workshops are organized where writing and reading sessions take place and where work in progress can be discussed. Poetry and autobiography are favoured forms of articulation for those writing within the movement. The form of autobiography has a number of advantages: firstly, for fledgling writers it suggests a mode of writing which provides a resource of already available material with which to shape a narrative; secondly, and more significantly, it constitutes a form which enables the subject to speak and to assert his or her presence in a specific time and place: in short, in history.

The working-class autobiographies produced through community publishers are not only marked by moments of 'self-definition', but often disclose what have been referred to as 'acts of *collective* recovery ... premised on notions of a collective past',[46] an emphasis rarely evident in bourgeois autobiography, and more often than not absent from the autobiographies of working-class people who have made the 'upward' transition from their class of origin. Thus, writing is associated with making sense of a life and defining these lived experiences as important, common or shared.

The narratives encode a desire – sometimes explicit, often implicit – to pass on past experiences to a younger generation: to generate and convey *useful knowledge*.

In *To Live It Is To Know It* (1987), Alfred Williams, a retired, black railway-worker, hopes that 'Maybe things from my life some use to younger people . . . I an ordinary man, but what I know, I did not learn in books, I did learn from living it.'[47] Williams values his experiences as a black man domiciled in Britain and as a worker; positions through which he has made sense of his life. Evident is an active class consciousness at work in the narrative, produced by his experiences and now mediating his account of them. Thus we hear that 'I learn during those years [of working for plantation owners]: the rich kind of people get rich, the rich kind of people stay rich. And I look about me today, in England, in 1987, and I think this; for the poor people this country is becoming like the West Indies' (p. 17).

Common to a number of working-class autobiographies is an important organizing principle which is found in the experiences of work and friendships and the significance of locality. Williams stresses the hardship of proletarian labour as he documents his early life in Jamaica, where work was close to the experience of slavery, but vital for survival; he describes emigration to England, where work was hard to come by because of prejudice. Finally settling in Yorkshire, he finds employment on the railways and gets married, but life is still not easy: 'All my life I work hard, sometime two job. When I get home I must sleep, or maybe I go to pub and try to forget work, try to forget how I treat for being coloured, try to find a little enjoyment' (p. 50). His memories of work in Jamaica are no better:

> This is one of the hardest and worst positions to be in; to work and to live in. Any time of the night and day the boss come and knock on your door. Any time. And when the boss knock, you work, because if you don't work, then you have no job . . . So I was semi-slave. (p. 13)

But as an immigrant living in Britain, Williams necessarily has a more ambiguous relationship with the significance of both locality and nation, which impinges also upon ideas of class-belongingness. The identity sustained for a working-class person by a sense of place is instead undercut by the complex experiences of diaspora. Williams reveals his own individual struggle over whether to leave Jamaica for the 'Mother-Country': 'All my life in Jamaica people is telling me, *Come to England. Come to Mother-Country, it flow with milk and honey.* Van come round with a film show in it: *Come to England. Come to England*' (p. 33). He nevertheless remains 'betwixt and between', wary of the rhetoric, yet finally enticed to leave his own culture for an alien one:

> I'm not going to hide the truth as I know it. When we come to England it was Hell here. Coloured *always* get worse. Some days I am blasted bitter about life. When I think of some of the things life give out to me ... Life is good and life is Hell and it the same life. (p. 39)

The language is seen to move ambivalently from 'I' to 'we' and back to 'I'. The shifting pronouns suggest that Williams understands his experiences not only on an individual level, but in a collective sense. However, here the mode of address is as a black person speaking to, with and for other black immigrants in a complex alignment. Vološinov, discussing verbal interaction and orientation, described this structure in terms of what he called the 'I-experience' and 'we-experience', and much of Williams's narrative corresponds to this formulation. Here the self is understood only in relation to others, in acts of both identification and disidentification. For Vološinov, language, or the 'word ... is the product of the reciprocal relationship between speaker and listener, addresser and addressee'; so that 'I give myself verbal shape from another's point of view, ultimately, from the point of view of the community to which I belong'.[48] But the utterance, or speech-act, takes its shape and its intelligibility within specific contexts and historical and social situations. The relevant historical situation here is the one of being 'betwixt and between', straddled between two cultures, a definition corresponding to Bhabha's 'Third Space'. However, the structure of the utterance thrusts towards Vološinov's more inclusive 'we-experience', so that the experience of diaspora for Williams is not something borne in isolation, or individually, but recognized through what Vološinov calls a 'united collective',[49] and this facilitates an utterance marked 'predominantly by overtones of active and self-confident protest with no basis for humble and submissive intonation'.[50] This structure of feeling characterizes Williams's writing throughout, though interestingly the speaking voice takes up a number of positions in the narrative, not only that of the migrant voice, but also that of a class-conscious worker, which he identifies and articulates also as a 'united collective'.

Nevertheless, the rhetoric of continuity, a convention predicated of types of autobiography, yields to the more ambivalent experience of *passage*, and thus of displacement. Identity is negotiated through a process of transition and transmigration, producing a structure of feeling which cannot always be successfully accommodated within traditional autobiographical forms. Williams tells the story of his displacement and his struggle to *replace* or re-situate himself within a 'Mother-Country' whose own selective history and invented traditions will marginalize or degrade his existence. Bakhtin suggested the term 'heteroglossia' to describe the multiple voices within a single language and culture; voices which express in tone and structure different evaluative accents and positions corresponding to social classes or groups, and in which the ideological struggles of the oppressed to resist incorporation within, or obliteration by, the dominant discourse and power occur. As Edward Said has argued, 'the power to narrate, or to block other narratives from forming and emerging'[51] represents a crucial mode of cultural hegemony, a view which I have stressed throughout this book. In both content and form, Williams's narrative resists the 'received' modes of expression, which he deems insufficient for articulating his self and his experiences. The vernacular of black (working-class) Britain instead constitutes a *purer* language which encodes the experience of struggle (his own and that of others – the 'we' he articulates), while striving to demystify the stories told 'to keep rich people rich and poor people poor' (p. 51). The autobiography disturbs the homogenization of experience which hegemonic modes of articulating stories of cultural belonging and national identity attempt to impose, whilst at the same time working to acknowledge and celebrate solidarities with others. Williams's view of Britain is a multicultural one, reflecting his experience as part of a generation of post-war immigrants to the country; though he understands that a person's place within the imagined community involves the various struggles of the subordinated for justice and recognition. The text represents, therefore, one man's attempt to rescue the black working-class experience from the enormous condescension of posterity; yet throughout, Williams identifies with those he terms 'ordinary people', disclosing what Raymond Williams once called a powerful desire for a 'common betterment'.[52]

He writes of his early world on the plantation as both intimate and 'Other': 'I don't know who Edwin Charley was, I think he was an Englishman, or American, but we didn't know him, we did not see him, he just like Tate and Lyle' (p. 14). Power relations such as these, Williams insists, oppress and degrade human lives. On one level, his motive for writing is to celebrate his own *agency*, the overcoming of these conditions, and to insist on his survival and his *presence*; but as a worker, he stresses also the need for a collective response against the rich and powerful, both then and in the present juncture. It was only the union's arrival that made any significant difference to the lives of the plantation workers: 'Things change when the Union form. The big plantation had to keep to the union rule' (p. 14). Back in the present, he warns, 'If Union broke in England, then you will come to know what is Hell' (p. 47). Williams's reference to the historic moment and, more specifically, to economic class-struggle, is a response to Thatcherism's attacks on trade unions in the 1980s, which he sees as attacks on working-class living conditions, its very existence. He warns that 'there is nothing I can do, or you can do, unless we get together' (p. 47). And the 'we' here points to a different referent, another 'we-experience', which illustrates my earlier point that the narrative itself is composed of a range of different but interconnected subject positions. Thus, there exists no insurmountable conflict between Williams's *difference* as a black man and his identity as a worker. And from this perspective, the imagined community of the nation is erected upon and is fractured by economic injustice; a condition which will be alleviated only by recognizing the inevitability of class struggle. Collective action by the workers themselves will prevent those who 'have money' from imposing their economy on others. The structure of feeling here explores difference whilst proposing solidarity as a remedy to the injustice and exploitation suffered by the subaltern and subordinate. While telling an individual story, the narrative's mode of address transcends individualism. To do this, it mobilizes collective modes of identification predicated on experiences refracted through the prisms of both race and class, and insists in the end not so much on the celebration of difference, but on the imperative of forming and recognizing complex solidarities.

The pluralism which posits the play of difference produces a politics which, in celebrating the plurality of identity among black people and others, neglects 'the material conditions of life and power struggle over resources'.[53] This is not the same as saying difference does not matter, however, but is to suggest that it is crucial to understand how such politics is employed strategically, and whether in the process these deployments and positions do not in fact essentialize, or reify – as Friedman suggests – these categories themselves, thus occluding social divisions and differences within them: divisions of, in this case, class. In her book *Where We Stand: Class Matters*, bell hooks argues that 'race and gender can be used as screens to deflect away from the harsh realities of class politics', and suggests that 'the neat binary categories of white and black and male and female are not there when it comes to class';[54] and in this sense, class itself becomes the 'Third Space' which disrupts and destabilizes any easy notions or bland celebrations of difference.

Conclusion

I began this book by suggesting that representations of working-class life in British culture are ubiquitous. It perhaps could not be any other way: class still structures and frames the social world we live in. Whether we accept this or not, will probably depend in large part on where we are located (or have been located) in that structure. It may also depend on the stories we tell ourselves (and that are told to us by others) about who we are and where we come from.

This book has examined representations of working-class life by focusing on key historical periods when class seemed an imperative to be addressed: the Hungry Thirties; the Age of Affluence; and, most particularly, the Thatcherite 1980s and their aftermath. My aim has been to analyse how these moments have been articulated in a range of narratives, mostly fictional, with the purpose of defining what seem to be the structures of feeling which inform and shape them, seeing these narratives then as socially symbolic acts around which converge the pressing historical and political questions of the time. What I am suggesting, then, is that these narratives — whether the product of working-class writers or not — tell us something vital about the lived experience of class during these particular historic junctures; at the same time, they may reveal the way the wider, hegemonic culture seeks to 'place', 'arrange' and displace the realities of class. I am not saying that the writing simply 'reflects reality', though in key ways it does, both shaping and defining reality in the process. Indeed, I have suggested throughout that the narratives are as significant for what they do not say, as for what they express. Under the tensions of the moment, such articulation might find uneasy expression through certain images and ideas — rhetorical devices, received conventions and modes, ideological positions – which, as Williams suggests in his discussion of structures of feeling, can hover at the very 'edge of semantic availability'.

The central focus of this book has been on the closing two decades of the twentieth century. There are clear reasons for this, already elaborated upon. This is partly derived, too, from my acceptance of Keating's 'crisis paradigm', outlined in chapter 1. Keating's suggestion that socio-economic crisis in the nineteenth century produced within writing a focus on the 'threat' of the working-class presence is persuasive. It is adaptable to discussions of the Hungry Thirties as well. My analysis of writing from the affluence period might, however, be seen to contradict the argument. This did not constitute a moment of capitalist economic crisis, but expansion. But crisis and threat of a *cultural* kind, as I have shown, is never far away in the narratives of cultural theorists and novelists alike, and this is also seen as a crisis for the wider society and the dominant culture. Thus, anxieties around class arise in the dialectic of simultaneous working-class absence and presence. The moral economy and culture of the working class are seen to disappear in Hoggart's amorphous image of the commercialized masses, or indeed in the Frankfurt School's duped proles, fodder for the insatiable appetite of the culture industry. But class reappears in the marketing ploys of capitalist advertising, in sub-cultural formations and in the novels and plays of writers like Wesker, Delaney and Sillitoe.

Though the 1980s see a return of harsh economic conditions, with a renewed laissez-faire capitalism intent on eroding welfare structures and job security (accompanied by a profound alteration in the mode of production itself), Keating's argument takes hold only tenuously because his referent (the working class) has finally dissolved. In the context of postmodernism and 'new times', Lyotard will argue that 'the social foundation of the principle of division . . . class struggle' has vanished, or been 'blurred to the point of losing all . . . radicality'. And in the hyper-real world of total mediation invoked by Jean Baudrillard, 'the social . . . does not exist any more', and thus neither does social class, so that 'the concept of class will have dissolved . . . into some parodic, extended double, like the "mass of workers" or simply into a retrospective simulation of the proletariat'.[1] For Baudrillard, then, at this late stage, class is really only about representation, a sign without a referent, in the endlessly simulated terrain of postmodernity. Encoded as a subtext in this view may well be a deeper narrative, where the working class has once again failed the intelligentsia by not living up to its historical role as capitalism's gravediggers.

One of the chief reasons that my focus on narrating class in recent times has fallen on those producers who could be labelled more definitively as working-class writers is to contradict such easy writing-off, or the writing-out, of class. Subaltern voices work at the margins of cultural production, as counter-hegemonic practices which remain vulnerable to incorporation, assimilation, disregard. Their purpose might be seen as an attempt to redress an imbalance and falsity of cultural representations; to challenge received ideas and stereotyped images. James Kelman, describing his own practice as a writer, suggests that traditionally 'the working class in English literature . . . were confined to the margins, kept in their place . . . You only ever saw them or heard them. You never got into their mind. You did find them in the narrative but from without, seldom from within.'[2] Here, Kelman suggests that it is not necessarily the absence of the working-class character from the English canon that counts; the working-class figures emerge, but in a range of strategies which deny their full humanity. Representations of working-class life may abound within literature and the media generally, but they need to be viewed, as Kelman suggests, sceptically. Raymond Williams has argued that conventions which organize dominant narratives and influence ways of seeing might entail that

> all other persons may be conventionally presented as instrumental (servants, drivers, waiters), as merely environmental (other people in the street), or indeed as essentially absent (not seen, not relevant). Any such presentation depends on the acceptance of its convention, but it is always more than a 'literary' or 'aesthetic' decision.[3]

These assumptions have a social and broadly political dimension which is often decisive. Kelman then – and a range of other writers examined here – attempt to contest the perceived inadequacy and the ideological status of dominant representations and, in doing so, contest the forms and conventions that place class within a particular regime of representation (the heroic proletariat, the assimilated and conciliated worker) derived from a range of discursive contexts and positions. Kelman's commitment to write the 'other side' of working-class identity is a political decision in its widest sense. Pat Barker's desire to recover imaginatively the lives of working-class women ignored in a male-dominated world represents another example of this tendency. As Alfred Williams says in his autobiography, *To Live It Is To Know It*, to understand the hidden injuries of class, 'it need everybody write a book'.

There is no doubt a real need to re-think – and re-present – what we now mean by class, rather than collude, by silence, with the myth of 'classlessness'. The profound processes of de-industrialization, which began in the 1980s in the west, and the ramifications for working-class identity, culture and politics, are still being felt – initiating what some have gladly called the 'unmaking' of the British working class. It is evident that new voices have entered the political arena, a fact identified and celebrated by Raymond Williams, for instance in his last book, *Towards 2000*. It has been these voices – the 'new social movements' – that those on the Left now identify as replacing the working class in any radical politics. This, though, was not Williams's view. He pointed instead to a potential dynamic between these new voices and the 'older' ones, as resources of hope in the making of complex solidarities which suggest a condition far more complex and potentially hopeful than some would be prepared to admit.

Notes

Notes to Introduction

¹ Sally Munt (ed.), *Cultural Studies and the Working Class: Subject to Change* (London, Cassell, 2000), p. 3.

² Andrew Milner, *Re-Imagining Cultural Studies: The Promise of Cultural Materialism* (London, Sage, 2002), p. 2.

³ Debates about Thatcherism in Britain and its impact on the working class are almost too numerous to mention. Hall's article is very much a paradigm piece in the context of new thinking about class. There have been some interesting counters to the view taken by Hall, Laclau and Mouffe and others on the Left in Britain: see, for instance, A. Sivanandan, 'All That Is Solid Melts Into Air – The Hokum of "New Times"', *Race and Class*, 31, 3 (1990), 1–31, and Eileen Meiksins Wood, *The Retreat from Class: A New 'True' Socialism* (London: Verso, 1986).

⁴ Stuart Hall, 'Brave New World', in *Marxism Today*, (August 1988), 36.

⁵ Ibid., 36.

⁶ Ernesto Laclau and Chantal Mouffe, *Hegemony and Socialist Strategy* (London, Verso, 1987), p. 58.

⁷ Quoted in Andrew Milner, *Class* (London, Sage, 1999), p. 11.

⁸ Munt (ed.), *Cultural Studies*, p. 11. Disquiet within the academy about the rejection of class and its significance can be found most recently in an article by Maria Elisa Cevasco, 'Whatever happened to Cultural Studies: Notes from the Periphery', *Textual Practice*, 14, 3 (2000), 433–8. But see also Michael Pickering, *History, Experience and Cultural Studies* (London, Macmillan, 1997); and Andrew Milner's *Literature, Culture and Society* (London, University College London Press, 1996).

⁹ Raymond Williams, *Marxism and Literature* (Oxford, Oxford University Press, 1977), p. 115.

¹⁰ Alan Sinfield, *Literature, Politics and Culture in Post-War Britain* (Oxford, Basil Blackwell, 1989); see chapter 3, 'Literature and cultural production', pp. 23–38.

¹¹ Raymond Williams, *The Long Revolution* (London, Pelican, 1965), p. 64.

¹² Andy Medhurst, 'If Anywhere: Class Identifications and Cultural Studies Academics', in Munt (ed.), *Cultural Studies*, p. 21.

¹³ Ibid., p. 26.

¹⁴ Ibid., p. 25.

¹⁵ Richard Hoggart, *The Uses of Literacy: Aspects of Working-Class Life with*

Special Reference to Publications and Entertainments (London, Penguin, 1966 edn), p. 294.

16 Barry Jackson and Dennis Marsden, *Education and the Working Class: Some General Themes Raised by a Study of Eighty-Eight Working-Class Children in a Northern Industrial City* (London, Routledge & Kegan Paul, 1962), p. 172.

17 Hoggart, *Uses of Literacy*, p. 291.

18 Annette Kuhn, *Family Secrets: Acts of Memory and Imagination* (London, Verso, 1995), p. 101.

19 This is E. P. Thompson's well-known definition of class in *The Making of the English Working Class* (London, Penguin, 1963), p. 8.

20 Kuhn, *Family Secrets*, p. 21.

21 Medhurst, 'If Anywhere', p. 23.

22 Kuhn, *Family Secrets*, p. 28.

23 Williams, *Marxism and Literature*, p. 132.

24 Carolyn Steedman, *The Radical Soldier's Tale* (London, Routledge, 1988), p. 2.

25 Kuhn, *Family Secrets*, p. 3.

26 Ibid., p. 3.

27 See Pierre Bourdieu, *Distinctions: A Social Critique of the Judgement of Taste* (London, Routledge, 1989).

28 Valerie Walkerdine, *Schoolgirl Fictions* (London, Verso, 1991), p. 158.

29 Ibid.

30 Beverley Skeggs explores these responses in her *Formations of Class and Gender: Becoming Respectable* (London, Sage, 1997). Pamela Fox makes a similar point in her discussion of 'class shame' in *Class Fictions: Shame and Resistance in the British Working-Class Novel, 1890–1945* (Durham, Duke University Press, 1994). In my analysis of some of the cultural fictions here, these themes emerge time and again and constitute examples of those 'hidden injuries of class'.

31 Joanne Lacey, 'Discursive Mothers and Academic Freedom: Class, Generation and the Production of Theory', in Munt (ed.), *Cultural Studies*, p. 42.

32 Beverley Skeggs, 'The Appearance of Class: Challenges in Gay Space', in Munt (ed.), *Cultural Studies*, p. 142.

33 Diane Coole, 'Is Class a Difference that Makes a Difference?', *Radical Philosophy*, 77 (May/June 1996), p. 22.

34 Milner, *Class*, p. 86.

35 bell hooks, *Where We Stand: Class Matters* (London, Routledge, 2000), p. 105.

36 See Terry Eagleton, *The Illusions of Postmodernism* (Oxford, Blackwell, 1996), pp. 56–60.

37 Roger Bromley, 'The Theme That Dare Not Speak Its Name: Class and Recent British Film', in Munt (ed.), *Cultural Studies*, p. 54.

38 Ibid., p. 56.

39 Chris Haylett, ' "This Is About Us, This Is Our Film!"': Personal and Popular Discourses of "Underclass"', in Munt (ed.), *Cultural Studies*, p. 80.

40 Glen Creeber, ' "Can't Help Lovin' That Man": Social Class and the Female Voice in *Nil by Mouth*', in Munt (ed.), *Cultural Studies*, p. 198.

41 Terry Lovell, 'Landscape and Stories in 1960s' British Realism', in Andrew Higson (ed.), *Dissolving Views: Key Writings on British Cinema* (London, Cassell, 1996), p. 168.

42 Creeber, ' "Can't Help Lovin' That Man" ', p. 202.

[43] Bromley, 'The Theme', p. 63.
[44] Terry Lovell, *Pictures of Reality* (London, BFI Publishing, 1980), p. 95.
[45] Bromley, 'The Theme', p. 67.
[46] Ibid. (quoting Raymond Williams in *Marxism and Literature*), p. 126.
[47] Terry Eagleton, *The Idea of Culture* (Oxford, Blackwell, 2000), p. 123.
[48] Jim McGuigan, *Culture and the Public Sphere* (London, Routledge, 1996), p. 136.
[49] Ibid., p. 138.
[50] Diane Reay, 'Children's Urban Landscape: Configurations of Class and Space', in Munt (ed.), *Cultural Studies*, p. 151.
[51] Ibid., p. 162.
[52] Raymond Williams, *Towards 2000* (London, Chatto & Windus, 1983), pp. 172–3.
[53] Stanley Aronowitz and William DiFazio, *The Jobless Future: Sci-Tech and the Dogma of Work* (Minneapolis, University of Minnesota Press, 1994), p. 294. Aronowitz and DiFazio use the phrase 'multidimensionality' in their discussion of class and insist on the plurality of class identities whilst refuting the notion of classlessness. Fresh perspectives on class within labour history can be found in, for instance, H. Beynon and T. Austrin, *Masters and Servants: Class and Patronage in the Making of a Labour Organization* (London, Rivers Oram, 1994); and in P. Alexander and R. Halpern (eds), *Racializing Class, Classifying Race: Labour and Difference in Britain, the USA and Africa* (London, Macmillan, 2000). The spatial relations of class are explored in Andrew Herod (ed.), *Organizing the Landscape: Geographical Perspectives on Labour Unionism* (London, University of Minnesota Press, 2000). I have already referred to a number of significant texts on class by women earlier in this chapter, and it is worth mentioning two recent publications on working-class life which represent significant, if somewhat controversial, contributions to debates on class: Simon J. Charlesworth's *A Phenomenology of Working Class Experience* (Cambridge, Cambridge University Press, 2000), and Royce Turner's *Coal Was Our Life* (Sheffield, Sheffield Hallam University Press, 2000).
[54] Kuhn, *Family Secrets*, p. 8.
[55] Ibid., p. 8.

Notes to Chapter 1

[1] See Pamela Fox, *Class Fictions: Shame and Resistance in the British Working-Class Novel, 1890–1945* (Durham, Duke University Press, 1994), p. 63.
[2] Robert Tressell, *The Ragged Trousered Philanthropists* (London, Paladin, 1991 [1914]), p. 13. All further references will be to this edition and will be made in the text.
[3] Gary Day, ' "Culture" in *The Ragged Trousered Philanthropists*', in H. Gustav Klaus and Stephen Knight (eds), *British Industrial Fictions* (Cardiff, University of Wales Press, 2000), p. 72.
[4] Ibid., p. 82.
[5] Raymond Williams, 'The Ragged-Arsed Philanthropists', in *Writing and Society* (London, Verso, 1987), p. 25.
[6] See Wim Neetens, *Writing and Democracy: Literature, Politics and Culture in Transition* (Brighton, Harvester/Wheatsheaf, 1991), p. 142.

[7] Gareth Stedman Jones, *Language of Class: Studies in English Working Class History 1832–1982* (Cambridge, Cambridge University Press, 1982), p. 188.
[8] Ibid., p. 182.
[9] Peter Keating, *The Working Classes in Victorian Fiction* (London, Routledge and Kegan Paul, 1971), p. 5.
[10] Harold Macmillan, quoted by J. Klugman in 'View of the Left', in J. Clark, M. Heinemann, D. Margolies and C. Snee (eds), *Culture and Crisis in the Thirties* (London, Lawrence & Wishart, 1979), p. 16.
[11] F. R. Leavis, 'Retrospect of a Decade', in *Scrutiny*, IX, 1 (June 1940), 71–2.
[12] Ibid., p. 71.
[13] George Orwell, 'Inside the Whale', in G. Orwell, *The Collected Essays, Journalism and Letters: Vol. I, 1920–1940* (London, Penguin, 1970), p. 568.
[14] H. Gustav Klaus, 'Socialist Fiction in the 1930s', in J. Lucas (ed.), *The 1930s* (Brighton, Harvester, 1978), p. 36.
[15] Walter Greenwood, *Love on the Dole* (London, Penguin, 1987 [1933]), p. 86. All further references will be to this edition and will be made in the text.
[16] Valentine Cunningham, *British Writers of the Thirties* (Oxford, Oxford University Press, 1988), p. 83.
[17] Quoted by Roger Webster in '*Love on the Dole* and the Aesthetics of Contradiction', in Jeremy Hawthorne (ed.), *The British Working Class Novel in the Twentieth Century* (London, Edward Arnold, 1984), p. 45.
[18] *Left Review*, 1, 1 (1934).
[19] See Raymond Williams, *Marxism and Literature* (Oxford, Oxford University Press, 1977), pp. 121–8.
[20] See Fox, *Class Fictions*, pp. 10–17.
[21] C. L. Mowat, *Britain Between the Wars* (London, Methuen, 1955), p. 486.
[22] George Orwell, *The Road to Wigan Pier* (London, Penguin, 1988 [1937]), p. 86.
[23] Walter Brierley, *Means Test Man* (London, Methuen, 1935), p. 155. All further references will be to this edition and will be made in the text.
[24] Graham Holderness, 'Miners and the Novel', in Hawthorne (ed.), *British Working Class Novel*, p. 26.
[25] Andy Croft, *Red Letter Days* (London, Lawrence & Wishart, 1988), p. 257.
[26] H. Gustav Klaus, *The Literature of Labour* (Brighton, Harvester, 1985), p. 117.
[27] Ibid., p. 149.
[28] John Sommerfield, *May Day* (London, Lawrence & Wishart, 1982), p. 170. All further references will be to this edition and will be made in the text.
[29] Bruce Robbins makes a similar point in his discussion of the rhetorical effects of such representations in some nineteenth-century fiction in *The Servant's Hand: English Fiction from Below* (New York, Columbia University Press, 1986), pp. 9–14.
[30] Croft, *Red Letter Days*, p. 91.
[31] Lewis Jones, *Cwmardy* (London, Lawrence & Wishart, 1937), p. 104. All further references will be to this edition and will be made in the text.
[32] Holderness, 'Miners', p. 29.
[33] Holderness makes a very similar point in 'Miners and the Novel', p. 31.
[34] Keith Laybourn, *The General Strike* (Manchester, Manchester University Press, 1993), p. 74.
[35] Ellen Wilkinson, *Clash* (London, Virago, 1989 [1929]), p. 288. All further references will be to this edition and will be made in the text.

[36] Lewis Grassic Gibbon, *A Scots Quair* (London, Penguin, 1986), p. 406. All further references will be to this edition and will be made in the text
[37] Walter Benjamin, 'Theses on the Philosophy of History', in *Illuminations* (New York, Schocken Books, 1969), p. 257.
[38] Ibid., p. 256.
[39] Cunningham, *British Writers*, p. 317.
[40] Quoted in Angus Calder, 'A Mania for Self-Reliance', in David Jefferson and Graham Martin (eds), *The Uses of Fiction: Essays on the Modern Novel in Honour of Arnold Kettle* (Milton Keynes, Open University, 1982), p. 109.
[41] George Orwell, 'The Proletarian Writer', in *The Collected Essays, Journalism and Letters of George Orwell, Vol. II, 1940–1943*, ed. Sonia Orwell and Ian Angus (London, Penguin, 1970), pp. 51–64.
[42] Quoted in Stuart Laing, *Representations of Working-Class Life: 1957–1964* (London, Macmillan, 1984), p. 19.
[43] Ibid.
[44] George Orwell, *The Road to Wigan Pier* (London, Penguin, 1988 [1937]), p. 62.
[45] Ibid., pp. 104–5.
[46] John Hill, *Sex, Class and Realism* (London, BFI Publishing, 1986), p. 5.
[47] Ibid., p. 5.
[48] Laing, *Representations*, p. 3.
[49] Ibid., p. 7.
[50] Ibid., p. 14.
[51] Hill, *Sex*, p. 10.
[52] Ibid.
[53] Ibid., p. 11.
[54] Ibid., p. 13.
[55] Richard Hoggart, *The Uses of Literacy* (London, Penguin, 1966 [1957]), p. 19.
[56] Ibid., p. 19.
[57] Ibid., p. 243.
[58] Ibid., p. 250.
[59] Raymond Williams, *Culture and Society* (London, Chatto & Windus, 1958), p. 300.
[60] Ibid., p. 300.
[61] The review of Hoggart appeared in *Essays in Criticism*, 7, iv (1957). Reprinted in John McIlroy and Sallie Westwood, *Border Country: Raymond Williams in Adult Education* (Leicester, NIACE, 1993), pp. 84–9.
[62] Williams, *Culture and Society*, p. 327.
[63] Colin MacInnes, *City of Spades* (London, Abacus, 1986 [1957]), p. 177. All further references will be to this edition and will be made in the text.
[64] Colin MacInnes, *Absolute Beginners* (London, Abacus, 1986 [1959]), p. 14. All further references will be to this edition and will be made in the text.
[65] Alan Sinfield, *Literature, Politics and Culture in Post-War Britain* (Oxford, Basil Blackwell, 1989), p. 170.
[66] Sam Selvon, *The Lonely Londoners* (London, Longman, 1972 [1956]), p. 72.
[67] This play is a rare example of working-class writing by a working-class woman. Very little working-class writing by women emerged in the 1930s; by the late 1950s and 1960s it seemed that this absence had not been rectified, despite the greater public visibility of women in British society generally.
[68] Shelagh Delaney, *A Taste of Honey* (London, Methuen, 1982 [1958]), p. 31.

⁶⁹ Laing, *Representations*, p. 61.
⁷⁰ John Braine, *Room at the Top* (London, Mandarin, 1989 [1957]), p. 19. All further references will be to this edition and will be made in the text.
⁷¹ Alan Sillitoe, *Saturday Night and Sunday Morning* (London, Longman, 1968 [1958]), p. 5. All further references will be to this edition and will be made in the text.
⁷² Alan Sillitoe, *The Loneliness of the Long Distance Runner* (London, W. H. Allen, 1985 [1959]), p. 8.
⁷³ See Peter Hitchcock, *Working-Class Fiction in Theory and Practice: A Reading of Alan Sillitoe* (Michigan, UMI Research Press, 1989), p. 70.
⁷⁴ See V. N. Vološinov, *Marxism and the Philosophy of Language* (New York, Seminar Press, 1973), p. 24. Also Williams, *Marxism and Literature*, pp. 21–44.
⁷⁵ Alan Sillitoe, *The Death of William Posters* (London, Pan Books, 1967 [1965]), p. 36. All further references will be to this edition and will be made in the text.
⁷⁶ Stuart Hall and Tony Jefferson, *Resistance Through Rituals: Youth Sub-Culture in Post-War Britain* (London, Hutchinson, 1975), pp. 9–75.
⁷⁷ Ibid., p. 55.
⁷⁸ Raymond Williams, *Politics and Letters* (London, New Left Books, 1979), p. 336.

Notes to Chapter 2

¹ Alan Sinfield, *Literature, Politics and Culture in Post-War Britain* (Oxford, Basil Blackwell, 1989), p. 254.
² Tom Nairn, *The Breakup of Britain* (London, New Left Books, 1981), p. 388.
³ These figures are taken from J. Anderson, S. Duncan and R. Hudson (eds), *Redundant Spaces in Cities and Region? Studies in Industrial Decline and Social Change* (London, Academia Press, 1982), pp. 4–7.
⁴ In *New Statesman and Society* (16 December 1988).
⁵ Ian Jack, *When the Oil Ran Out: Britain 1977–1987* (London, Fontana, 1987), p. 222.
⁶ For debates on Williams's use of 'structure of feeling' and for discussions of what some writers see as the problematic status of associated terms such as 'experience' and 'community', see T. Eagleton (ed.), *Raymond Williams: Critical Perspectives* (Cambridge, Polity Press, 1989); D. L. Dworkin and G. Roman (eds), *Views Beyond the Border Country: Raymond Williams and Cultural Politics* (New York, Routledge, 1993), esp. ch. 1; J. Eldridge and E. Eldridge, *Raymond Williams: Making Connections* (London, Routledge, 1994), pp. 111–45. Feminist perspectives are provided in Jane Miller, *Seduction: Studies in Reading and Culture* (London, Virago, 1990), ch. 2; Jenny Bourne Taylor, 'Raymond Williams: Gender and Generation', in Terry Lovell, *British Feminist Thought: A Reader* (Oxford, Blackwell, 1990), pp. 296–308. Andrew Milner provides a lucid and largely positive retrospective on aspects of Williams's work in 'Cultural Materialism, Culturalism and Post-Culturalism: The Legacy of Raymond Williams', *Theory, Culture and Society*, 11, 1 (1994), 43–75.
⁷ Peter Middleton, 'Why Structure of Feeling?', in *News from Nowhere*, 6 (1989), 30–42.

[8] Ibid., 34.
[9] Ibid., 35.
[10] Raymond Williams, *Marxism and Literature* (Oxford, Oxford University Press, 1977), p. 132.
[11] Ibid.
[12] Raymond Williams, *Writing and Society* (London, Verso, 1981), p. 163.
[13] Williams, *Marxism and Literature*, p. 131.
[14] Williams, *Politics and Letters* (London, New Left Books, 1979), p. 162.
[15] Eldridge and Eldridge, *Raymond Williams*, p. 140.
[16] Ibid., p. 141.
[17] Right-wing politicians and the right-wing press made concerted efforts, at this time, to construct the unemployed as scroungers or layabouts, refusing to work. Beatrix Campbell has described what she calls the 'witch hunt' which accompanied this process in *Wigan Pier Revisited* (London, Virago, 1984), pp. 22–30.
[18] In Bob Millington and Ray Nelson, *'Boys from the Blackstuff': The Making of a TV Drama* (London, Comedia, 1986), p. 33
[19] Bob Millington, 'Boys from the Blackstuff', in George Brandt (ed.), *British Television Drama in the 1980s* (Cambridge, Cambridge University Press, 1992), p. 120.
[20] David Lusted, *What's Left of Blackstuff?* (London, BFI Publishing, 1984), p. 43.
[21] Walter Benjamin, on Brechtian technique and ideological effects, in *Illuminations* (New York, Schocken Books, 1968), p. 149.
[22] Ibid., p. 150.
[23] Alan Bleasdale, *Boys from the Blackstuff: Studio Scripts*, ed. David Self (London, Hutchinson, 1985), p. 26. All further references will be to this edition and will be made in the text.
[24] See John Tulloch, *Television Drama: Agency, Audience and Myth* (London, Methuen, 1990), p. 271.
[25] Lusted, *What's Left?*, p. 44.
[26] Benjamin, *Illuminations*, p. 255.
[27] Tulloch, *Television Drama*, p. 273.
[28] Luke Spencer, 'British Working-Class Fiction: The Sense of Loss and Potential for Transformation', in *Socialist Register* (London, Merlin Press, 1988), p. 376.
[29] Barry Hines, *The Price of Coal* (London, Penguin, 1982), p. 23.
[30] Barry Hines, *Looks and Smiles* (London, Penguin, 1983), p. 67.
[31] Barry Hines, *The Heart of It* (London, Michael Joseph, 1994), p. 80.
[32] Tony Harrison, *Selected Poems* (London, Penguin, 1987), p. 155. All further references will be to this edition and will be made in the text.
[33] John Lucas, 'Speaking for England?', in Neil Astley (ed.), *Tony Harrison* (Newcastle, Bloodaxe, 1991), p. 352.
[34] Williams, *Politics and Letters*, p. 164.
[35] Williams, *Marxism and Literature*, p. 137.
[36] Quoted in Tulloch, *Television Drama*, p. 272.
[37] Ibid., p. 278.
[38] Stuart Hall, 'Notes on Deconstructing the Popular,' in Raphael Samuel (ed.), *People's History and Socialist Theory* (London, Routledge & Kegan Paul, 1981), p. 232.

Notes to Chapter 3

1 James Kelman, *Not Not While The Giro* (London, Minerva, 1989), p. 72.
2 Edward Soja, *Postmodern Geographies* (London, Verso, 1988), p. 24.
3 David Harvey, *Consciousness and the Urban Experience* (Oxford, Basil Blackwell, 1985), p. ix.
4 Doreen Massey, 'A Place Called Home', in *New Formations*, 171 (1992), p. 5.
5 Ibid., p. 14.
6 David Harvey, *The Condition of Postmodernity* (Oxford, Basil Blackwell, 1989), p. 284.
7 Fredric Jameson, *Postmodernism, or, the Cultural Logic of Late Capitalism* (London, Verso, 1990), p. 51.
8 Patrick Wright, *A Journey Through the Ruins: The Last Days of London* (London, Radius, 1991), p. 75.
9 Ibid., p. 75.
10 Peter Dunn and Lorraine Leeson, 'The Art of Change in London', in John Bird, Barry Curtis, George Robinson and Lisa Tickner (eds), *Mapping the Futures* (London, Routledge, 1993), p. 138.
11 Ibid., p. 121.
12 Bill Lancaster, 'What Sort of Future?', in Robert Colls and Bill Lancaster (eds), *Geordies: The Roots of Radicalism* (Edinburgh, Edinburgh University Press, 1992), p. 50.
13 Irvine Welsh, *Trainspotting* (London, Secker & Warburg, 1993), pp. 308–9.
14 See Ian A. Bell, 'Scottish Fiction and the Experience of Industry', in H. Gustav Klaus and Stephen Knight (eds), *British Industrial Fictions* (Cardiff, University of Wales Press, 2000), p. 190.
15 Christopher Meredith, *Shifts* (Bridgend, Seren, 1988), p. 106.
16 In John MacClean, 'James Kelman Interview', *Edinburgh Review*, 71 (1985), p. 72.
17 James Kelman, *The Burn* (London, Polygon, 1984), p. 239. All further references will be to this edition, and will be made in the text.
18 In MacClean, 'James Kelman', p. 73.
19 James Kelman, *Greyhound for Breakfast* (London, Secker & Warburg, 1987), p. 113. All further references will be to this edition, and will be made in the text.
20 Jurgen Habermas, 'Modernity: An Incomplete Project', in H. Foster (ed.), *Postmodern Culture* (London, Pluto, 1985), pp. 3–16.
21 Ken Worpole, *Dockers and Detectives* (London, Verso, 1984), p. 65.
22 Kristen Ross, 'Watching the Detectives', in Francis Barker, Peter Hulme and Margaret Iverson (eds), *Postmodernism and the Re-reading of Modernity* (Manchester, Manchester University Press, 1992), p. 57.
23 Malcolm Bradbury, 'The Cities of Modernism', in Malcolm Bradbury and James MacFarlane (eds), *Modernism* (London, Penguin, 1976), p. 100.
24 Raymond Williams, *The Politics of Modernism* (London, Verso, 1989), p. 36.
25 James Kelman, *The Busconductor Hines* (London, J. M. Dent, 1984), p. 80. All further references will be to this edition and will be made in the text.
26 Walter Benjamin, *Illuminations* (New York, Schocken Books, 1969), p. 141.
27 Ross, 'Watching', p. 61.
28 Cairns Craig, 'Resisting Arrest: James Kelman', in Randall Stevenson and Geoff Wallace (eds), *The Scottish Novel since the Seventies* (Edinburgh, Edinburgh University Press, 1993), pp. 99–112.

[29] James Kelman, *A Disaffection* (London, Secker & Warburg, 1989), p. 72. All further references will be to this edition, and will be made in the text.
[30] For instance, see Marx on money in Tom Bottomore and Marc Rubel (eds), *Karl Marx: Selected Writings in Sociology and Social Philosophy* (London, Penguin, 1973), pp. 179–83.
[31] Fredric Jameson, *The Geopolitical Aesthetic* (London, BFI Publishing, 1991), p. 38.
[32] Raymond Williams, *The Country and the City* (London, Chatto & Windus, 1975), p. 245.
[33] James Kelman, *How Late It Was, How Late* (London, Secker & Warburg, 1994), p. 4. All further references will be to this edition and will be made in the text.
[34] See Geoff Gilbert, 'Can Fiction Swear? James Kelman and the Booker Prize', in Rob Mengham (ed.), *An Introduction to Contemporary Fiction* (Cambridge, Polity Press, 1999), p. 228.
[35] In Gilbert, 'Can Fiction Swear?', p. 231.
[36] Stuart Hall and Paul DuGay (eds), *The Question of Identity* (London, Sage, 1996), p. 5.
[37] A term used by Edward Said in discussing colonial writing, in *Yeats and Decolonization* (Derry, Field Day, 1988), p. 12.
[38] Ross, 'Watching', p. 61.
[39] Said, *Yeats*, p. 12.

Notes to Chapter 4

[1] Ian Haywood, *Working-Class Fiction: From Chartism to Trainspotting* (Plymouth, Northcote House, 1997), p. 151.
[2] Steph Lawler, 'Escape and Escapism: Representing Working-Class Women', in Sally Munt (ed.), *Cultural Studies and the Working Class: Subject to Change* (London, Cassell, 2000), p. 123.
[3] For a discussion of Owens's fiction see Ingrid Von Rosenberg, 'People Like That: The Fiction of Agnes Owens', in H. Gustav Klaus and Stephen Knight, *British Industrial Fictions* (Cardiff, University of Wales Press, 2000), pp. 193–206.
[4] Quoted in Simon Dentith, *Bakhtinian Thought: An Introductory Reader* (London, Routledge, 1995), p. 184
[5] Livi Michael, *Under a Thin Moon* (London, Secker & Warburg, 1992), p. 116. All further references will be to this edition and will be made in the text.
[6] Edward Said, *Orientalism* (London, Penguin, 1978), p. 18.
[7] See Dentith, *Bakhtinian Thought*, p. 196.
[8] Books and articles dealing with these issues included Michele Barrett's *Women's Oppression Today: The Marxist-Feminist Encounter* (London, Verso, 1989), and Beatrix Campbell's less theoretically informed *Wigan Pier Revisited* (London, Virago, 1984). For a response to tendencies within British feminism to evacuate issues of class from its relation to gender, see A. Weir and E. Wilson, 'The British Women's Movement', *New Left Review*, 1, 148 (Nov.–Dec. 1984), 74–103. Terry Lovell's reader, *British Feminist Thought* (Oxford, Blackwell, 1990), covers debates within British feminism during the 1970s and 1980s. Cora Kaplan has made an important contribution to the argument in her article 'Pandora's Box: Subjectivity, Class and Sexuality in Socialist Feminist Criticism', in *Sea Changes* (London, Verso, 1986).

[9] Elaine Showalter, *A Literature of Their Own: British Women Novelists from Brontë to Lessing* (London, Virago, 1978), p. 314.
[10] Stuart Tannock, 'Nostalgia Critique', *Cultural Studies*, 9 (1995), p. 454.
[11] Ibid., p. 456.
[12] Ibid., p. 459.
[13] In Suzie MacKenzie, 'Out of the Past', review of *Another World*, by Pat Barker, in the *Guardian* [London], 24 October 1998.
[14] Antonio Gramsci, *Selection from Prison Notebooks*, trans. and ed. Quintin Hoare and Geoffrey Nowell-Smith (London, Lawrence and Wishart, 1971), p. 324.
[15] John Fentress and Chris Wickham, *Social Memory* (Oxford, Blackwell, 1992), p. 25.
[16] Ibid., p. 134.
[17] Ibid.
[18] Ibid.
[19] Gina Wisker (ed.), *It's My Party: Reading Twentieth Century Women's Writing* (London, Pluto, 1994), p. 8.
[20] Carolyn Steedman, *Landscape for a Good Woman: A Tale of Two Lives* (London, Virago, 1986), p. 13.
[21] Ibid., p. 12.
[22] Ibid., p. 16. In this quote Steedman is also referencing Jeremy Seabrook's *A Working-Class Childhood* (London, Gollancz, 1982).
[23] Ibid., p. 11.
[24] Ibid., p. 21.
[25] Ibid., p. 123.
[26] Annette Kuhn, *Family Secrets: Acts of Memory and Imagination* (London, Verso, 1995), p. 8.
[27] Lyn Pykett, 'The Century's Daughter: Recent Women's Fiction and History', *Critical Quarterly*, 29, 3 (1987), p. 72.
[28] Peter Hitchcock, 'Radical Writing', in Dale M. Bauer and Susan Jaret McKistry (eds), *Feminism, Bakhtin and the Dialogic* (Albany, SUNY Press, 1991), p. 91.
[29] Pat Barker, *Union Street* (London, Virago, 1982), p. 249. All further references will be to this edition and will be made in the text.
[30] Pat Barker, *Blow Your House Down* (London, Virago, 1984), p. 125. All further references will be to this edition and will be made in the text.
[31] Ibid., p. 98.
[32] Pat Barker, *The Century's Daughter* (London, Virago, 1984), p. 33.
[33] Pykett, 'The Century's Daughter', p. 73
[34] Hitchcock, 'Radical Writing', p. 108.
[35] Richard Johnson and Gregor McLennan (eds), *Making Histories: Studies in History-Writing and Politics* (London, Hutchinson, 1982), p. 232.
[36] I am referring here to Habermas's critique of the postmodernists' rejection of modernity, and I am suggesting that Barker (or, rather, her character Liza) sees modernity as an 'incomplete project' too. See J. Habermas, 'Modernity: An Incomplete Project', reprinted in H. Foster (ed.), *Postmodern Culture* (London, Pluto, 1985).
[37] This is a term developed by Julia Kristeva, and discussed by Toril Moi in *Sexual, Textual Politics* (London, Methuen, 1985), pp. 150–74.
[38] Pykett, 'The Century's Daughter', p. 74.
[39] See Patrick Wright, *On Living in an Old Country: The National Past in Contemporary Britain* (London, Verso, 1985), p. 62.

Notes to Chapter 5

[1] Salman Rushdie, *The Satanic Verses* (London, Penguin, 1989), p. 353. All further references will be to this edition and will be made in the text.

[2] Homi Bhabha (ed.), *Nation and Narration* (London, Routledge, 1990), p. 318.

[3] Ibid., p. 318.

[4] Timothy Brennan, 'The National Longing for Form', in Bhabha (ed.), *Nation*, p. 47.

[5] Bhabha (ed.), *Nation*, p. 48.

[6] Jim McGuigan, *Culture and the Public Sphere* (London, Routledge, 1996), p. 136.

[7] Cornel West, quoted in McGuigan, *Culture and the Public Sphere*, p. 138.

[8] Andy Medhurst, 'If Anywhere: Class Identifications and Cultural Studies Academics', in Sally Munt (ed.), *Cultural Studies and the Working Class: Subject to Change* (London, Cassell, 2000), p. 23.

[9] Eric Hobsbawm and Terence Ranger (eds), *The Invention of Tradition* (Cambridge, Cambridge University Press, 1983), p. 1.

[10] Stuart Hall, *The Hard Road to Renewal* (London, Verso, 1988), p. 4.

[11] See the Chatto CounterBlast series, Jonathan Raban, *God, Man and Mrs Thatcher* (London, Chatto & Windus, 1989).

[12] See G. Seidel and Rose Levitas (eds), *The Ideology of the New Right* (London, Polity Press, 1986), pp. 107–36.

[13] Ibid., p. 108.

[14] Ibid., p. 112.

[15] Ibid., pp. 113–14. This comment invokes, of course, Norman Tebbitt's infamous cricket-match test.

[16] Ibid., p. 113.

[17] Ibid., p. 117.

[18] See Paul Gilroy, *There Ain't No Black in the Union Jack* (London, Hutchinson, 1987). Gilroy argues that blacks in Britain are deemed inherently criminal and unable to adhere to British law. This argument contains the Lockean distinction between individuals 'freed' by acceptance of the law, and the 'barbarians' who remain outside civilized practice by an inability to conform to and accept such institutions and values.

[19] Paul Gilroy, 'You Can't Fool the Youth', *Race and Class*, XXIII (Autumn 1981/Winter 1982), 22 (2–3), 210.

[20] Ibid., 212, 218.

[21] Ibid., 218. Gilroy emphasizes the cross-race alliance characterizing Two-Tone music in the early 1980s. He uses as an example the Midlands-based group, the 'Specials', whose hit in July 1981, 'Ghost Town', came at the high point of inner-city rioting. The record spent several weeks at the top of the British hit parade. The lyrics are openly polemical:

> This town is coming like a ghost town
> Why must the youth fight against themselves?
> Government's leaving youths on the shelf
> this town is coming like a ghost town
> No job to be found in this country,
> Can't go on no more, people getting angry
> this town is coming like a ghost town.

²² Kobena Mercer, 'Recoding Narratives of Race and Nation', in *Black Film British Cinema* (London, ICA, 1988), p. 5.
²³ Ibid.
²⁴ Ibid., p. 13.
²⁵ See Andrew Higson in *British Cinema and Thatcherism*, pp. 105–29. Also, Patrick Wright, *On Living in an Old Country: The National Past in Contemporary Britain* (London, Verso, 1985), especially the introduction, and also his book on London referred to in chapter 3. The heritage critique is taken up further by Keith Walsh in *The Representation of the Past: Museums and Heritage in the Post-Modern World* (London, Routledge, 1992).
²⁶ Higson, *British Cinema*, p. 29.
²⁷ Susan Torry-Barber, 'Insurmountable Difficulties and Moments of Ecstacy: Crossing Class, Ethnic and Sexual Barriers in the Films of Stephen Frears', in Lawrence Friedman (ed.), *Fires were Started: British Cinema and Thatcherism* (London, University College London Press, 1993), pp. 221–36.
²⁸ John Hill, *British Cinema in the 1980s* (Oxford, Oxford University Press, 1999), p. 136.
²⁹ Ibid., p. 218.
³⁰ The New Right historian, Norman Stone, responded to these films in typical fashion in an article in *The Sunday Times*, 10 January 1988. In 'Through a Lens Darkly', he took exception to what he perceived as the uniformly bleak, and inaccurate, representations in these films of modern (Thatcherite) Britain. He concludes that the film-makers (Kureishi among them) were under the pernicious influence of the 1960s' 'protest' culture, itself a throwback to the lamentably 'Marxist' 1930s. To find a more fitting representation of what it might be to be British, Stone points us in the direction of David Lean's adaptation of Forster's *A Passage to India*.
³¹ Hanif Kureishi, *My Beautiful Laundrette and The Rainbow Sign* (London, Faber & Faber, 1986), p. 29.
³² See Pierre Bourdieu for a discussion of these categories in *Distinctions: A Social Critique of the Judgement of Taste*, trans. Richard Nice (London, Routledge, 1986).
³³ In Torry-Barber, 'Insurmountable Difficulties', p. 232.
³⁴ Salman Rushdie, from 'Inside the Whale', in Lisa Appignanesi and Sara Maitland (eds), *The Rushdie File* (London, ICA, 1989), p. 175.
³⁵ Kureishi, *My Beautiful Laundrette*, p. 78.
³⁶ Homi Bhabha, *The Location of Culture* (London, Routledge, 1994), pp. 38–9.
³⁷ Ian Chambers, *Migrancy, Culture and Identity* (London, Routledge, 1994), p. 110.
³⁸ Jonathan Friedman, 'Global Crises, the Struggle for Cultural Identity and Intellectual Porkbarrelling: Cosmopolitans versus Local, Ethnics and Nationals in an Era of De-hegemonization', in Pnina Werbner and Tariq Modood (eds), *Debating Cultural Hybridity: Multicultural Identities and the Politics of Anti-Racism* (London, Zed, 2000), p. 75.
³⁹ Aijaz Ahamad, 'The Politics of Literary Post-coloniality', *Race and Class*, 33, 3 (1995), 18.
⁴⁰ Meera Syal, *Anita and Me* (London, Flamingo, 1997), p. 112. All further references will be to this edition and will be made in the text.
⁴¹ See Roger Bromley's *Narratives for a New Belonging: Diasporic Cultural Fictions* (Edinburgh, Edinburgh University Press, 2000), p. 145.

⁴² Ibid., p. 144.
⁴³ Ibid., p. 101.
⁴⁴ Friedman, 'Global Crises', p. 81.
⁴⁵ David Morley and Ken Worpole, *The Republic of Letters* (London, Comedia, 1981), p. 17.
⁴⁶ Simon Dentith and Philip Dodd, 'The Uses of Autobiography', *Literature and History*, 14, 1 (Spring 1988), 9.
⁴⁷ Alfred Williams, *To Live It Is To Know It* (Yorkshire, Yorkshire Arts Circus, 1987), p. 7. All further references will be to this edition and will be made in the text.
⁴⁸ V. N. Vološinov, 'Language, Speech and Utterance [and] Verbal Interaction', in Simon Dentith (ed.), *Bakhtinian Thought: An Introductory Reader* (London, Routledge, 1995), p. 130.
⁴⁹ Ibid., p. 133.
⁵⁰ Ibid.
⁵¹ Edward Said, *Culture and Imperialism* (London, Vintage, 1993), p. viii.
⁵² Raymond Williams, *Culture and Society* (London, Chatto & Windus, 1958), p. 331.
⁵³ McGuigan, *Culture*, p. 147.
⁵⁴ bell hooks, *Where We Stand: Class Matters* (London, Routledge, 2000), p. 6.

Notes to Conclusion

¹ Quoted in Andrew Milner, *Class* (London, Sage, 1999), p. 10.
² James Kelman, *Some Recent Attacks: Essays Cultural and Political* (Stirling, AK Press, 1992), p. 81.
³ Raymond Williams, *Marxism and Literature* (Oxford, Oxford University Press, 1977), p. 175.

Bibliography

Primary Sources

Barker, Pat, *Union Street* (London, Virago, 1982).
——, *The Century's Daughter* (London, Virago, 1984).
——, *Blow Your House Down* (London, Virago, 1986).
Billy Elliot (2000, dir. Stephen Daldry).
Bleasdale, Alan, *Boys from the Blackstuff*, first shown BBC2, October–November 1982.
——, *Boys from the Blackstuff: Studio Scripts*, ed. David Self (London, Hutchinson, 1985).
Brassed Off (1996, dir. Mark Herman).
Braine, John, *Room at the Top* (London, Mandarin, 1989 [1957]).
Brierley, Walter, *Means Test Man* (London, Methuen, 1935).
Delaney, Shelagh, *A Taste of Honey* (London, Methuen, 1982 [1958]).
Grassic Gibbon, Lewis, *A Scots Quair* (London, Penguin, 1986).
Greenwood, Walter, *Love on the Dole* (London, Penguin, 1987 [1933]).
Harrison, Tony, *Selected Poems* (London, Penguin, 1987).
Hines, Barry, *A Kestrel for a Knave* (London, Michael Joseph, 1968).
——, *The Price of Coal* (London, Penguin, 1982).
——, *Looks and Smiles* (London, Penguin, 1983).
——, *The Heart of It* (London, Michael Joseph, 1994).
Jones, Lewis, *Cwmardy* (London, Lawrence & Wishart, 1937).
——, *We Live* (London, Lawrence & Wishart, 1939).
Kelman, James, *The Burn* (London, Polygon, 1984).
——, *The Busconductor Hines* (London, J. M. Dent, 1984).
——, *Greyhound for Breakfast* (London, Secker & Warburg, 1987).
——, *A Disaffection* (London, Secker & Warburg, 1989).
——, *Not Not While The Giro* (London, Minerva, 1989).
——, *How Late It Was, How Late* (London, Secker & Warburg, 1994).
MacInnes, Colin, *City of Spades* (London, Abacus, 1986 [1957]).
——, *Absolute Beginners* (London, Abacus, 1986 [1959]).
Meredith, Christopher, *Shifts* (Bridgend, Seren, 1988).

Michael, Livi, *Under a Thin Moon* (London, Secker & Warburg, 1992).
My Beautiful Laundrette (1985, dir. Stephen Frears).
Nil by Mouth (1997, dir. Gary Oldman).
Rushdie, Salman, *The Satanic Verses* (London, Penguin, 1989).
Sammy and Rosie Get Laid (1986, dir. Stephen Frears).
Selvon, Sam, *The Lonely Londoners* (London, Longman, 1972 [1959]).
Sillitoe, Alan, *Saturday Night and Sunday Morning* (London, Longman, 1968 [1958]).
——, *The Loneliness of the Long Distance Runner* (London, W. H. Allen, 1959).
——, *The Death of William Posters* (London, Pan Books, 1967 [1965]).
Sommerfield, John, *May Day* (London, Lawrence & Wishart, 1982).
Syal, Meera, *Anita and Me* (London, Flamingo, 1997).
The Full Monty (1997, dir. Peter Cattaneo).
Tressell, Robert, *The Ragged Trousered Philanthropists* (London, Paladin, 1991 [1914]).
Welsh, Irvine, *Trainspotting* (London, Secker & Warburg, 1993).
Williams, Alfred, *To Live It is to Know It* (Yorkshire, Yorkshire Arts Circus, 1987).
Wilkinson, Ellen, *Clash* (London, Virago, 1989 [1929]).
Winterson, Jeannette, *Oranges are Not the Only Fruit* (London, Vintage, 1985).

Secondary Sources

Ahamad, Aijaz, 'The Politics of Literary Postcoloniality', *Race and Class*, 33, 3 (1995), 1–20.
Alexander, P. and Halpern, R. (eds), *Racialising Class, Classifying Race: Labour and Difference in Britain, the USA and Africa* (London, Macmillan, 2000).
Anderson, J., Duncan, S and Hudson, R. (eds), *Redundant Spaces in Cities and Region? Studies in Industrial Decline and Social Change* (London, Academia Press, 1982).
Aronowitz, Stanley and DiFazio, William, *The Jobless Future: Sci-Tech and the Dogma of Work* (Minneapolis, University of Minnesota Press, 1994).
Astley, Neil (ed.), *Tony Harrison* (Newcastle, Bloodaxe, 1991).
Barker, Francis, Hulme, Peter and Iverson, Margaret (eds), *Postmodernism and the Re-reading of Modernity* (Manchester, Manchester University Press, 1992).
Barrett, Michele, *Women's Oppression Today: The Marxist/Feminist Encounter* (London, Verso, 1989).
Bauer, Dale M. and McKistry, Susan Janet (eds), *Feminism, Bakhtin and the Dialogic* (Albany, SUNY Press, 1991).
Bell, Ian A., 'Scottish Fiction and the Experience of Industry', in H. Gustav

Klaus and Stephen Knight (eds), *British Industrial Fictions* (Cardiff, University of Wales Press, 2000).

Benjamin, Walter, 'Theses on the Philosophy of History', in idem, *Illuminations* (New York, Schocken Books, 1969).

Beynon, H. and Austrin, T., *Masters and Servants: Class and Patronage in the Making of a Labour Organization* (London, Rivers Oram, 1994).

Bhabha, Homi (ed.), *Nation and Narration* (London, Routledge, 1990).

——, *The Location of Culture* (London, Routledge, 1994).

Bird, John, Curtis, Barry, Robertson, George and Tickner, Lisa (eds), *Mapping the Futures* (London, Routledge, 1993).

Bottomore, Tom and Rubel, Marc (eds), *Karl Marx: Selected Writings in Sociology and Social Philosophy* (London, Penguin, 1973).

Bourdieu, Pierre, *Distinctions: A Social Critique of the Judgement of Taste*, trans. Richard Nice (London, Routledge, 1986).

Bradbury, Malcolm and MacFarlane, James (eds), *Modernism* (London, Penguin, 1976).

Bradbury, Malcolm, 'The Cities of Modernism', in Malcolm Bradbury and James MacFarlane (eds), *Modernism* (London, Penguin, 1976).

Brandt, George (ed.), *British Television Drama in the 1980s* (Cambridge, Cambridge University Press, 1992).

Brennan, Timothy, 'The National Longing for Form', in Homi Bhabha (ed.), *Nation and Narration* (London, Routledge, 1990).

Bromley, Roger, *Narratives for a New Belonging: Diasporic Cultural Fictions* (Edinburgh, Edinburgh University Press, 2000).

——, 'The Theme That Dare Not Speak its Name: Class and Recent British Film', in Sally Munt (ed.), *Cultural Studies and the Working Class: Subject to Change* (London, Cassell, 2000).

Calder, Angus, 'A Mania for Self-Reliance', in David Jefferson and Graham Martin (eds), *The Uses of Fiction: Essays on the Modern Novel in Honour of Arnold Kettle* (Milton Keynes, Open University, 1982).

Campbell, Beatrix, *Wigan Pier Revisited* (London, Virago, 1984).

Cevasco, Maria Elisa, 'Whatever Happened to Cultural Studies: Notes from the Periphery', *Textual Practice*, 14, 3 (2000), 433–8.

Chambers, Ian, *Migrancy, Culture and Identity* (London, Routledge, 1994).

Charlesworth, Simon J., *A Phenomenology of Working Class Experience* (Cambridge, Cambridge University Press, 2000).

Clark, J., Heinemann, M., Margolies, D. and Snee, C. (eds), *Culture and Crisis in the Thirties* (London, Lawrence & Wishart, 1979).

Colls, Robert and Lancaster, Bill (eds), *Geordies: The Roots of Radicalism* (Edinburgh, Edinburgh University Press, 1992).

Coole, Diane, 'Is Class a Difference That Makes a Difference?', *Radical Philosophy*, 77 (May/June 1996), 17–25.

Cosgrave, S. and Campbell, D., 'Behind the Wee Smiles', *New Statesman and Society*, 16 December 1988.

Craig, Cairns, 'Resisting Arrest: James Kelman', in Randall Stevenson and Geoff Wallace (eds), *The Scottish Novel since the Seventies* (Edinburgh, Edinburgh University Press, 1993).
Creeber, Glen, ' "Can't Help Lovin' That Man": Social Class and the Female Voice in *Nil by Mouth*', in Sally Munt (ed.), *Cultural Studies and the British Working Class: Subject to Change* (London, Cassell, 2000).
Croft, Andy, *Red Letter Days* (London, Lawrence & Wishart, 1988).
Cunningham, Valentine, *British Writers of the Thirties* (Oxford, Oxford University Press, 1988).
Day, Gary, ' "Culture" in *The Ragged Trousered Philanthropists*', in H. Gustav Klaus and Stephen Knight (eds), *British Industrial Fictions* (Cardiff, University of Wales Press, 2000).
Dentith, Simon, *Bakhtinian Thought: An Introductory Reader* (London, Routledge, 1995).
Dentith, Simon and Dodd, Philip, 'The Uses of Autobiography', *Literature and History*, 14, 1 (Spring, 1988), 4–19.
Dunn, Peter and Leeson, Lorraine, 'The Art of Change in London', in John Bird, Barry Curtis, George Robinson and Lisa Tickner (eds), *Mapping the Futures* (London, Routledge, 1993).
Dworkin, D. L. and Roman, G. (eds), *Views Beyond the Border Country: Raymond Williams and Cultural Politics* (New York, Routledge, 1993).
Eagleton, Terry, *The Illusions of Postmodernism* (Oxford, Blackwell, 1996).
——, *The Idea of Culture* (Oxford, Blackwell, 2000).
—— (ed.), *Raymond Williams: Critical Perspectives* (Cambridge, Polity Press, 1989).
Eldridge, J. and Eldridge, E., *Raymond Williams: Making Connections* (London, Routledge, 1994).
Fentress, John and Wickham, Chris, *Social Memory* (Oxford, Blackwell, 1992).
Foster, Hal (ed.), *Postmodern Culture* (London, Pluto, 1985).
Fox, Pamela, *Class Fictions: Shame and Resistance in the British Working-Class Novel, 1890–1945* (Durham, Duke University Press, 1994).
Friedman, Jonathan, 'Global Crises, the Struggle for Cultural Identity and Intellectual Porkbarrelling: Cosmopolitans versus Local, Ethnics and Nationals in an Era of De-hegemonization', in Pnina Werbner and Tariq Modood (eds), *Debating Cultural Hybridity: Multi-cultural Identities and the Politics of Anti-racism* (London, Zed, 2000).
Friedman, Lawrence (ed.), *Fires Were Started: British Cinema and Thatcherism* (London, University College London Press, 1993).
Gilbert, Geoff, 'Can Fiction Swear? James Kelman and the Booker Prize', in Rob Mengham (ed.), *An Introduction to Contemporary Fiction* (Cambridge, Polity Press, 1999).
Gilroy, Paul, *There Ain't No Black in the Union Jack* (London, Hutchinson, 1987).

——, 'You Can't Fool the Youth', *Race and Class*, XXIII (Autumn 1981/Winter 1982), 23 (2–3), 207–22.
Gramsci, Antonio, *Selections from Prison Notebooks*, trans. and ed. Quintin Hoare and Geoffrey Nowell-Smith (London, Lawrence & Wishart, 1971).
Habermas, Jurgen, 'Modernity: An Incomplete Project' in Hal Foster (ed.), *Postmodern Culture* (London, Pluto, 1985).
Hall, Stuart, *The Hard Road to Renewal* (London, Verso, 1988).
—— and Jefferson, T., *Resistance Through Rituals: Youth Sub-Culture in Post-War Britain* (London, Hutchinson, 1975).
—— and DuGay, Paul (eds), *The Question of Identity* (London, Sage, 1996).
——, 'Notes on Deconstructing the Popular', in Raphael Samuel (ed.), *People's History and Socialist Theory* (London, Routledge & Kegan Paul, 1981).
——, 'Brave New World', *Marxism Today* (August 1988), 34–7.
Harvey, David, *Consciousness and the Urban Experience* (Oxford, Basil Blackwell, 1985).
——, *The Condition of Postmodernity* (Oxford, Basil Blackwell, 1989).
Hawthorne, Jeremy (ed.), *The British Working Class Novel in the Twentieth Century* (London, Edward Arnold, 1984).
Haylett, Chris, ' "This Is About Us, This Is Our Film!": Personal and Popular Discourses of "Underclass" ', in Sally Munt (ed.), *Cultural Studies and the Working Class: Subject to Change* (London, Cassell, 2000).
Haywood, Ian, *Working-Class Fiction: From Chartism to Trainspotting* (Plymouth, Northcote House, 1997).
Herod, Andrew (ed.), *Organizing the Landscape: Geographical Perspectives on Labor Unionism* (London, University of Minnesota Press, 2000).
Higson, Andrew (ed.), *Dissolving Views: Key Writings on British Cinema* (London, Cassell, 1996).
Hill, John, *Sex, Class and Realism* (London, BFI Publishing, 1986).
——, *British Cinema in the 1980s* (Oxford, Oxford University Press, 1999).
Hitchcock, Peter, *Working-Class Fiction in Theory and Practice: A Reading of Alan Sillitoe* (Michigan, UMI Research Press, 1989).
——, 'Radical Writing', in Dale M. Bauer and Susan Janet McKistry (eds), *Feminism, Bakhtin and the Dialogic* (Albany, SUNY Press, 1991).
Hobsbawm, Eric and Ranger, Terence (eds), *The Invention of Tradition* (Cambridge, Cambridge University Press, 1983).
Hoggart, Richard, *The Uses of Literacy: Aspects of Working-class Life with Special Reference to Publications and Entertainments* (London, Penguin, 1966 [1957]).
Holderness, Graham, 'Miners and the Novel', in Jeremy Hawthorne (ed.), *The British Working-Class Novel in the Twentieth Century* (London, Edward Arnold, 1984).
hooks, bell, *Where We Stand: Class Matters* (London, Routledge, 2000).

Jack, Ian, *When the Oil Ran Out: Britain 1977–1987* (London, Fontana, 1987).
Jackson, Barry and Marsden, Dennis, *Education and the Working Class: Some General Themes Raised by a Study of Eighty-Eight Working-class Children in a Northern Industrial City* (London, Routledge & Kegan Paul, 1962).
Jameson, Fredric, *Postmodernism, or, the Cultural Logic of Late Capitalism* (London, Verso, 1990).
——, 'Class and Allegory in Contemporary Mass Culture', in idem, *Signatures of the Visible* (New York, Routledge, 1991).
——, *The Geopolitical Aesthetic* (London, BFI Publishing, 1991).
Jefferson, David and Martin, Graham (eds), *The Uses of Fiction: Essays on the Modern Novel in Honour of Arnold Kettle* (Milton Keynes, Open University, 1982).
Johnson, Richard and McLennan, Gregor (eds), *Making Histories: Studies in History-writing and Politics* (London, Hutchinson, 1982).
Kaplan, Cora, *Sea Changes* (London, Verso, 1986).
Keating, Peter, *The Working Classes in Victorian Fiction* (London, Routledge & Kegan Paul, 1971).
Kelman, James, *Some Recent Attacks: Essays Cultural and Political* (Stirling, AK Press, 1992).
Klaus, H. Gustav, *The Literature of Labour* (Brighton, Harvester, 1985).
—— and Knight, Stephen (eds), *British Industrial Fictions* (Cardiff, University of Wales Press, 2000).
——, 'Socialist Fiction in the 1930s', in John Lucas (ed.), *The 1930s* (Brighton, Harvester, 1978).
Klugman, Jack, 'View of the Left', in J. Clark, M. Heinemann, D. Margolies and C. Snee (eds), *Culture and Crisis in the Thirties* (London, Lawrence & Wishart, 1979).
Kuhn, Annette, *Family Secrets: Acts of Memory and Imagination* (London, Verso, 1995).
Kureishi, Hanif, *My Beautiful Laundrette and the Rainbow Sign* (London, Faber & Faber, 1986).
Lacey, Joanne, 'Discursive Mothers and Academic Fandom: Class, Generation and the Production of Theory', in Sally Munt (ed.), *Cultural Studies and the Working Class: Subject to Change* (London, Cassell, 2000).
Laclau, Ernesto and Mouffe, Chantal, *Hegemony and Socialist Strategy* (London, Verso, 1987).
Laing, Stuart, *Representations of Working-Class Life: 1957–1964* (London, Macmillan, 1986).
Lancaster, Bill, 'What Sort of Future?', in Robert Colls and Bill Lancaster (eds), *Geordies: The Roots of Radicalism* (Edinburgh, Edinburgh University Press, 1992).
Lawler, Steph, 'Escape and Escapism: Representing Working-Class Women', in

Sally Munt (ed.), *Cultural Studies and the Working Class: Subject to Change* (London, Cassell, 2000).

Laybourn, Keith, *The General Strike* (Manchester, Manchester University Press, 1993).

Leavis, F. R., 'Retrospect of a Decade', *Scrutiny*, IX, 1 (June 1940), 71–2.

Left Review, 1, 1 (1934).

Lovell, Terry, *Pictures of Reality* (London, BFI Publishing, 1980).

——, *British Feminist Thought: A Reader* (Oxford, Blackwell, 1990).

——, 'Landscape and Stories in 1960s British Realism', in Andrew Higson (ed.), *Dissolving Views: Key Writings on British Cinema* (London, Cassell, 1996).

Lucas, John (ed.), *The 1930s* (Brighton, Harvester, 1978).

——, 'Speaking for England?', in Neil Astley (ed.), *Tony Harrison* (Newcastle, Bloodaxe, 1991).

Lusted, David, *What's Left of Blackstuff?* (London, BFI Publishing, 1984).

MacClean, John, 'James Kelman Interview', *The Edinburgh Review*, 71 (1985), 70–9.

McGuigan, Jim, *Culture and the Public Sphere* (London, Routledge, 1996).

McIlroy, John and Westwood, Sallie (eds), *Border Country: Raymond Williams in Adult Education* (Leicester, NIACE, 1993).

MacKenzie, Suzie, 'Out of the Past', review of Pat Barker's *Another World* in the *Guardian* [London], 24 October 1998.

Massey, Doreen, 'A Place Called Home', *New Formations*, 171 (1992), 3–19.

Medhurst, Andy, 'If Anywhere: Class Identifications and Cultural Studies Academics', in Sally Munt (ed.), *Cultural Studies and the Working Class: Subject to Change* (London, Cassell, 2000).

Mercer, Kobena, 'Recoding Narratives of Race and Nation', in idem, *Black Film British Cinema* (London, ICA, 1988).

Middleton, Peter, 'Why Structure of Feeling?', *News from Nowhere*, 6 (1989), 30–42.

Millington, Bob and Nelson, Ray, *'Boys from the Blackstuff': The Making of a TV Drama* (London, Comedia, 1986).

Millington, Bob, 'Boys from the Blackstuff', in George Brandt (ed.), *British Television Drama in the 1980s* (Cambridge, Cambridge University Press, 1992).

Milner, Andrew, 'Cultural Materialism, Culturalism and Post-Culturalism: The Legacy of Raymond Williams', *Theory, Culture and Society*, 11, 1 (1994), 43–75.

——, *Literature, Culture and Society* (London, University College London Press, 1996).

——, *Class* (London, Sage, 1999).

——, *Re-Imagining Cultural Studies: The Promise of Cultural Materialism* (London, Sage, 2002).

Moi, Toril, *Sexual Textual Politics* (London, Methuen, 1985).
Morley, David and Worpole, Ken, *The Republic of Letters* (London, Comedia, 1981).
Mowat, C. L., *Britain Between the Wars* (London, Methuen, 1955).
Munt, Sally (ed.), *Cultural Studies and the Working Class: Subject to Change* (London, Cassell, 2000).
Nairn, Tom, *The Breakup of Britain* (London, New Left Books, 1981).
Neetens, Wim, *Writing and Democracy: Literature, Politics and Culture in Transition* (Brighton, Harvester Wheatsheaf, 1991).
Orwell, George, *The Road to Wigan Pier* (London, Penguin, 1988 [1937]).
——, 'Inside the Whale', in George Orwell, *The Collected Essays, Journalism and Letters of George Orwell: Vol. I, 1920–1940*, ed. Sonia Orwell and Ian Angus (London, Penguin, 1970).
——, 'The Proletarian Writer', in George Orwell, *The Collected Essays, Journalism and Letters of George Orwell: Vol II, 1940–1943*, ed. Sonia Orwell and Ian Angus (London, Penguin, 1970.)
——, *The Penguin Essays of George Orwell* (London, Penguin, 1984).
Pickering, Michael, *History, Experience and Cultural Studies* (London: Macmillan, 1997).
Pykett, Lyn, 'The Century's Daughter: Recent Women's Fiction and History', *Critical Quarterly*, 29, 3 (1987), 71–7.
Raban, Jonathan, *God, Man and Mrs Thatcher* (London, Chatto & Windus, 1989).
Reay, Diane, 'Children's Urban Landscape: Configurations of Class and Space', in Sally Munt (ed.), *Cultural Studies and the Working Class. Subject to Change* (London, Cassell, 2000).
Robbins, Bruce, *The Servant's Hand: English Fiction from Below* (New York, Columbia University Press, 1986).
Ross, Kristen, 'Watching the Detectives', in Francis Barker, Peter Hulme and Margaret Iverson (eds), *Postmodernism and the Re-reading of Modernity* (Manchester, Manchester University Press, 1992).
Rushdie, Salman, 'Outside the Whale', in Lisa Appignanesi and Sara Maitland (eds), *The Rushdie File* (London, ICA, 1989).
Said, Edward, *Orientalism* (London, Penguin, 1978).
——, *Yeats and Decolonization* (Derry, Field Day, 1988).
——, *Culture and Imperialism* (London, Vintage, 1993).
Seabrook, Jeremy, *Working-class Childhood* (London, Gollancz, 1982).
Seidel, G. and Levitas, Rose (eds), *The Ideology of the New Right* (London, Polity Press, 1986).
Showalter, Elaine, *A Literature of Their Own: British Women Novelists from Brontë to Lessing* (London, Virago, 1978).
Sinfield, Alan, *Literature, Politics and Culture in Post-War Britain* (Oxford, Basil Blackwell, 1989).

Sivanandan, A., 'All That is Solid Melts into Air: The Hokum of "New Times"', *Race and Class*, 31, 3 (1990), 1–31.
Skeggs, Beverley, *Formations of Class and Gender: Becoming Respectable* (London, Sage, 1997).
——, 'The Appearance of Class: Challenges in Gay Space', in Sally Munt (ed.), *Cultural Studies and the Working Class: Subject to Change* (London, Cassell, 2000).
Soja, Edward, *Postmodern Geographies* (London, Verso, 1988).
Spencer, Luke, 'British Working-Class Fiction: The Sense of Loss and Potential for Transformation', in Ralph Miliband, Leo Panitch and John Saville (eds), *Socialist Register* (London, Merlin Press, 1988), pp. 367–85.
Stedman Jones, Gareth, *Language of Class: Studies in English Working Class History 1832–1982* (Cambridge, Cambridge University Press, 1982).
Steedman, Carolyn, *Landscape for a Good Woman: A Tale of Two Lives* (London, Virago, 1986).
——, *The Radical Soldier's Tale* (London, Routledge, 1988).
Stevenson, Randall and Wallace, Geoff (eds), *The Scottish Novel since the Seventies* (Edinburgh, Edinburgh University Press, 1993).
Stone, Norman, 'Through a Lens Darkly', *Sunday Times*, 10 January 1988.
Tannock, Stuart, 'Nostalgia Critique', *Cultural Studies*, 9 (1995), 453–64.
Taylor Bourne, Jenny, 'Raymond Williams: Gender and Generation', in Terry Lovell, *British Feminist Thought: A Reader* (Oxford, Blackwell, 1990).
Thompson, E. P., *The Making of the English Working Class* (London, Penguin, 1963).
Torry-Barber, Susan, 'Insurmountable Difficulties and Moments of Ecstacy: Crossing Class, Ethnic and Sexual Barriers in the Films of Stephen Frears', in Lawrence Friedman (ed.), *Fires Were Started: British Cinema and Thatcherism* (London, University College London Press, 1993).
Tulloch, John, *Television Drama: Agency, Audience and Myth* (London, Methuen, 1990).
Turner, Royce, *Coal was Our Life* (Sheffield, Sheffield Hallam University Press, 2000).
Vološinov, V. N., *Marxism and the Philosophy of Language* (New York, Seminar Press, 1973).
——, 'Language, Speech and Utterance [and] Verbal Interaction', in Simon Dentith (ed.), *Bakhtinian Thought: An Introductory Reader* (London, Routledge, 1995).
Walkerdine, Valerie, *Schoolgirl Fictions* (London, Verso, 1991).
Walsh, Keith, *The Representation of the Past: Museums and Heritage in the Post-modern World* (London, Routledge, 1992).
Webster, Roger, '*Love on the Dole* and the Aesthetics of Contradiction', in Jeremy Hawthorne (ed.), *The British Working Class Novel in the Twentieth Century* (London, Edward Arnold, 1984).

Weir, A. and Wilson, E., 'The British Women's Movement', *New Left Review*, 1, 148 (Sept.–Dec. 1984), 74–103.

Werbner, Pnina and Modood, Tariq (eds), *Debating Cultural Hybridity: Multi-cultural Identities and the Politics of Anti-racism* (London, Zed, 2000).

Williams, Raymond, *Culture and Society* (London, Chatto & Windus, 1958).

——, *The Long Revolution* (London, Pelican, 1965).

——, *The Country and the City* (London, Chatto & Windus, 1975).

——, *Marxism and Literature* (Oxford, Oxford University Press, 1977).

——, *Politics and Letters* (London, New Left Books, 1979).

——, *Writing and Society* (London, Verso, 1981).

——, *Towards 2000* (London, Chatto & Windus, 1983).

——, *The Politics of Modernism* (London, Verso, 1989).

——, 'A Kind of Gresham's Law', a review of Hoggart's *The Uses of Literacy*, reprinted in John McIlroy and Sallie Westwood (eds), *Border Country: Raymond Williams in Adult Education* (Leicester, NIACE, 1993), 82–9.

Wisker, Gina (ed.), *It's My Party: Reading Twentieth Century Women's Writing* (London, Pluto, 1994).

Wood, Eileen Meiksins, *The Retreat from Class: The New 'True' Socialism* (London, Verso, 1986).

Worpole, Ken, *Dockers and Detectives* (London, Verso, 1984).

Wright, Patrick, *On Living in an Old Country: The National Past in Contemporary Britain* (London, Verso, 1985).

——, *A Journey Through the Ruins: The Last Days of London* (London, Radius, 1991).

Index

affluence 2, 52, 53, 54, 55, 58, 62, 64, 69, 71, 74, 76, 91
'Affluence and After' 29, 51
affluence discourse 68
affluent worker 54
Age of Affluence 3, 7, 31, 35
agency 8, 38, 43, 54, 76, 95, 100, 110, 111, 113, 121, 127, 133, 134, 138, 140, 183, 188
  and migrant agency 182
Ahamad, Aijaz 183, 205 n.39
ambivalence 161
Anderson, J. 199 n.3
Aronowitz, Stanley 196 n.53
Attlee administration 173

Bakhtin, Mikhail 136, 137–8, 187
  Bakhtinian 50, 149, 154, 165
  and carnivalesque 50
  and dialogic(s) 72, 129, 136, 138
  and grotesque 133
  and heteroglossia 187
  and inner-voice discourse 72
Baldwin, Stanley 46
Barke, James 114
  Major Operation 114
Barker, Pat 12, 13, 30, 108, 109, 112, 136, 141–60, 193
  Blow Your House Down 141, 142, 149, 152–3
  Century's Daughter, The 108, 141, 148, 151–2, 153–60

Regeneration, The Eye in the Door, The Ghost Road 144
  Union Street 141, 142, 148–52, 159
Barstow, Stan 65
Baudrillard, Jean 191
Bell, A. Ian 109
belonging 163, 178–82, 183
Benjamin, Walter 49, 85–6, 90, 200 n.26
Bhabha, Homi 161–2, 165, 178, 179, 186
Billy Elliot 26–8
black film-making 169
'Blair's Britain' 18
Blairism 19
Bleasdale, Alan 18, 30, 83–90, 103, 104, 156
  Boys from the Blackstuff 18, 30, 83–90, 100, 101, 102, 103, 109, 156
  and 'complex seeing' 86
  and formal strategies 85–6
Blonde Fist 140
Booker Prize 131, 133
Bourdieu, Pierre 13, 205 n.32
  and cultural capital 1, 9, 27, 171, 182
  and disposition 13
  and habitus 8, 52, 57, 80, 108
Braine, John 29, 54, 65–9
  Room at the Top 65–9, 73
Brassed Off 19, 20, 22, 23, 24, 25, 26, 28

Brecht, Bertolt 85–6
    and alienation effect 85–6
    and Brechtian 22
    and Epic Theatre 85
Brennan, Timothy 204 n.4
Brierley, Walter 29, 40–2, 50, 103
    Means Test Man 40–2, 84, 103, 135
Britain 18
'Britishness' 25, 166
Bromley, Roger 18–24, 28, 181, 205 n.41, 206 n.43
Business as Usual 140

Campbell, Beatrix 200 n.17
Canary Wharf 176
capitalism 17, 179
    consumer capitalism 3
    laissez-faire capitalism 191
    late capitalism 106
    welfare capitalism 53, 62, 74, 139
'cartographic impulse' 133
Casey, John 176
Chambers, Ian 205 n.37
citizenship 98, 163
class
    as academic and political issue 2–5
    belongingness 19, 23, 25, 185
    classless/classlessness 7, 14, 19, 28, 51, 53, 54, 61, 62, 76, 183, 193
    class geographies 113
    'classism' 17
    conflict 35, 59
    as economic/political category 59, 164
    and gender 11–16, 20–8, 29, 30, 135–41
    and gender and race 80, 179
    mobility 9, 28
    and multidimensionality 28
    and 'personal politics' 11–17
    and political economy of 5, 25
    politics 4, 18, 24, 74, 87
    and race 162–70, 170–89
    shame 25, 40, 103, 195 n.30
    as 'style' 59–63
    see also working class
cognitive mapping 17, 22, 101, 112, 155
commodity fetishism 126
community/communities 18, 22, 23, 25, 27, 30, 74, 79–84, 93, 112, 134
    see *also* working class 18, 22–8, 143–60, 180–2
Communist Party, British 4
complex solidarities 28, 31, 188, 193
consumer culture 109
consumers 2, 54, 74
'Cool Britannia' 18
Craig, Cairns 51, 124
Creeber, Glen 21
Crosland, Anthony 54
cultural identity 2, 8, 29, 59, 113, 184
    and sub-cultures 60, 61, 62
    and sub-cultural 64, 73, 100
    and transgression 162
    see also working-class identity
Cultural Studies 2, 3, 5, 7, 10, 16, 25
culture industry 26
culture industries 57
Cunningham, Valentine 38, 50

Day, Gary 33
Delaney, Shelagh 63–4, 136, 191 198 n.67
    Taste of Honey, A 63–5, 136
de-industrialization 20, 30, 78, 88, 104, 105, 113, 124, 133, 156, 176, 193
Di Fazio, William 196 n.53
diaspora 25, 63, 178, 186
    diaspora culture 168
    diaspora structure of feeling 180, 183
    diasporic workforce 118, 124, 179

difference 2, 4, 14, 28, 30, 163–5, 176, 183, 189
  and 'logic of difference' 28, 178
  and 'politicization of difference' 24–5
  and politics of difference 164–5, 167, 170, 178–9
Dostoevsky, Fyodor 136
Dunbar, Andrea 136
  Arbor, The 136
  Rita, Sue and Bob Too 136
  Shirley 136
Duncan, S. 199 n.3
Dunn, Peter 107

Eagleton, Terry 17, 24
Eliot, T. S. 36
'Englishness' 25, 163, 166–7, 174, 178
ethnicity 4, 24, 31, 63

Fanon, Franz 172
Federation of Worker Writers and Community Publishers 184
feminism 140–1
feminist 2, 11, 16, 135, 154
Fentress, J. 144–5
Fordism 2
  and post-Fordism 2
  and post-Fordist 4
Foucault, Michel 122
Fox, Pamela 40, 195 n.30, 196 n.1
Frankfurt School 54, 191
Friedman, Jonathan 183, 184, 189, 205 n.38
Full Monty, The 11, 20, 22, 23, 25, 26

General Strike (1926) 45
Gilbert, Geoff 133
Gilroy, Paul 168, 194 n.18
  There Ain't No Black in the Union Jack 168
Glasgow 79, 113, 114, 122
globalization 2, 18, 179

Gramsci, Antonio 144, 177
Grassic Gibbon, Lewis 29, 48, 51, 114
  Cloud Howe 48
  Grey Granite 48, 49
  Scots Quair, A 114, 122
  Sunset Song 48
Greenham Common 167
Greenwood, Walter 29, 37–9, 51, 64
  Love on the Dole 37–9, 42, 44, 51, 64, 72, 135

Habermas, J. 117, 203 n.36
Hall, Stuart 4, 101–2, 133, 165, 169, 199 n.76
  'Brave New World' 4
  'Notes on Deconstructing the Popular' 101–2
Handsworth Songs 169
Harrison, Tony 30, 95–9, 100, 163
  'Marked with D' 95
  'National Trust' 96
  'Working' 96–7
  'V' 97–9
Harvey, David 105, 106
Haylett, Chris 20
heritage film 169, 176
heritage industry 5, 143
'heritagization' 169
Hill, John 29, 198 n.46, 198 n.47, 198 n.51
  Sex, Class and Realism 29
Hines, Barry 30, 90, 100
  Blinder, The 90
  Heart of It, The 93–5
  Kestrel for a Knave, A 91
  Looks and Smiles 91, 92–3
  Price of Coal, The 91–2
Hitchcock, Peter 72, 148, 150, 154, 199 n.73
Hobsbawm, Eric 165
Hoggart, Richard 7–10, 12, 13, 25, 29, 54, 55–7, 64, 65, 68, 145, 146, 191

Uses of Literacy, The 7–12, 29, 55–7, 58, 72
Holderness, G. 197 n.24, 197 n.32
hooks, bell 17, 189
   Where We Stand: Class Matters 189
Hudson, R. 199 n.3
hybrid 162
   and hybridity 170, 176, 178, 180–2
   and 'formal hybridity' in Kureishi 175

identity politics 4, 16, 162, 163, 164, 179
ideology 1, 12, 16, 50, 64, 76, 77, 80–2, 95, 100, 104, 128, 138, 162 165–7, 171
imagined community 162, 167, 174, 178, 183, 187, 188

Jack, Ian 199 n.5
Jameson, Fredric 19, 22, 106, 112, 127, 158
   'Class and Allegory in Contemporary Mass Culture' 19
Jenkins, Simon 133
Johnson, Richard 155
   Making Memories 155
Jones, Lewis 29, 44, 51, 110
   Cwmardy 44–5
   We Live 44–5

Kaplan, Cora 141, 202 n.8
Keating, Peter 35, 79, 191
Kelman, James 19, 30, 105, 113–34, 136, 148, 163, 179, 192, 193
   Busconductor Hines, The 120–5
   Burn, The 118, 119, 129
   'By the Burn' 114–15
   Disaffection, A 125–31
   'Governor of the Situation' 120
   Greyhound for Breakfast 117–18

How Late It Was, How Late 131–3
   'Situation, A' 118–19
Klaus, H. Gustav 36, 197 n.26
Kristeva, J. 203 n.37
Kuhn, Annette 10, 11, 13, 30
   Family Secrets 10, 13
Kureishi, Hanif 169–78
   My Beautiful Laundrette 169, 170–5, 177, 180
   Sammy and Rosie Get Laid 169, 170, 175–7

Labour, 'New' 28
labourism 125
Labour Party, British 2
Lacey, Joanne 16
Laclau, Ernesto 4
   Hegemony and Socialist Strategy 4
Laing, Stuart 64, 198 n.42, 198 n.48, 198 n.49, 198 n.50
Lawler, Steph 202 n.2
Lawrence, D. H. 36, 111
Leavis, F. R. 36
Leeson, Lorraine 107
Left Book Club 39
Left Review 39
Letter to Brezhnev 140
Liverpool 78, 79, 84, 89
Liverpudlians 101
Loach, Ken 19, 26, 76, 91
   Cathy Come Home 76
   Kes 26, 91
   Ladybird, Ladybird 19, 20
   My Name is Joe 19
London 42, 47, 48, 62, 79, 107, 170, 171
   East End 106–7
   Docklands Development Corporation 107
   Isle of Dogs/Docklands 107
   Londoners 177
   Poplar 79
Lovell, Terry 21, 23

Lucas, John 97
Lusted, David 200 n.20, 200 n.25
Lyotard, J. F. 191

Macauley 162
MacInnes, Colin 29, 59, 64, 65, 73, 110
   Absolute Beginners 60–3, 64, 110
   City of Spades 59–61, 64
Macmillan, Harold 36
McGuigan, Jim 24–5, 204 n.6
Marx, Karl 17, 87, 111, 127, 173
   alienation 111
   money 126
   and surplus value 87
Marxism 16
Marxism Today 4
Marxist 18, 36, 114, 131, 179
Massey, Doreen 106
master-narratives 1, 3, 12, 32, 154
means test 40, 49, 50
Medhurst, Andy 7, 8, 10, 11, 204 n.8
memory 12, 13, 16, 17, 30, 142, 143, 145, 147, 154
   class memory 145, 154
   and 'memory-texts' 13, 16
   popular 155
   social memory 144
   see also 'nostalgic memory'
Mercer, Kobena 169
Meredith, Christopher 30, 110
   Shifts 110–13
Michael, Livi 136
   Under a Thin Moon 136–40
middle class 7, 9, 13, 16–17, 27, 34, 124
   and academics 13
   conscience 46
   'movements' 16
   novelists 35
   readership 38, 72
   values 19
Middleton, Peter 80

migrant experience 178–88
Milner, Andrew 3, 5, 16–17
   Class 16
Miner's Strike (1984–5) 5, 27, 93, 97, 99, 167
mining industry 91
Morrison, Toni 159
Mouffe, Chantal 4
Mowat, C. L. 40
multi-ethnic 24
Munt, Sally 194 n.8

Nairn, Tom 78, 106
nation 98, 162, 164
national belonging 31, 98
national identity 24, 162–8, 174, 176, 177
Neetens, Wim 34
Newcastle 108
   and north-east of England 108
New Brutalism 136
New Right 24, 137, 165, 170, 174
new social movements 4
Nil by Mouth 25
north/south divide 22, 47, 79
nostalgia 15–16, 142, 143, 144, 158, 160, 169
   and 'nostalgic memory' 142–5, 147, 154, 158, 160

Oldman, Gary 21
Orwell, George 36, 40, 51, 52, 56, 71
   Nineteen Eighty-Four 71
   Road to Wigan Pier, The 40, 51, 52, 56
Owens, Agnes 136

Passions of Remembrance 169
Playing Away 169
'pleasure of identification' 23, 85
popular culture 101–2
post-colonial 31, 60, 161, 163, 171
   intellectuals 183

and multicultural 165, 178, 188
and post-colonialism 178
subjectivity 183
theory 170
post-industrialism 30, 105, 109, 118, 141
postmodern 2, 106, 109, 110, 126, 127, 144, 154, 158, 178, 179
  condition 2, 14
  cultural theory 2, 17
  and performance 16
  and performative act 109
postmodernism 2, 13, 17, 30, 122, 191
postmodernity 192
poststructuralist 3, 12, 16, 80
Powell, Enoch 166
Powellism 173
poverty 18, 39, 116
proletarian literature 3
proletarian writing 25
proletarian fiction 32, 110
  see also working-class writing
Pykett, Lyn 148, 153, 159

race 4, 24, 30, 31, 60, 61, 165, 168
  and race and class dialectic 31, 167, 170
  race/class/gender/sexual orientation 17
  race problem 167
Reaganism 2
Reay, Diane 26, 28
representation(s)
  aesthetic/cultural and political importance of 102
  and discursive struggle 35, 59
  of 'escaper-paradigm' in working-class writing 26–8
  of place/space 105–8; see also community/communities
  politics of 124, 169
  and reality 40–1, 50, 94

  and representational strategies 19–20, 139
  significance of 5–6, 102
  and working class 1–3
Ross, Kristen 119, 122
Rushdie, Salman 161–3, 165, 177
  Satanic Verses, The 161–2

Said, Edward 134, 137, 187, 202 n.37
Salford, Manchester 37, 64
Salisbury Review, The 166
Sartre, J. P. 127
Scargill, Arthur 97
Scotland 109
Scruton, Roger 166
Seabrook, Jeremy 146
Selvon, Sam 63
  Lonely Londoners, The 63
sexual orientation 172
sexuality 4, 13, 21, 65
Showalter, Elaine 141
  Literature of their Own, A 141
Sillitoe, Alan 29, 54, 69–76, 191
  Death of William Posters, The 74–6
  Loneliness of the Long Distance Runner, The 69–70, 72
  Saturday Night and Sunday Morning 69–74, 75, 135
Sinfield, Alan 6, 63, 78
Skeggs, Beverley 11, 16
Social Darwinist 137
social realism/realist 21, 22, 26, 85, 170
  British cinema and the 'male norm' 21, 27
  British New Wave 21, 22, 26, 29
  'classic realist' 149
  and documentary realism 44
  provincial realists 69
  and psychological realism 40
  'reality-effect' 43
Soja, Edward 105
Sommerfield, John 42–3, 51

May Day 42–3
Spencer, Luke 200 n.28
Spivak, G. 9, 14
Stedman Jones, Gareth 34–5
Steedman, Carolyn 11, 12, 13, 30, 145–7, 203 n.22
  Landscape for a Good Woman 12, 13, 145–7
Stone, Norman 205 n.30
'strategic essentialism' 14
structure(s) of feeling 1, 3, 6, 8, 11, 19, 22, 23, 25, 29, 35, 37, 38, 39, 43, 44, 52, 53, 58, 63, 70, 71, 72, 74, 75, 79–102, 108, 109, 112, 136, 142, 143, 154, 156, 157, 160, 164, 171, 173, 178, 187, 190, 191
Syal, Meera 180–2
  Anita and Me 180–2

Thatcher, Margaret 18, 77, 84, 165–6, 167, 175
Thatcher era 133
Thatcherism 2, 77, 78, 83, 93, 164, 165, 170, 188
Thatcherite 18, 19, 53, 153, 155, 158, 162, 165, 169, 170, 175
Thatcher's Britain 30, 97, 177
theory 10–11
Thompson, E. P. 144, 195 n.9
'Third-Space' 181, 186, 189
Tressell, Robert 29, 32–4, 38, 42, 50, 51, 121
  Ragged Trousered Philanthropists, The 32–5, 38, 72, 121
Tulloch, John 101, 200 n.24, 200 n.27

underclass 20, 136, 173
unemployment 40, 78–9, 84, 85, 87, 89, 103, 109, 114, 131
United States 2, 164
useful knowledge 185

'utopian impulse' 43, 44, 50, 63, 90, 122, 125, 133, 143, 175

Victorian values 96, 165, 173
Vološinov, Valentin 72, 186

Wales 110
Walkerdine, Valerie 11, 13–14, 16
welfare state 25, 89, 147, 150
Welsh, Irvine 108, 110
  Trainspotting 108–10
Wesker, Arnold 54, 191
West, Cornel 164
Wickham, C. 144–5
Wilkinson, Ellen 29, 45, 51, 135
  Clash 45–8
Williams, Alfred 185–8, 193
  To Live It Is To Know It 185–8
Williams, Raymond 3, 6, 8, 9, 15, 23, 28, 29, 30, 33, 35, 39, 57–9, 72, 77, 79–83, 86, 90, 100, 120, 129, 184, 188, 191, 192, 193
  and community 82–3
  Country and the City, The 16
  and cultural formations 39, 184
  Culture and Society 57–9, 77
  and experience 79–83
  and 'knowable community' 35, 79–83, 85, 90, 100
  Marxism and Literature 72, 80
  and modernism 120
  Politics and Letters 77
  residual, dominant, emergent 23–4, 83; *see also* structure of feeling 79–102
  selective tradition 6
  Towards 2000 193
Winterson, Jeanette 136, 140
  Oranges are Not the Only Fruit 136, 140
Wisker, Gina 145
Woolf, Virginia 11
work 30, 91–2, 98–9, 103–4, 119, 152–3

working class
  academics 16
  consciousness 5, 19, 34, 38, 71, 72, 146, 168, 185
  culture 10, 12, 52, 57–8, 72, 99
  disappearance/demise of 2, 53, 56, 59
  fragmentation 19, 30, 108, 124
  identity 5, 7, 17, 19, 20, 22, 24, 26, 28, 72, 98, 109, 141, 193
  in recent film 18–25
  masculinity 20, 21, 26, 27, 40–2, 104
  stereotypes 124, 169, 170, 175, 182, 192
  stratification 28, 196
  subjectivity 10, 16, 30
  and uses of autobiography 7–17, 154, 184–5
  and uses of experience 7–15
  women 39, 45, 56, 65, 73, 94, 104, 129, 135, 135–160, 198 n.67
  see also class
working-class writers 5, 29, 39, 79, 83, 192
working-class writing 29, 30–4
  and dialogics 72
  feminization of 30, 135
  and language 72, 95, 99, 115, 127, 129, 133, 187
  on 'multiaccentuality of the sign' 72
  see also representation(s)
Worpole, Ken 117
Wright, Patrick 106, 107, 159–60
  Journey Through the Ruins, A 106–7

youth 55, 60, 62, 63